D1071376

THE
SPEECHES
IN
THUCYDIDES

THE
SPEECHES
IN
THUCYDIDES

A COLLECTION OF
ORIGINAL STUDIES
WITH A BIBLIOGRAPHY

Edited by Philip A. Stadter

THE UNIVERSITY OF NORTH CAROLINA PRESS
CHAPEL HILL

Copyright © 1973 by The University of North Carolina Press
All rights reserved
Manufactured in the United States of America
Printed by Heritage Printers, Inc., Charlotte, North Carolina
ISBN 0–8078–1213–7
Library of Congress Catalog Card Number 73–7816

Library of Congress Cataloging in Publication Data
Main entry under title:

The Speeches in Thucydides.

   Papers presented at a colloquium sponsored by the Dept. of Classics of the
University of North Carolina at Chapel Hill, March 26–27, 1972.
   Bibliography: p.
   1. Thucydides—Congresses. I. Stadter, Philip A., ed. II. North Carolina. University.
Dept. of Classics.
PA4461.S6   938   73–7816
ISBN 0–8078–1213–7

CONTENTS

Preface   [vii]

Introduction   [ix]
*George Kennedy, The University of North Carolina
at Chapel Hill*

The Speeches in Thucydides: A Description and Listing   [3]
*William C. West III, The University of North Carolina
at Chapel Hill*

Pathology of Power and the Speeches in Thucydides   [16]
*Henry R. Immerwahr, The University of North Carolina
at Chapel Hill*

The Speech of the Athenians at Sparta   [32]
A. E. Raubitschek, Stanford University

The Particular and the Universal in the Speeches in Thucydides
with Special Reference to That of Hermocrates at Gela   [49]
N. G. L. Hammond, University of Bristol

Speeches and Course of Events in Books Six and Seven
of Thucydides   [60]
Hans-Peter Stahl, Yale University

The "Non-Speeches" of Pisander in Thucydides, Book Eight [78]
*W. James McCoy, The University of North Carolina at
Chapel Hill*

The Settings of Thucydidean Speeches   [90]
H. D. Westlake, University of Manchester

[v]

Thucydidean Orators in Plutarch   [109]
    Philip A. Stadter, The University of North Carolina at
    Chapel Hill

A Bibliography of Scholarship on the Speeches in Thucydides,
1873–1970   [124]
    William C. West III, The University of North Carolina
    at Chapel Hill

Index of Names and Passages   [167]

PREFACE

On March 26–27, 1972, the Department of Classics of The University of North Carolina at Chapel Hill sponsored a colloquium on the speeches in Thucydides. The high quality of the papers presented there, the evident profit gained by the audience and participants, and the unity and importance of the subject persuaded the Department of Classics to present the papers in book form, with such modifications as seemed necessary and appropriate.

The department is indebted to The University of North Carolina Research Council for a publication grant, and to all those who by word or deed encouraged and supported the production of the colloquium and this book.

Special thanks are due to Professor Douglas C. C. Young, who read the book in proof and caught various errors, and to the department secretaries, Miss Nancy J. Honeycutt, Miss Jane Paris, and Mrs. Carol Smarr.

INTRODUCTION

by George Kennedy

This book is a study of the most striking literary feature of the greatest Greek historian, the "speeches" which constitute a large and integral part of Thucydides' *History* of the Peloponnesian War. Most ancient historians include speeches of some sort, varying from full-scale debates to reports of conferences, conversations, letters, messages, and other forms of verbal expression. The original model was doubtless furnished by the "speeches" of characters in the *Iliad*, which the Greeks regarded as a work of history. This practice was taken up by Herodotus and continued later, indeed down into the nineteenth century, when it succumbed to the concept of scientific historiography. But within the tradition, Thucydides' speeches are remarkable and unique. To them, as Sir Richard Claverhouse Jebb and John Malcolm Mitchell put it, "is due in no small measure the imperishable interest of the *History*, since it is chiefly by the speeches that the facts of the Peloponnesian War are so lit up with keen thought as to become illustrations of general laws and to acquire a permanent suggestiveness for the student of politics."[1] A similar statement could be found in many discussions of Thucydides. Werner Jaeger wrote that the speeches "are the most direct expression of Thucydides' thought, which rivals the work of the greatest Greek philosophers both in obscurity and in profundity."[2]

Thucydides hoped that his *History* would be useful, and this

1. *Encyclopedia Britannica*, 11th ed., s.v. "Thucydides."
2. *Paideia: The Ideals of Greek Culture*, trans. Gilbert Highet (New York, 1945), 1:392.

book is an attempt to put together a selection of material which may be useful in approaching the speeches, through the speeches the thought of Thucydides, and through Thucydides the mind of the Greeks. We have assembled a brief description and list of the speeches, a comprehensive bibliography of scholarly work on them over the last hundred years, with some comments on the direction that research has taken, and a series of essays on aspects of the subject which we hope bring out some of the major issues and problems involved and illustrate some of the possible points of view or methods which may be useful in approaching Thucydides. These essays are in all cases the results of original research not previously published; they are, however, intended to be read not only by scholars but by a wider audience. Greek words where they seemed necessary are printed in transliterated forms and quotations are translated into English. That the writers of the various chapters are not always in agreement seemed to us rather a virtue. At least it is honest; it shows the continuing interest of a topic which has remained controversial and refused to be settled once for all. That the chapters do not systematically cover every bit of ground may also be a virtue: though we believe Thucydidean scholars will be interested in them, we hope that students can be persuaded to take some of the approaches or ideas here suggested and work out the application of them to other parts of Thucydides' work.

Some other distinctive features of these chapters are, first, that they deal with the speeches not in isolation, but in their contexts and in their relationship to preceding and following events. Hans-Peter Stahl, for example, attempts a reading of Thucydides in which the narrative comes to elucidate the thought of the speeches, rather than the other way around as might be expected, while H. D. Westlake examines the preambles and postscripts which characteristically introduce and conclude the speeches and relate them to the specific contexts. Second, to a greater degree than most who study Thucydides' speeches we have attempted to include both the speeches dramatically presented in direct discourse and those longer or shorter remarks stated indirectly; indeed, our concept of "speech" is deliberately made as wide as possible. Third, although most major speeches are touched upon—Henry Immerwahr and Philip Stadter, for example, both consider Pericles' Funeral Oration, A. E. Raubitschek examines the speech of the Athenians at Sparta, N. G. L. Hammond the speech of Hermocrates at Gela—no portion of Thucydides' work is neglected. Thus James McCoy examines some speeches in indirect discourse from Book Eight, a book which is commonly said to have no speeches!

Clearly Thucydides' speeches cannot simply be labeled ornaments primarily intended to make the history more readable or to bring out the character of the actors in events. Occasionally that may result, but in general the speeches are too difficult, too highly intellectual, too rarely personal. Are they perhaps best seen as expositions of the issues of the times or even as Thucydides' own comments? Certainly they are part of his attempt to write a history which will be useful to future readers trying to understand events. But what method has he followed? What is the relationship of these speeches to what was actually said at the time? Why does the historian sometimes attribute speeches to specific individuals, sometimes to groups such as "the Athenians," "the Corinthians"? How did he select the occasions which were to have speeches? Does his use of speeches change or vary in the course of the work? Some of these questions can in part be answered, others can at least be better understood on the basis of the chapters that follow.

Thucydides himself comments on his speeches in a celebrated passage near the end of his preface (1.22). For the convenience of readers I quote the passage in full, using the translation of R. Crawley, originally published in 1874:

With reference to the speeches in this history, some were delivered before the war began, others while it was going on; some I heard myself, others I got from various quarters; it was in all cases difficult to carry them word for word in one's memory, so my habit has been to make the speakers say what was in my opinion demanded of them by the various occasions, of course adhering as closely as possible to the general sense of what they really said. And with reference to the narrative of events, far from permitting myself to derive it from the first source that came to hand, I did not even trust my own impressions, but it rests partly on what I saw myself, partly on what others saw for me, the accuracy of the report being always tried by the most severe and detailed tests possible. My conclusions have cost me some labour from the want of coincidence between accounts of the same occurrences by different eye-witnesses, arising sometimes from imperfect memory, sometimes from undue partiality for one side or the other. The absence of romance in my history will, I fear, detract somewhat from its interest; but if it be judged useful by those inquirers who desire an exact knowledge of the past as an aid to the interpretation of the future, which in the course of human things must resemble if it does not reflect it, I shall be content. In fine, I have written my work, not as an essay which is to win the applause of the moment, but as a possession for all time.

On first reading this passage may seem to make clear the historian's practice and assist the reader's interpretation. In fact, it has satisfied almost no one. The translation of several key words in the Greek text is highly uncertain. The words here rendered "what was in my opinion demanded of them," *ta deonta* in Greek, might perhaps be better translated "the essentials," recognizing the common Greek view of human nature by which thought, actions, and words were predictable in accordance with human probability. Another difficult phrase is that here translated "the general sense (*gnômês*) of what they really said," a phrase on which A. E. Raubitschek has some suggestions in his essay. And there are other problems: the structure of the passage and its relation to what precedes and what follows it have equally been debated. Although Thucydides' remarks may help us to define the problems involved, a more complex methodology of interpretation is essential for full understanding of the historian's art. The actual speeches and their contexts have to be examined in themselves, in relation to other speeches, and in terms of the remarks in the preface just quoted. The following chapters show that it is possible to come to some specific conclusions and to point toward some probable principles. We offer them not as a possession for all time, but as a contribution to the next stage in elucidation of the fascinating and difficult mind of the greatest Greek historian.

THE
SPEECHES
IN
THUCYDIDES

THE SPEECHES
IN THUCYDIDES

A DESCRIPTION AND LISTING

by William C. West III

The earliest work that gives a list of the speeches is the first edition of Blass's *Die attische Beredsamkeit* (1868). Blass's list of forty-one speeches does not include those in indirect discourse, but it imposes a kind of continuing influence, as the number of forty-one speeches appears again in Jebb's list, in his essay published in 1880. Categorizing the speeches broadly as deliberative, judicial, and epideictic, Blass and Jebb note one epideictic oration (Pericles' *epitaphios*); two judicial speeches (those of the Plataeans and Thebans at the trial of the Plataeans, 3.53–67); and thirty-eight deliberative speeches. Noted, but not included in the forty-one, are two dialogues, that between the Plataeans and Archidamus, 2.71–74, and the Melian dialogue. Certain speeches are recognized as "military speeches" but are included among the thirty-eight deliberative orations.

The consideration of what constitutes a proper list of the speeches in Thucydides may therefore justify a few words on the question of what constitutes a speech. Speech and narrative characterize broadly the contrasting methods by which Thucydides reports the action of his history. When verbal communication represents significant action, worthy of record, the historian is confronted with the possibility of reporting such action by direct speech or indirect statement, thereby deepening the issues involved and providing the reader with the means of interpreting the events. It is also possible, however, that the action prompted by speech may be viewed in terms of its result. In such cases he may use an objective statement, that a discussion took place and that a decision was reached, and so forth. Obvious examples include decrees of the assembly, and instances where one man, or a group, persuades another, or a group. Verbal communication indeed took place, but the historian focuses upon its result, not the communication itself. With this distinction in mind, I would suggest that a speech be defined as the report, in direct or indirect discourse, of what was said (or its substance) in any particular instance; this definition is intended to draw the distinction between a speech and the narrative statement of the occurrence of an event which involved the use of discourse. One must beware of formulating a definition too rigidly in the absence of the actual text, however. The eighth book shows readily how complicated the problem of definition is. As a working hypothesis it at least has the merit of directing attention to the words used, the arguments employed to influence the course of events, and allows one to conceive of speech, apart from narrative, as action significant in itself.

Luschnat (cf. Bibliography, 37, cols. 1146 ff.) calls attention to the ambiguity of the categories of deliberative, judicial, and epideictic for reference to the speeches in Thucydides. The speech in the public assembly and the general's speech of encouragement before battle are both deliberative only in the sense that they are concerned with the attitude of the audience to a future event, but there the similarity ends. The former represents advice to the assembly, which may be accepted or rejected, and the speaker's aim is to be persuasive. In the latter, however, the general need simply be encouraging to his troops. He must say "what the situation demands" in a convincing manner but need not fear that his exhortation must be ratified. Hence, as a point of method, the general's speech should be recognized as a distinct class. This subject has been amply dealt with by Luschnat in a monograph (133).

P. Moraux (279) uses the speeches of Cleon and Diodotus in the Mytilene debate to show that further precision of definition is possible in classifying the deliberative speech before the assembly.

He argues that these speeches can be analyzed in terms which demonstrate their construction according to principles described by the author of the *Rhetorica ad Alexandrum*. Cleon's speech combines the elements of dissuasion (*apotreptikos logos*) and accusation (*kategorikos logos*), both of which are suitable for an oration in the assembly. He attempts to dissuade the assembly from rescinding its earlier decision to put the Mytileneans to death and then sharply accuses the Mytileneans themselves for their revolt from Athens. Diodotus first finds fault with Cleon's accusation and then recommends what the situation demands for the best interests of Athens. It is, therefore, at first apotreptic, then deliberative in the true sense.

Mme de Romilly has drawn attention to extended sections of the narrative where no speech occurs but which suggest a speech as their immediate background (cf. Bibliography, 69, pp. 21 ff., in reference to 6.96–7.9). Luschnat (37, cols. 1163 ff.) presents an elaborate chart of the different types of speeches one finds in Thucydides. He expands noticeably the old lists of Blass and Jebb, organizing the spoken *logoi* along the lines of direct and indirect speech, delivered by one person or by a group, to one person or a group. He presents more than sixty examples of such spoken units but intends his catalogue as a detailed illustration of the variety of speech in Thucydides, not as a list definitive in itself.

My own listing, too, cannot claim to be comprehensive. There are too many instances where a distinction between speech and narrative is not feasible in objective terms. I have sought to include all examples of those cases where the history seems to focus upon what was said, but have usually excluded brief narrative statements suggesting that a speech took place, that a decision was made, and the like. Consequently, in addition to the Melian dialogue, I would list fifty-two speeches in direct discourse, eighty-five in indirect discourse, and three in which there is a combination of direct and indirect speech.[1] As the audience of an oration is important, these have been listed in each case.

---

1. The list of direct speeches compiled by Blass contains eleven fewer speeches than mine. This difference is accounted for in the fact that it does not contain four short speeches (1.53.2 and 4, 1.87.2, 1.139.3), two letters (1.128.7, 1.129.3), and a dialogue (2.71–74 [five speeches]).

As one considers the relationship between the speech and the audience, it becomes evident that this is an area where other useful distinctions might be made. For instance, Thucydides' marked tendency to group speeches in pairs appears in every book, although there are some interesting variations to the practice of grouping. Readily recognizable examples of paired speeches are those delivered in a public assembly. Here different speakers address themselves to handling the same subject before the same audience. There are, counted individually, eight paired speeches in Book One; one dialogue, which serves this purpose, in Book Two; four paired speeches in Book Three; seven in Book Four; three, and one dialogue, in Book Five; fourteen in Book Six; four in Book Seven; and four in Book Eight.[2]

Contrasted to paired speeches, however, on the same subject, before the same audience, complementary speeches might also be distinguished. These are speeches by different speakers and to different audiences, but on the same kind of topic. Good examples would be 1.120–24 (the speech of the Corinthians to the Peloponnesians on the need for war against Athens) and 1.140–44 (Pericles' first speech, to the Athenians on the coming war with Sparta and her allies); and 2.11 (the speech of Archidamus to the Spartans, on resources for the war and expectations of success) and 2.13.2–9 (Pericles' speech, in indirect discourse, on Athenian resources). Of the complementary speech there are two examples in Book One; four in Two; two in Four; two in Five; two in Six; and three in Seven.[3] The distinction between paired and complementary speeches emphasizes, of course, not the speaker, but the literary activity of Thucydides in arranging his speeches for maximum effect.

Finally, there is one example of speeches grouped together in

2. Paired speeches include: Book One (a) 32–36, 37–43 (b) 53.2, 53.4 (c) 68–71, 73–78, 80–85, 86 [cf. 87.2]; Book Two 71–74; Book Three (a) 37–40, 42–48 (b) 53–59, 61–67; Book Four (a) 17–20, 21.3, 22.1, 22.2 (b) 97.2–4, 98, 99; Book Five (a) 44.3–45.1, 45.2–4, 46 (b) 85–113; Book Six (a) 9–14, 16–18, 19.1, 20–23, 25.1, 25.2 (b) 33–34, 36–40, 41.2–4 (c) 47, 48, 49 (d) 76–80, 82–87; Book Seven 47.3–4, 48, 49 (bis); Book Eight (a) 86.3, 86.6–7 (b) 89.1, 89.2.

3. Complementary speeches include: Book One 120–24, 140–44; Book Two (a) 11, 13.2–9 (b) 87, 89; Book Four 10, 11.4; Book Five 69.1, 69.2; Book Six 68, 72.2–5; Book Seven 61–64, 66–68, 69.2.

what might be called a parallel situation: the speeches of Themistocles, in indirect discourse, at 1.90.3 and 91.4–7. The first is delivered to the Athenians and stresses the need for rebuilding the walls, after the Persian wars, and directs how it should be done. I think that the activity of speech in the public assembly should be recognized in terms of phrases of ring composition: *ekeleuen* ... *Themistoklês* and *tauta didaxas*, followed by *hupeipôn talla*, suggesting private remarks in contrast to the public statements. The speech parallel to this is delivered to the Spartans, after the walls have been built, and stresses the fact that, because of the walls, Athens and Sparta can now deliberate from positions of equal strength. These are speeches by the same speaker to different audiences, but on the same kind of subject: the proper attitude of each city to the walls of Athens.

A LIST OF THE SPEECHES

	1.31–44	Assembly at Athens
1]	32–36	Speech of the Corcyraeans
2]	37–43	Speech of the Corinthians
	1.52–53	Exchange of messages at Sybota
3]	53.2	Message of the Corinthians
4]	53.4	Reply of the Athenians
	1.67–88	Conference of the Peloponnesian League at Sparta
5]	68–71	Speech of the Corinthians
6]	73–78	Speech of the Athenians
7]	80–85.2	Speech of Archidamus
8]	86	Speech of Sthenelaïdas
9]	87.2	Motion of Sthenelaïdas
10]	1.90.3	Speech of Themistocles at Sparta, indirect discourse
11]	1.91.4–7	Speech of Themistocles at Sparta, indirect discourse
	1.119–125.2	Conference of the Peloponnesian League at Sparta
12]	120–124	Speech of the Corinthians

13]   1.128.7   Pausanias' letter to Xerxes

14]   1.129.3   Xerxes' letter to Pausanias

15]   1.136.4   Speech of Themistocles to Admetus of Mo-
                    lossus, indirect discourse

16]   1.137.2   Remarks of Themistocles to the captain of
                    a ship, indirect discourse

17]   1.137.4   Letter of Themistocles to Artaxerxes, di-
                    rect and indirect discourse

        1.139.3–145 Assembly at Athens
18]   139.3   Speech of the Spartan ambassadors
19]   140–144   Speech of Pericles

        2.2–6   Theban attack on Plataea
20]   2.4   Proclamation of the Theban herald,
                         indirect discourse
21]   3.1   Response of the Plataeans, indirect dis-
                         course
22]   4.7   Remarks of the Theban embassy at
                         Plataea, indirect discourse
23]   5.5   Remarks of the Plataean herald, in-
                         direct discourse

        2.10.2–11   Assembly of the Peloponnesian army at the
                     Isthmus
24]   11   Speech of Archidamus

        2.13   Assembly at Athens
25]   13.2–9   Speech of Pericles, indirect discourse

        2.34–46   Public burial at Athens
26]   35–46   Funeral oration of Pericles

        2.59.3–65.2 Assembly at Athens
27]   60–64   Speech of Pericles

        2.71–74   Preparations for seige of Plataea by Sparta
28]   71.2–4   Speech of the Plataeans
29]   72.1   Speech of Archidamus
30]   72.2   Reply of the Plataean ambassadors, in-
                         direct discourse
31]   72.3   Reply of Archidamus

32]	73.1	Consultation, indirect discourse
33]	73.2–3	Message to the Plataeans
34]	74.1	Reply of the Plataeans to Archidamus, indirect discourse
35]	74.2	Reply of Archidamus
	2.86–89	Preparations for a naval battle near Rhium
36]	87	Speech of the Spartan generals, Cnemus and Brasidas
37]	89	Speech of Phormio
	3.8–15	Conference of the Peloponnesians at Olympia
38]	9–14	Speech of the Mytileneans
	3.29.2–31	Conference of the Peloponnesians at Embatum in the territory of Erythrae
39]	30	Speech of Teutiaplus of Elis
	3.36–49.1	Assembly at Athens
40]	37–40	Speech of Cleon
41]	42–48	Speech of Diodotus
	3.52–68	Trial of the Plataeans
42]	52.4	Question of the Spartan judges, indirect discourse
43]	53–59	Speech of the Plataeans
44]	61–67	Speech of the Thebans
45]	68.1	Response of the Spartan judges, indirect discourse
	3.113	Exchange of messages between the Ambraciot herald and the Acarnanians and Amphilochians
46]	113	Dialogue and indirect discourse
47]	4.10	Speech of Demosthenes to Athenian troops on Sphacteria
48]	4.11.4	Speech of Brasidas to Spartan trierarchs and helmsmen, indirect discourse
	4.16–22	Assembly at Athens
49]	17–20	Speech of the Spartans
50]	21.3	Reply of Cleon, indirect discourse

51]   22.1   Response of the Spartan ambassadors, indirect discourse

52]   22.2   Speech of Cleon to the Spartan ambassadors, indirect discourse

       4.27–29.1   Assembly at Athens
53]   27–28   Exchange between Nicias and Cleon, indirect discourse

54]   4.40.2   Conversation between an Athenian ally and a Spartan prisoner at Athens, indirect discourse

55]   4.50.2   Letter of Artaxerxes to the Spartans, indirect discourse

       4.58–65.2   Assembly of Sicilian cities at Gela
56]   59–64   Speech of Hermocrates

       4.84–88   Assembly at Acanthus
57]   85–87   Speech of Brasidas

       4.91–93.1   Assembly of Boeotian army at Tanagra
58]   92   Speech of Pagondas the Boeotarch

59]   4.95   Speech of Hippocrates to the Athenians at Delium

       4.97.2–99   Exchange between Athenian and Boeotian heralds, after the battle of Delium
60]   97.2–4   Speech of the Boeotian herald, indirect discourse
61]   98   Reply of the Athenians, indirect discourse

62]   99   Reply of the Boeotians, indirect discourse

       4.114.3–5   Assembly at Torone
63]   114.3–5   Speech of Brasidas, indirect discourse

       4.120.3   Assembly at Scione
64]   120.3   Speech of Brasidas, indirect discourse

65]   4.126   Speech of Brasidas to Peloponnesians at Lyncus

66]   5.9   Speech of Brasidas at Amphipolis

67]   5.27.2   Advice of Corinthian ambassadors at Argos, indirect discourse

68]   5.30.1   Speech of Spartan ambassadors at Athens, indirect discourse

      5.44.2–46.3   Assembly at Athens
69]   44.3–45.1   Speech of the Spartan ambassadors, indirect discourse
70]   45.2–4   Speech of Alcibiades, indirect discourse
71]   46   Speech of Nicias, indirect discourse

      5.55.1   Assembly of the Peloponnesians at Mantinea
72]   55.1   Speech of Euphamidas of Corinth, indirect discourse

73]   5.60.2–3   Criticism of Agis by the Peloponnesian army, indirect discourse

74]   5.61.2   Speech of the Athenian ambassadors at Argos, indirect discourse

75]   5.65.2   Criticism of generals by the Argive army, indirect discourse

      5.69.1–2   Generals' speeches before Mantinea
76]   69.1   Speech of the Mantineans, Argives, and Athenians, indirect discourse
77]   69.2   Speech of the Spartans, indirect discourse

78]   5.85–113   Melian dialogue

      6.8–26   Assembly at Athens
79]   9–14   Speech of Nicias
80]   16–18   Speech of Alcibiades
81]   19.1   Speech of the ambassadors of Leontini and Segesta, indirect discourse
82]   20–23   Speech of Nicias
83]   25.1   Remark of an Athenian, indirect discourse
84]   25.2   Speech of Nicias, indirect discourse

      6.32.3–41   Assembly at Syracuse

85]   33–34   Speech of Hermocrates
86]   36–40   Speech of Athenagoras
87]   41.2–4   Speech of a general

           6.46.5–50.1   Conference of Athenian generals at Rhe-
                      gium
88]   47   Speech of Nicias, indirect discourse
89]   48   Speech of Alcibiades, indirect discourse
90]   49   Speech of Lamachus, indirect discourse

91]   6.68   Speech of Nicias at Syracuse

92]   6.72.2–5   Speech of Hermocrates at Syracuse, indi-
                      rect discourse

           6.75.3–88   Assembly at Camarina
93]   76–80   Speech of Hermocrates
94]   82–87   Speech of Euphemus

           6.88.9–93   Assembly at Sparta
95]   89–92   Speech of Alcibiades

96]   7.5.3–4   Speech of Gylippus at Syracuse, indirect
                      discourse

           7.10–15.2   Assembly at Athens
97]   11–15   Letter of Nicias

           7.47–49   Council of generals at Epipolae
98]   47.3–4   Speech of Demosthenes, indirect dis-
                      course
99]   48   Speech of Nicias, indirect discourse
100]   49   Response of the two to the proposals,
                      indirect discourse

           7.60.5–69.2   Speeches before the battle in the harbor at
                      Syracuse
101]   61–64   Speech of Nicias
102]   66–68   Speech of Gylippus and Syracusan gen-
                      erals
103]   69.2   Speech of Nicias, indirect discourse

104]   7.77   Speech of Nicias to the Athenian survivors
                      at Syracuse

105]   8.12   Advice of Alcibiades to the Spartan ephors, indirect discourse

106]   8.14.2   Speech of Alcibiades and Chalcideus in the assembly at Chios, indirect discourse

107]   8.27.1–5   Speech of Phrynichus to other generals, indirect discourse

108]   8.32.3   Speech of Astyochus to the Chians and Pedaritus, indirect discourse

109]   8.40.1–3   Speech of the Chians and Pedaritus to Astyochus, indirect discourse

110]   8.41.3   Advice of the Cnidians to Astyochus, indirect discourse

111]   8.43.2–4   Criticism of Tissaphernes by the Peloponnesian generals, indirect discourse

112]   8.45.1   Letter of Spartans to Astyochus, indirect discourse

113]   8.45.2–3   Advice of Alcibiades to Tissaphernes, indirect discourse

114]   8.45.4–6   Advice of Alcibiades to island cities, indirect discourse

115]   8.46   Advice of Alcibiades to Tissaphernes, indirect discourse

116]   8.48.4–7   Phrynichus' criticism of Alcibiades, indirect discourse

117]   8.50.2   Letter of Phrynichus to Astyochus, indirect discourse

118]   8.52   Advice of Alcibiades to Tissaphernes, indirect discourse

119]   8.53   Speech of Pisander in the Athenian assembly, direct and indirect discourse

120]   8.55.2   Report of Xenophantidas to the Rhodians, indirect discourse

121]   8.56.4   Demands of Tissaphernes, presented by
                      Alcibiades, to the Athenians, indirect dis-
                      course

122]   8.63.4   Consultation of Athenian oligarchs on Sa-
                      mos, narrative and indirect discourse

123]   8.65.3   Public demands of Athenian oligarchs, in-
                      direct discourse

124]   8.67.1   Motion of Pisander in the Athenian assem-
                      bly, indirect discourse

125]   8.73.4   Entreaties of the Samians to Leon, Diome-
                      don, Thrasybulus, and Thrasylus, narra-
                      tive and indirect discourse

126]   8.74.3   Speech of Chaereas to the soldiers in Sa-
                      mos, indirect discourse

127]   8.76.2–7   Discussion of Athenian soldiers in Samos,
                      indirect discourse

128]   8.78   Complaints of the Peloponnesian fleet
                      against Astyochus and Tissaphernes, indi-
                      rect discourse

129]   8.81.2   Speech of Alcibiades to the soldiers in Sa-
                      mos, indirect discourse

        8.86   Assembly at Delos
130]   86.3   Speech of the envoys of the Athenian
                           oligarchs, narrative and indirect dis-
                           course
131]   86.6–7   Speech of Alcibiades, indirect discourse

132]   8.89.1   Speech of Athenian ambassadors to Samos
                      in the Athenian assembly, indirect dis-
                      course

133]   8.89.2   Speech of Athenian oligarchs in the Athe-
                      nian assembly, narrative and indirect dis-
                      course

134]   8.90.3   Private remarks (cf. 92.2) of Theramenes
                      and his supporters, indirect discourse

135]   8.91.1–2   Private remarks (cf. 92.2) of Theramenes
                      and his supporters, indirect discourse

136]   8.92.2–4   Accusations of Theramenes and others,
                      narrative and indirect discourse

137]   8.92.6   Reply of Theramenes to the four hundred,
                      indirect discourse

138]   8.92.9–11   Dialogue between Athenian hoplites and
                      Theramenes, indirect discourse

139]   8.93.2–3   Remarks of some of the four hundred to
                      some of the Athenian hoplites, indirect
                      discourse

140]   8.98.3   Remarks of Aristarchus to the Athenian
                      garrison in Oenoe, indirect discourse

141]   8.108.1   Remarks of Alcibiades to the Athenians, in-
                      direct discourse

PATHOLOGY OF POWER AND THE SPEECHES IN THUCYDIDES

by Henry R. Immerwahr

The speeches in Thucydides are often considered as independent political essays from which the reader derives an understanding of the forces operative in the Peloponnesian War if not in history in general. More recently the connection of the speeches with the narrative has been more heavily emphasized, and this view has led some to interpret the speeches merely as narrative elements. I believe that neither view is correct, but that the speeches are both part of the story of the war and complementary to it. In what follows I shall place the speeches in an overall pattern for the *History* constructed on the basis of the theme of the pathology of power as developed in the prooemium and further described in the rest of the work. The changes that political power underwent in the course of the Peloponnesian War were to Thucydides indicative of deterioration as in disease, and an important symptom of this deterioration was the suffering which power inflicted. The reader may think of "pathology" first of all as an account of the corruption of power and secondarily as an "account of suffering."

I

Thucydides' work is a fragment, although an extensive one: the lack of completion is apparent not only at the end, but also in some places within the work. The unity of conception is therefore a special problem. It has been attacked brilliantly by Mme de Romilly in her book on Athenian imperialism in Thucydides: according to her, the idea of imperialism developed consistently during the time of composition.[1] I shall take a somewhat different path and ask whether the prooemium furnishes a clue to the unity of the work. The problem of composition does not, I think, prejudice this question at all, for it is possible for an author to hold to the same notions during a lifetime. Even if the *History* is made up of a series of separate compositions, we may still inquire to what extent they hang together.

I must first show, however, that chapters 1–23 of the first book form a unified prooemium.[2] The proof for this assumption consists of two parts. First, these chapters deal with certain standard topics found in historical prooemia both before and after Thucydides. After giving his name and the subject of his work, Thucydides points to his competence by saying that he began to write as soon as the war broke out. The statement that he is a contemporary historian takes the place of Herodotus' statement that his work is based on *historiē*. Thucydides goes on to claim that the Peloponnesian War was greater than previous wars—a comparison familiar to us from Herodotus' comparison of the Persian War with certain preceding wars (Hdt. 7.20). At the end of the prooemium, Thucydides marks the beginning of the conflict (Herodotus begins with Croesus) and defines its causes. It is important to realize that these topics are entirely conventional.

The second proof of the unity of the prooemium is formal. The statement of the greatness of the present war leads to a digression in which previous military operations are compared with the Peloponnesian War, the so-called *Archaeology*.[3] At the end, in the

1. J. de Romilly, *Thucydides and Athenian Imperialism*, trans. P. Tody (Oxford, 1963).

2. On the proem, see A. W. Gomme, *A Historical Commentary on Thucydides* (Oxford, 1945), 1:154–57; O. Luschnat, s.v. "Thukydides" in Pauly-Wissowa-Kroll, *Real-Encyclopädie der klassischen Altertumswissenschaft*, suppl. 12 (1970), passim; H. Patzer, *Das Problem der Geschichtsschreibung des Thukydides und die Thukydideische Frage* (Berlin, 1937), pp. 1–79. See also following note.

3. N. G. L. Hammond, "The Composition of Thucydides' History," *Classical Quarterly* 34 (1940):146, and 46 (1952):127–41.

chapters on method (1.20–22), Thucydides combines the reaffirma-
tion of the greatness of the present war with the justification of his
authority by means of his accuracy as a contemporary historian.
This is done by interlarding statements about the war with sections
that together form an extensive critique of historical method, including the famous distinction of how he treated speeches and
events in the war (1.22).[4]

The principal idea of the prooemium is thus the greatness of the
Peloponnesian War. In trying to demonstrate this point, Thucydides develops an entirely novel definition of what constitutes this
greatness. The *Archaeology* develops as its main theme the growth
of power, *dynamis*, in Greece, with special reference to Sparta and
to Athenian naval power. The theme is not imperialism, but the
force that lies behind it. The *Archaeology* gives some indications
about the factors which encourage concentration of power: fertility
of soil (1.2.4), influx of capital from commerce (1.15.1, etc.), and
victorious wars (1.15.2). The analysis recognizes historical differences to some extent: Sparta's early power was due to her constitution (1.18.1); the policies of the tyrants on the whole prevented
increases in power (1.17.1). Absence of good land and foreign con-
quests could limit the development of power. But in general, increase in power is based on certain recurrent phenomena that are
connected with the development of seafaring. The effect of the
exercise of power is the concentration of resources and the spread
of civilization. Power enables people to act in concert and to mix
with one another (1.15). The most distinguishing characteristic of
power is that it leads to constant activity: at an early time popula-
tions migrated to Attica (1.2.6); piracy was a primitive form of
dynamis (1.5); and larger wars resulted in ever greater concentration of power for the victors.[5] Thucydides sees power as a force
which nourishes, perpetuates, and increases itself in constant pro-
gression. The concept of *dynamis* as a progressive force is new in
Greek thought at this time. In Herodotus, to name only one exam-

4. H. R. Immerwahr, "Ergon: History as a Monument in Herodotus and
Thucydides," *American Journal of Philology* 81 (1960):278.
5. On the theme of the development of power in the proem see also J. de
Romilly, *Histoire et raison chez Thucydide* (Paris, 1956), pp. 261 ff. Cf. in general
A. G. Woodhead, *Thucydides on the Nature of Power* (Cambridge, Mass., 1970),
pp. 37 ff.

ple, *dynamis* is a static quality, an aspect of wealth which does not automatically lead to action.[6] In Thucydides wealth, *periousia chrêmatôn*, becomes *paraskeuê*, preparation for action for the purpose of self-preservation or further expansion. These activities lead in turn to experience, *empeiria*, in the use of resources, especially in war. By *empeiria* the practical intelligence tries to control the progress of power when it comes in conflict with other sources of power, which it assimilates unless it is weakened or destroyed by them. We may go a little further in the analysis of *dynamis* as sketched in the *Archaeology*. There is a certain ambiguity in the definition of power, which may be considered a concrete phenomenon—in this sense we may speak of troops as a *dynamis*—or an abstract force which lies behind the phenomena, as the force of gravity causes the apple to fall. A similar ambiguity exists between the concrete manifestations of *dynamis* and the activity of the mind, or *polypragmosynê*, which is a psychological aspect of *dynamis*. The truth is that *dynamis* is both concrete and abstract, and both factual and psychological. Now the late Adam Parry established in his unpublished doctoral dissertation that Thucydides operates consistently with the antithesis of the rational faculty, *logos*, and the external world, *ergon*.[7] It is, however, necessary to introduce a further antithesis into this scheme, for Thucydidean psychology recognizes two aspects of the mind, practical intelligence or *logos*, and emotion, for which we find a number of terms, *orgê, tolma, phobos*, etc., but for which the most inclusive is *anthrôpeia physis*. In Thucydides, the term "human nature" refers only to the irrational factor in man.[8] Now it seems of fundamental importance that *dynamis* is not confined to any one of these three areas—*logos*,

6. H. R. Immerwahr, *Form and Thought in Herodotus*, American Philological Association, Monograph 23 (Cleveland, 1966), pp. 206–8.

7. A. M. Parry, "Logos and Ergon in Thucydides" (Ph.d. diss., Harvard University, 1957). For a similar antithesis, *gnômê — tychê*, see Schmid-Stählin, *Geschichte der griechischen Literatur* 1, 5, (Munich, 1948):31.

8. See 1.76.2; 3.45; 3.82.2 (cf. perhaps 1.22.4); somewhat differently 5.105.1–2. The different concept in 3.84.2 is not Thucydidean. In general, see P. Shorey, *Transactions of the American Philological Association* 24 (1893): 66 ff.; W. Jaeger, *Paideia*,[2] trans. G. Highet (Oxford, 1945), 1:389 and 485, note 21; J. H. Finley, *Thucydides* (Cambridge, Mass., 1947), pp. 54 ff.; K. von Fritz, *Die griechische Geschichtsschreibung* (Berlin, 1967), 1:545 ff. and 807.

anthrôpeia physis, and *ergon*—but that it belongs to all three. *Dynamis* is first an attempt of the mind to control the environment, a control which is achieved by the rational *logos* which calculates resources, prepares military forces, and plans strategy and tactics in war. But power also works through the emotions, where it arouses a deep commitment, which Thucydides calls *erôs* and which we might call patriotism.[9] This commitment expresses itself in extreme daring, restless activity (*polypragmosynê*) and fear of other powers. In both the rational and the irrational aspects, *dynamis* is an instrument to achieve security against enemies and the realm of *tychê* (chance). At the same time, *dynamis* appears as a concrete element like money, military forces, and more generally empire, *archê*. It should be evident, then, that we have in the concept of *dynamis* (rather than in the phenomenon of imperialism) the main unifying theme in the work: all other elements in the *History* are somehow related to it.

To return to the prooemium: the delineation of power, as we have said, aims at substantiating the greatness of the Peloponnesian War. Power and war are intimately connected by the desire for security (*phobos*), the desire for expansion (*pleonexia*), and more generally by what Thucydides calls "necessity" (*anankê*), which means that in power politics a mechanism develops in the relations between the antagonists, which regularly, although not automatically, leads to war.[10] In the prooemium, Thucydides makes a number of statements about the greatness of the Peloponnesian War. In chapter 1, he says that at the outset the resources of the contestants were greater than ever before and that a great movement resulted from Greek states joining one or the other side. The greatness of *paraskeuê* is repeated at the end of the *Archaeology* (1.19). In the chapters on method (1.20–22), Thucydides declares

9. *Erôs* in Thucydides: 6.24.3 (narrative), cf. 6.13 (Nicias). 2.43.1 (Funeral Oration), 3.45.5 (speech of Diodotus). F. M. Cornford, *Thucydides Mythistoricus* (London, 1907), pp. 201–20.

10. On the Thucydidean concept of historical necessity, which is not absolute, see now J. de Romilly, "La notion de nécessité dans l'histoire de Thucydide," *Science et Conscience de la Société, Mélanges Raymond Aron* (Paris, 1971), 1:109–28, especially 124 ff. Differently (and wrongly, I think) D. Grene, *Man in His Pride* (Chicago, 1950, reissued as *Greek Political Theory*, Chicago, 1965), pp. 56–79, and D. Kagan, *The Outbreak of the Peloponnesian War* (Ithaca, 1969), pp. 357–74.

that this greatness will be apparent from the facts (*ta erga*) themselves. But in the following chapter (1.23) Thucydides introduces two wholly new ideas when he says that the war differed from the Persian War by its length and that it caused more suffering than previous wars. The difficulty of this chapter is notorious: it introduces a different point of view, and its connection with the preceding is obscure. Some have thought that it is part of an older prooemium.[11]

The following considerations, however, argue for the unity of the prooemium as a whole. First, the statements in chapters 1 and 19 refer to the situation at the outbreak of the war rather than to the war itself, and the chapters on method do not explain what the events were that made the war so great. Chapter 23 for the first time gives us specifics. Second, it would have been impossible for Thucydides to claim that the Peloponnesian War had produced greater *deeds* than the Persian Wars. He answers the claim that the Persian War was the greatest by shifting his ground and substituting length and suffering (*pathêmata*) for great deeds. A third argument for the unity of the prooemium is the unspoken, but evident, connection of suffering with the concept of *dynamis*. The length of the Peloponnesian War was in part due to the magnitude of the *paraskeuê* on both sides, especially the Athenian reserves in ships and money. This enabled Pericles to plan a war of some length. But the main reasons for the length of the war were irrational, namely the Athenian fear of the consequences of losing the war and Athenian *pleonexia* after the death of Pericles. It must be admitted that the connection between power and the length of the war is not made absolutely clear in the prooemium, but it becomes evident from the analysis of the work itself. Furthermore, Thucydides says in chapter 23 that the misfortunes of the Peloponnesian War were due not only to its length, but to the density of disasters in that length of time. This frequency had two sources: first, the activities of the belligerents with regard to external and internal enemies, and second the natural phenomena which could not be foreseen, such as the plague.[12] The density of suffering has

---

11. E. Schwartz, *Das Geschichtswerk des Thukydides* (Munich, 1929, reprinted Hildesheim, 1960), pp. 170–75. Luschnat, "Thukydides," cols. 1201–4.

12. It must be admitted that the emphasis on *natural* causes of suffering has no

thus a partial cause in the power of the belligerents. This too will become apparent from the analysis of the work.

II

I shall now proceed to sketch briefly some features of the body of the work in order to substantiate the suggestion that the pro-oemium gives us the principal theme in the relation of power and suffering. Here the narrative rather than the speeches seems at first glance to furnish more compelling proofs. As Professor Stahl has shown, the narrative frequently stresses the irrational nature of events and the helplessness of man in confronting them.[13] This irrationality appears in the narrative of decisive events such as the plague, the battle of Delium, the affair of Pylos, and the events in Sicily. It is even more apparent in the dramatic development of events which did not influence the outcome of the war decisively, such as the Mytilenean affair, the story of the Plataeans, and the events at Corcyra and Melos, to name only the most conspicuous examples. Thucydides even dramatizes events that concern only small states, and which have a purely emotional impact upon the reader. Here the destruction of Mycalessus in Boeotia by Thracian mercenaries comes to mind immediately (7.29-30). In all these dramatic compositions, whether they show power affected by un-controllable situations or by situations that are misunderstood by the belligerents, whether they show the effect of power or of acci-dent upon the weak, there is a common, we might say, humani-tarian, factor, which is expressed by a technical device that I have elsewhere called "*pathos* statements," that is, the accounts are closed by a remark that such and such was the greatest misfortune of its kind.[14] Power then, in addition to its effect in the political

direct connection with the concept of power. It has been claimed that this element is due to rhetorical *auxêsis* and thus indicates that the proem is early; see Luschnat, "Thukydides." Yet the influence of *tychê* (of which natural disasters are a part) is much evident in the work. In 1.23 Thucydides specifies only the earliest disaster (the plague), but this is in the manner of prooemia. In the *Iliad* and *Odyssey* too only the earlier events of the poems are mentioned in the prooemia.

13. H.-P. Stahl, *Thukydides: die Stellung des Menschen im geschichtlichen Prozess* (Zetemata 40, Munich, 1966).

14. Immerwahr, "Ergon," p. 284.

field, has a human import which is tragic. In this sense, Thucydides does indeed paint a desperate picture of the human situation in his narrative.

How do the speeches fit into the picture created by the narrative? It is clear from 1.22 that they have at least an equal importance with the narrative in Thucydides' account. I shall claim in what follows that so far as power politics is concerned the speeches are not simply elements in the narrative, but that they have four different functions in the work: (1) they give a rational analysis of the main ideas of the *History*, including the analysis of *dynamis* in basic agreement with the ideas developed in the prooemium. (2) They give a description of the irrational commitment to power. (3) They furnish a number of demonstrations (as seen by the speakers) of the relations of these intellectual perceptions to the individual actions in the war. (4) The speeches always stand in a dramatic relationship to the scenes of which they are a part and to the rest of the work. I omit a fifth point, namely that the speeches may reflect the actual words of the speakers: this is a problem I would like to disregard here except to say that in my opinion the dramatic and intellectual functions of the speeches do not exclude their authenticity. The treatment of the concept of *dynamis* in the speeches may serve as a test case of how we are to interpret them in general.

A first group of speeches in Book One gives a full analysis of the different aspects of *dynamis* in a political, psychological, and concrete sense. This group—I am not classifying the speeches by their occasions—consists of the Corcyraean speech, the first Corinthian speech, and the speech of the Athenians at Sparta. The fact that these speeches express what we might call philosophical truths—truths adapted in each case to the circumstances—shows that the belligerents entered the war in full knowledge of the nature of power, a knowledge similar to Thucydides' own. Thucydides' conception that the speakers shared with the author the same power of analysis has often troubled scholars, but Thucydides conceived of his own ideas not as private thoughts, but as common ideas of the period, and indeed as ideas which the mind would naturally form when confronted with certain situations. The Corcyraean speech (1.32–36) has some reference to the question of power as it affects alliances. The main advantage of an alliance of Athens and Corcyra will be an increase in Athenian sea power in the coming war (1.33.2-3). In addition Corcyra lies conveniently on the route to Sicily and Italy (36.2). These two arguments are accepted by the Athenians (44.2) who conclude a defensive alliance with Corcyra on the basis of a correct estimate of the situation. These points must not be overlooked, even if the Athenians were mistaken, as it turned out, in believing that they could avoid a direct conflict with Corinth.

The first speech of the Corinthians (1.68-71) and the Athenian speech at Sparta (1.73-78) have in common the purpose of frightening the Spartans; the Corinthians hope to frighten them into war, the Athenians into refraining from war. The Corinthian contrast of Spartan *hêsychia* with Athenian *polypragmosynê*, by which the Athenians are called daring "beyond their *dynamis*" (1.70.3), is based on the Thucydidean definition of power as an activity. But the principal analysis of *dynamis* is found in the Athenian speech.[15] This speech borrows a number of topics from the epideictic genre of oratory: the Athenians are worthy of praise (their polis is *axia logou*, 1.73.1) because of their deeds in the Persian Wars and because they are worthy of empire. The apology of imperialism is a development of the *topos* of praise. Of the three motives for empire—fear, honor, and self-interest—fear and self-interest are basic elements in the exercise of power. These forces are here represented as irrational, for the Athenians declare themselves "defeated" by them (*nikêthentes*, 1.76.2), since they are related to the natural law that the stronger must rule over the weaker. But the irrational base of power politics leads to a rational analysis of empire as the concrete manifestation of power. That this analysis is true should be clear from Thucydides' own analysis of empire in the *Archaeology*. Nevertheless, the speech does not have the intended effect, for the Spartan reaction, as shown by the short speech of Sthenelaïdas, is purely emotional, and Sparta decides on war. The truth could not prevail against Sparta's fear of the growing power of Athens. This is perhaps the first inkling of a tragic dimension in the work. But in addition to its immediate and dra-

---

15. The Athenian speech is fully analyzed by Professor Raubitschek in his paper in this book.

matic function, the speech has also an intellectual function, for it furthers an understanding of Athens' position.[16] We must therefore accept the praise of Athens as a valid feature of the work. Athens is more than an example of the futility of reason in the world.

The definitions given in these speeches suit their position at the beginning of the *History*. As we move closer to the outbreak of war, a second group of speeches (again not delivered on a single occasion) deals with the situation that will arise once war has broken out. From this point of view, we may group together the speech of Archidamus, the second Corinthian speech, and the first speech of Pericles. Archidamus (1.80–86) uses the question of the ability of the Spartans to wage protracted war in a futile attempt to prevent Sparta from declaring war. The Corinthians (1.120–24) and Pericles (1.140–44) describe the concrete elements of power on both sides, their *paraskeuê*, with the Corinthians giving a false picture of Peloponnesian power and Pericles giving a true one. Both speakers have the same aim—to make their audience accept war—and both the true and the false picture appear to be effective. Despite their various purposes, the three speeches give a consistent analysis of *paraskeuê*, a picture that is reinforced by cross references between the speeches. These references are made possible by the Thucydidean principle that speakers would say *ta deonta*, that is, what the situation required both in their own view and in the view of Thucydides himself. By and large, we have in Book One two groups of speeches which represent the *logos* or rational power of the belligerents, who have a clear understanding of the causes and nature of the coming war. Their knowledge is not identical with, but very similar to, Thucydides' own understanding of power politics.

With the beginning of the second book, we come to the outbreak of the war and the emotional picture of the enthusiasm for war at this time. In addition, the irrationality of war made itself felt from the beginning, especially in the Theban attack on Plataea so well analyzed by Professor Stahl,[17] and in the appearance of the plague. But if we conclude from these accounts that the bel-

16. Differently Stahl, *Thukydides*, pp. 43–50.
17. Ibid., pp. 65–74.

ligerents, and in particular the Athenians, are in a position of ignorance as to the possible course of the war, a very serious problem arises with respect to the Funeral Oration and the last speech of Pericles, which are usually interpreted as Thucydidean praise of Periclean Athens. Hellmut Flashar, in a recent monograph on the Funeral Oration, has drawn the logical conclusion from a view which subordinates the speeches to the narrative.[18] He argues that since the speech was written after the defeat of Athens in 404 B.C., the praise of the city can only be ironical, as the reader must realize when he compares the speech with the narrative, especially the account of the plague. Pericles' demand for a deep Athenian commitment to power politics in both of Pericles' speeches in Book Two is used ironically by Thucydides and proved to be a mistake by the outcome of events.

I believe this interpretation to be a serious error, since it denies the elements of praise and of rational argument in favor of a purely dramatic analysis. Since this view of the Funeral Oration affects our whole view of Thucydides' purposes, I shall discuss this oration at somewhat greater length in order to show that it contains, in addition to its dramatic function, a rational analysis that is truly Thucydidean, a description of the irrational commitment to power, and a demonstration of how these intellectual perceptions relate to the beginning of the war.

The Funeral Oration follows the tradition of funeral speeches in Athens which, we must assume, had been formed prior to the time it was written, since its general plan agrees with the later orations that have come down to us and which are not dependent on it. As in the Athenian speech in Book One, the conventional epideictic topics have a certain persuasive power. Nevertheless, it might be argued that such patterns could be used ironically, somewhat in the Euripidean manner. But the Funeral Oration, as I have suggested elsewhere, departs from the conventional pattern in ways which bring it closer to Thucydidean ideas.[19] To cite only

---

18. H. Flashar, *Der Epitaphios des Perikles: seine Funktion im Geschichtswerk des Thukydides* (Heidelberger Akademie der Wissenschaften, Sitzungsberichte, Philos.-Histor. Klasse, 1969, Abhandlung 1, Heidelberg, 1969).

19. Immerwahr, "Ergon," pp. 284 ff.

a few examples, Pericles concerns himself mainly with the present rather than the past, he praises attitudes rather than deeds, and he shows an intellectual pride that is characteristic of Thucydides himself. This intellectual adaptation of traditional patterns forces the reader to accept the speech as something more than conventional jingoism. The rational element consists in the description of the benefits the individual citizen derives from democracy, in the ties established between community and individual and between debate and action, and in the definition of the adaptable individual whose courage is knowledge of *ta deonta* (2.43.1). The transition from the praise of democracy to the praise of imperialism is also a logical one, because in fifth-century thought democracy is by nature imperial democracy.[20] Since freedom is an acquired benefit rather than a human right, it can exist only when supported by power. Thus Pericles demands the citizens "fall in love" with their powerful city: *tên tês poleôs dynamin kath' hêmeran theômenous kai erastas gignomenous autês* (2.43.1). The word *erastas*, to be sure, raises misgivings, since *erôs* is characteristic of tyrants.[21] Yet the emotional commitment to power, dangerous as it is, is unavoidable, as Pericles points out in his last oration, in which he calls the empire a tyranny which cannot be relinquished. This commitment involves the recognition that some day power will come to an end: *panta gar pephyke kai elassousthai*, as Pericles says in his last speech (2.64.3). In both speeches, the commitment to *dynamis* is delineated as a heroic (not to say, Homeric) attitude. Although this attitude comes in conflict with the realities of war, this does not mean that the Athenian commitment is seen only ironically. The *erôs* of the imperial city is basic to Pericles' plan for a long war and was operative for twenty-seven years. But it also

20. Imperial democracy: de Romilly, *Imperialism*, pp. 74–75. Flashar, *Der Epitaphios*, pp. 17 ff., claims that Pericles' description of Athenian democracy is idealizing and in conflict with reality. But the purpose of the Funeral Oration (as of epideictic orations in general) is didactic: by describing an ideal state Pericles tries to persuade his audience to live accordingly. This function of funeral orations was well understood by Plato when he makes the fathers address the children in *Menexenus* (246 D ff.). The didactic purpose of the Thucydidean Funeral Oration is to achieve the unity of state and individual (note the alternation of *koinon* and *idion* throughout the oration).

21. See above note 9.

led to the *pleonexia* of Pericles' successors, which Thucydides so strongly condemned.[22] The Athenian love of power is thus ambiguous; in part, it is a necessary foundation for the conduct of Athenian power politics, and in part it grew to that irrationality that became more and more apparent in the course of the war. From the dramatic point of view, Thucydides' work has the form of tragedy, but not of that kind of Euripidean tragedy in which human character is seen as basically disordered and corrupt. We cannot deny the Athenians in Thucydides a certain heroic quality, which is expressed in speeches as self-praise. The speeches show that Thucydides' work is heroic tragedy, whereas the narrative alone might lead us to interpretation closer to that valid for certain plays of Euripides.

The concept of power is further discussed in the speeches that follow in the remaining books, but the later speeches come more and more under the influence of specific situations and therefore show on the whole a degeneration of the *logos* under the influence of war and suffering. Space does not permit a full discussion of these speeches and I shall confine myself to a rapid survey by grouping a few of them under certain headings.

It has often been noted that in the later speeches we find statements on the nature of power which are very similar to the statements found in the first two books. For example, in the Mytilenean debate Cleon defines the Athenian empire as a tyranny, as Pericles had done in his last speech (3.37.2, cf. 2.63.2). The difference, however, does not lie in the definition, but in the context in which it is given. For Cleon departs from the Periclean idea of democratic imperialism by arguing against democratic debate in phrases which, in their stress on *sōphrosynē* and the blind reliance on *nomos*, recall Archidamus rather than Pericles (3.37.3-4, cf. 1.84.2 and 3). Cleon adopts this position merely for the convenience of the moment, for he wants to shut off further discussion of the decision regarding the fate of Mytilene. His position is basically dishonest. Equally false is the position of Diodotus, who speaks in favor of democratic debate merely because he wishes the assembly to change its mind.[23] *His* definition of power is embedded in the

22. Cf. Thuc. 2.65.7 and 10.
23. Differently Stahl, *Thukydides*, pp. 121 ff.

argument that the death penalty cannot act as a deterrent since human nature acts blindly when compelled by strong irrational factors, such as poverty, surfeit of means (*exousia*), and good luck. *Exousia* leads to *pleonexia* and pride (3.45.4). External situations like poverty, resources, and fortune arouse a blind commitment through *elpis* and *erôs* (3.45.5), which reason cannot overcome, whence punishment is futile. The definition of power is here reduced to the aspect of *pleonexia* (*dynamis* is not mentioned in this passage), a reduction caused by the involvement of the speaker with his specific argument. The intellectual attitude of both Cleon and Diodotus is determined by their immediate purposes, and their speeches are essentially dishonest. The two antagonists agree on one point, that no pity must be shown to the Mytileneans. But the reader surely has a gut reaction to the threatening fate of the Mytileneans, as he does also to the fate of the Plataeans and the treatment of the factions in Corcyra. We may call this reaction pity (a quality conspicuously absent in all three compositions), or outrage, but at any rate, Thucydides asks us to apply a common standard of humanity. Within this framework, the *logos* is indeed powerless, and the definitions of power are reduced for the convenience of the speakers.

Another repetition of the Periclean definition of power occurs in the Melian Dialogue, where the idea is much more fully and honestly stated than in the Mytilenean Debate. The Athenians tell the Melians that justice is used only when the power of adversaries is nearly equal; that they are not afraid of the end of their empire; that the hatred of the allies is proof of their power; that both *pleonexia* and security are reasons for conquest; that the rule by the stronger was not invented by them; and that it is not dishonorable to submit to a great city (5.89 ff.). All these statements are repetitions of ideas expressed in the speeches in the first two books, and all but the mention of *pleonexia* are Periclean.[24] But this does not mean that the Athenians are right, and that the Melians with their passionate reliance on hope, the gods, and the Spartans are wrong. The emotion aroused in the reader by the

24. Justice and power: cf. 1.76.2. End of empire: 2.64.3. Hatred of allies: 1.75 ff., 2.63.1–2, etc. *Pleonexia* and security: cf. 1.75–76 (*ôphelia* and *deos*). Rule of stronger: 1.76.2. Submission to a great city: 2.41.3.

fate of the Melians is so strong that we realize the falseness of the Athenian arguments. The Athenians use the philosophy of power politics to destroy a weak and, as Thucydides has it, innocent people.[25] The Melian incident is an example of the misuse of power. This element is even stronger in the speech of Euphemus in Sicily, in which Periclean power politics is used to persuade the Camarineans that Athens does *not* want to subject them (6.82–86).

The analysis of power is thus placed in dramatic situations by which it is distorted and shown to be invalid under the existing circumstances. One such distortion is the misunderstanding of the relation of *tychê* and *dynamis* in Athens during and after the Pylos affair, a relation which Pericles had outlined in his last speech (2.64.1–2). The climax of these misunderstandings is the Sicilian expedition, in which Pericles' policy of moderation was disregarded. Here it is in particular Alcibiades who exaggerates the idea of *polypragmosynê* to such a degree that he declares the state will wear itself out if it is not in *constant* activity (6.18.6). The application to the prevailing situation was of course wrong. Yet this did not mean that Athens was bound to be defeated in Sicily any more than power politics meant that she had to lose the war. It did mean that these policies increased the risks enormously and thus made defeat more likely than Pericles' plans, which had taken *tychê* and the enemy's strength more into account. Power does not inevitably lead to defeat, but in time of war the control of power becomes weakened and defeat becomes ever more likely.[26] The Sicilian disaster closes with a *pathos* statement: "this was the greatest event in this war, and it seems to me the greatest of all Hellenic events of which we hear, the most glorious for the victors and the most disastrous for the vanquished" (7.87.5). The statement no doubt foreshadowed a similar statement that was to come at the end of the whole war, of which we have some reflections in Xenophon's *Hellenica* (2.2.3, 10, 23).

Thus the pathetic element becomes stronger in the course of the *History*. The destruction in these cases is not only physical, but is

25. On the question whether Melos was actually a tributary member of the Athenian empire, see A. W. Gomme, etc., *A Historical Commentary on Thucydides* (Oxford, 1970), 4:156 ff.

26. On historical necessity, see above note 10.

accompanied by the corruption of reason and an excess of passion. In so far as the speeches are meant to represent the intellectual factor, they become less and less reasonable, and the speakers can no longer be said to say *ta deonta* in an objective sense. The subjective element is greater in the speeches during the war than at the beginning. The best example of this deterioration are certain speeches which are spoken in extreme situations of suffering. The speakers give themselves over to false notions and aim at a purely emotional effect. In the speech of the Plataeans before the Spartans as judges (3.53 ff.), the arguments are largely from the past services of the Plataeans to the Panhellenic cause without a real acknowledgment of their actions in the present war. The Melian answers to the Athenian statements in the Melian Dialogue are full of wild speculations which are based on false hopes, as the Athenians do not fail to point out. In his last speech to the troops, Nicias falls back on personal and conventional considerations, which are useless in the circumstances (7.77). The height of absurdity is reached when Nicias modifies a famous saying of Themistocles, and says that men are the city and not walls or ships empty of men (7.77.7, cf. Hdt. 8.61). These speeches express the pathetic element in the *History*; they have little intellectual validity.

I hope that this brief survey of power and *pathos* in some of the speeches has demonstrated that Thucydides' work has indeed a dramatic structure that emanates from the proem with its double emphasis on power and suffering. In this development speeches and narrative express the same basic ideas, namely that power becomes corrupted in the course of war. But certain aspects of the analysis of power appear primarily in the speeches, especially in the first two books. The twin ideas that power can be exercised and controlled by reason, and that the irrational commitment to power is heroic, determine the tragic conception of the work. The *logoi* of the speakers and the *logos* of Thucydides are bound up in a single interpretation. Thucydidean speakers do not give us merely a psychological picture of what was in their minds—although they do this too—nor are the speeches rhetorical exercises that have significance only for the moment in which they are delivered. In Thucydides, rhetoric tells us the truth.

THE SPEECH
OF THE
ATHENIANS AT SPARTA

by A. E. Raubitschek

Concerning the speech of the Athenians at Sparta (1.72–78)
Gomme and de Romilly[1] have already called attention to most of
the questions which have puzzled me and which I should like to
discuss, although I may not be able to answer them. The problems
concern the occasion of the speech, its content, its intention, and
its effect.

The occasion for the presence of the Athenian embassy in Sparta
has not been explained either by Thucydides (1.72) or by any of his
ancient and modern readers. The embassy happened to be there
already and it was concerned with other matters, that is, it was not
sent to reply to the charges made by Sparta's allies. Later, namely
after the allies of the Spartans had departed, the ambassadors

1. A. W. Gomme, *A Historical Commentary on Thucydides* (Oxford, 1945),
1:252. Full discussions of this passage are given by Gomme, pp. 233–46 and 252–
55, E. Schwartz, *Das Geschichtswerk des Thukydides* (Bonn, 1929), pp. 102–16,
J. de Romilly, *Thucydide et l'impérialisme athénien* (Paris, 1947), pp. 205–29,
H.-P. Stahl, *Thukydides: Die Stellung des Menschen im geschichtlichen Prozess*
(Zetemata 40, Munich, 1966), pp. 43–54. Since this manuscript was submitted to
the editor, I have been able, through the kindness of Peter Herrmann, to consult
L. Reich, "Die Rede der Athener in Sparta" (Ph.D. diss., Hamburg University,
1956). It is a good and detailed study which reaches the startling conclusion "dass
die Reden in Sparta, wie wir sie lesen, in Wirklichkeit nie gehalten worden sind,
sondern dass sie eine freie Schöpfung des Thukydides sind, der seine Leser mit der
alêthestatê prophasis des Peloponnesischen Krieges bekannt machen wollte."

of the Athenians returned home after having completed their negotiations.

The authoritative tone of the speech delivered by the Athenian embassy is indicated not only by the words used (which after all may be those of Thucydides) but also by the summary[2] with which the historian introduces the speech and which is bound to be a reasonably accurate account. This means that the Athenians present at Sparta were competent and responsible and could take it upon themselves to state their city's position without fear of repudiation at home or disbelief in Sparta.

My first suggestion is the claim that the Athenian embassy described by Thucydides is the very one which was sent according to Plutarch (*Per.* 30) at the motion of Pericles with the purpose of denouncing the Megarians for having cut down the trees of the "sacred field" between Eleusis and Megara, and of justifying the so-called Megarian Decree which was Athens' reply to the sacrilege.

It has been said[3] that this embassy cannot have taken place so early because the Athenian herald Anthemocritus died or was killed in Megara and the Athenians replied to this alleged criminal act of impiety with the famous decree of Charinus which provided for "two invasions annually" into Megarian territory. It is claimed accordingly that this deterioration of relations between Megara and Athens could not have taken place while negotiations between Sparta and Athens were still going on. This argument ignores the fact that the Athenian charges against the Megarians were religious and not political and therefore not subject to negotiations between Athens and Sparta. The matter had become political when the Athenians passed the so-called Megarian Decree which excluded the Megarians from the Attic markets. To explain the political punishment for a religious offense Pericles evidently asked an embassy to be sent to Megara and Sparta, and it was at this point that the Athenian ambassadors appeared in Sparta, and that Anthemocritus died or was killed in Megara. This time, the Athenian response was unpolitical: "enmity without truce and declaration" (*aspondos kai akēryktos echthra*), "death to any Me-

2. Or preamble, as Westlake names them in his article in this book.
3. W. R. Connor, *American Journal of Philology* 83 (1962):231.

garian found in Attica," and "twice every year" an "invasion" of the Megarid. That this was a demonstration and not war is made clear by the fact that it was to take place twice a year and was not to be announced nor to be concluded by a truce.

There is another link between the speech of the Athenian embassy reported by Thucydides and the decree of Pericles according to which an embassy was sent to Sparta and Megara. Plutarch remarks that the decree contained "a reasonable and humane justification" (*eugnômonos kai philanthrôpou dikaiologias echomenon*) which the herald was to convey. These adjectives seem to be eminently fitted to describe the speech of the Athenians in Sparta. Notice the two main themes: we are worthy to rule and we rule worthily.

To sum up, we may assume that the Athenian embassy which happened to be in Sparta when Sparta's allies made their first accusations against Athens had come at the request of Pericles in order to explain to the Spartans the Megarian Decree, and that this embassy was charged with giving a reasonable and humane justification of Athenian policy.

The next question concerns the relationship of the speech as given by Thucydides in his own words, the preamble (1.72), and the words put by him into the mouth of the embassy (1.73–78).

The purpose of the speech summarized by Thucydides is twofold: not to make a defense against the accusations raised by the cities but to show in general that the Spartans should not quickly make a decision but look at the situation at greater length. In the second place, the Athenians want to show the Spartans their power and to remind the older ones of something they knew and to tell the younger ones something of which they were ignorant; in this way they believed they would persuade both groups to be quiet rather than to make war. One could easily claim that Thucydides' summary of what the Athenians plan on saying does not quite agree with what they do say, or at any rate that the summary does not suggest the kind of speech quoted in direct oration.[4]

This argument may be carried a step further. Gomme already observed[5] that Archidamus' speech seems to ignore completely the

4. See de Romilly, *Thucydide*, pp. 224–27.
5. Gomme, *Commentary on Thuycydides*, 1:252.

preceding speech of the Athenians, and we may add that the speech of Sthenelaïdas refers to it in a peculiar way (1.86.1). The ephor says three things about it: a) they spent a long time praising themselves but did not claim that they did not do harm to our allies and to the Peloponnesus. This criterion, that they did not do harm (*hôs ouk adikousi*), recurs in the Plataean Debate (3.52–54) where the Spartans ask the prisoners "whether they had done anything good for the Spartans and their allies" (3.52.4) which is rephrased by the Plataeans "that they did no harm" (*ouk adikeisthai*, 3.54.2). Evidently, this is a standard argument of the Spartans.

The second point made by the ephor is also interesting: b) if they were noble then fighting against the Medes, but are now bad towards us, they deserve double punishment (*diplasias zêmias*) because they turned out bad having been good. This is exactly what the Thebans tell the Spartans about the Plataeans who had recounted their noble deeds during the Persian Wars (3.67.2). A good record, the Thebans say, ought to help those who are being injured, but for people who behave shamefully it should double their punishment (*diplasias zêmias*). The third point to which Sthenelaïdas replies (1.86.4) occurs also both in the summary (1.72.1) and in the speech itself (1.78.1): take time over your decision; c) let no one tell us how we must make our decision. All these are conventional responses which illustrate the famous remark of Thucydides about his speeches (1.22.1): "as each seemed to me to say *ta deonta* concerning the various circumstances." On the other hand, the next sentence of the speech of Sthenelaïdas is decisive (1.86.5): "vote for war." If he did not say that, Thucydides was lying; but he did say it, and Thucydides refers to this part of the speech with the words (1.22.1) "keeping as close as possible to the entire *gnômê* of what was really said."

The speech of Sthenelaïdas, and perhaps all the speeches of Thucydides, consists of two parts: a) what the man really said which has to be absolutely reliable—"vote for war," b) what Thucydides thought he was rather bound to say—"the Athenians are unreliable hypocrites."

We may now return to the speech of the Athenians and ask whether the summary (1.72) contains what they really said, the speech itself (1.73–78) what they were bound to say. If this is true, the summary contains what Thucydides heard them say (1.22.1, *autos êkousa*) or heard that they said (1.22.1, *emoi apangellousin*) or thought that they really meant (1.22.1, *tôn alêthôs lechthentôn*), namely, a) do not rush making your decision, b) remember or consider how we gained our power and how great it is. The speech itself (1.73–78) should then contain not only these two points, which in a way it does, but also others which the Athenians were bound to make because they represent the view which they had of themselves and especially, to judge from the historical situation, the views held by Pericles. This speech merits, therefore, our closest attention.

The first and the main theme of the speech of the Athenians is the Justification of their Empire: "we do not hold what we possess unreasonably (*apeikotôs*)" they say at the beginning (1.73.1) and "we are worthy (*axioi*) of the empire we hold" they say at the conclusion of their account of their achievements during the Persian Wars (1.75.1). Similarly, Euphemus begins his speech at Camarina, more than fifteen years later, with the same observation (6.82.1). "It is necessary as well to state that we hold the empire reasonably (*eikotôs*)," and he closes his argument concerning the Athenian actions during the Persian Wars with the statement (6.83.1), "therefore we are worthy (*axioi*) to rule."

The similarity between these two statements is so great that one has seen in them two expressions of one and the same attitude without appreciating the contrast between the idealism of the earlier speech and the realism of the later.

This is most clearly shown by the fact that Euphemus disclaims during the Sicilian Expedition what the Athenians assert before the outbreak of the war. "We do not speak in fine phrases (*kalliepoumetha*)" says Euphemus (6.83.2)—echoing the famous words of the Athenians at Melos (5.89). "We are not using fine phrases (*onomata kala*)"—such as "we rule reasonably (*eikotôs*) because we overthrew the barbarian singlehanded" (or "we rule justly [*dikaiôs*] because we put down the Mede," 5.89); but before the beginning of the war, the Athenians in their speech at Sparta used precisely this argument when they said (1.73.4) "we say that at Marathon we alone fought in the forefront against the barbarians," an argument which the Spartans had turned against the Athenians in their speech at Athens before the battle of Plataea (Hdt.8.142.2), "you stirred up this war, when we wanted nothing of it and the contest began for your territory," and which had been first suggested by the closing remarks of Miltiades' speech to Callimachus (Hdt. 6.109.6): "If you come over to my opinion, your country will be free, and the first state in Greece."

Euphemus refuses to use not only the argument based on the glory of Marathon but also the more striking one: we rule "because we risked our lives for the freedom of these men more than for that of all, and for our own." The meaning of this claim becomes clear from a passage in the speech of the Athenians at Sparta (1.73.4–74.3) which culminates in the assertion "therefore we state that we conferred on you no less than we received." The reason why the Athenians dare assert that they did more (they actually say "no less") for the Peloponnesians than for themselves was the fact that Athens had been captured but the Athenians continued to fight for the freedom of those Greeks who had not yet been overrun by the Persians. The full force of this point is made by the Athenians in their remarks closing this first argument (1.74.4): "But if we had yielded to the Mede, like the others, out of fear for our territory, or if we had refused afterwards to embark in our ships (like people already defeated), your naval inferiority would have made a sea fight unnecessary, and the enemy's objectives would have been obtained at leisure." The very same argument is made more forcefully in that famous passage in which Herodotus declares (7.139.5): "If a man should now say that the Athenians were the saviors of Greece, he would not miss the truth." How closely Thucydides follows Herodotus in the very words he uses will be pointed out presently; at the moment it suffices to become aware that Herodotus knows that his argument is liable to envy (*epiphthonon*, 7.139.1) while Euphemus glibly declares, after saying that he would not use the two claims mentioned above (Th. 6.83.2), "all are free from envy (*anepiphthonon*) who provide for their own safety."

It has become clear from this comparison of the speeches of the Athenians in Sparta (1.73–78) and of Euphemus in Camarina (6.82–87) that they represent two different stages in the development of the claim of the Athenians to be entitled to rule: in the first speech the claim is based on virtuous conduct, in the second on power. We notice in passing that in this respect the Euphemus speech agrees with the Athenian position in the Melian Dialogue (5.85–113) and with that of Alcibiades in his two great speeches in Athens (6.16–18) and in Sparta (6.89–92). On the other hand, the speech of the Athenians at Sparta (1.73–78) agrees with the famous praise of Athens which Herodotus must have written about the same time that the Athenians delivered their speech (Hdt. 7.139). The two statements agree not only in sentiment but also in content and may indeed represent the view which the Athenians held of their position in the world on the eve of the outbreak of the Peloponnesian War.

The Athenians, at the beginning of their speech (1.73.2), not unlike Thucydides himself (1.20.1), refuse to talk about the distant past because of the unreliability of mere hearsay. But they consider it necessary to speak of the Persian Wars although the events are well known and bothersome to hear again and again; the Athenians do not admit (as Herodotus does, 7.139.1) that what they have to say may be *epiphthonon*, but they later complain (1.75.1) that they do not deserve to be viewed invidiously (*epiphthonôs diakeisthai*). After Marathon, the famous decision to embark (*esbantes es tas naus pandêmei*) is mentioned (1.73.4) in words recalling the Themistocles Decree (*eisbainein eis tas . . . naus*).[6] The battle of Salamis kept Xerxes from attacking and destroying the individual cities of the Peloponnesus which could not have defended themselves and each other against the great Persian fleet. The same points are made by Herodotus (7.139.3: "taken city by city") and in Herodotus by Mnesiphilus (8.57.2: "they will scatter each to his city"), but the argument is different because Herodotus emphasizes the importance of the Athenian decision neither to flee nor to surrender but to fight. The Athenians speaking at Sparta assert that the fleet was the decisive part of the Greek armed forces (1.74.1), a view already expressed by Themistocles to Eurybiades, Hdt. 8.62.1: "The ships are the decisive factor of the war." They further assert that they made the three most useful contributions to the success of the battle: the largest number of ships (a little

6. R. Meiggs and D. Lewis, *A Selection of Greek Historical Inscriptions* (Oxford, 1971), no. 23, ll. 13–14.

less than half of the four hundred; see Hdt. 8.42–48), the most intelligent general, and the most unflinching enthusiasm; only the first and the third of these three contributions are repeated by Euphemus (6.83.1). The most intelligent (*xynetôtaton*) general, namely Themistocles, is not mentioned either by Euphemus or by Herodotus in his praise of Athens (7.139), although Herodotus later (8.124) reports that Themistocles was acclaimed as most intelligent (*sophôtatos*) and honored by the Spartans on account of his intelligence (*sophiê*) and cleverness (*dexiotês*).[7]

To sum up, the first and major theme of the speech of the Athenians, the Justification of their Empire, is presented in the same spirit as the famous praise of Athens by Herodotus, but the two passages do not directly depend on each other. They represent what Thucydides called (1.22.1) *peri tôn aiei parontôn ta deonta malista eipein* and thus reveal to us the view which the Athenians held of themselves at this important moment of their history.

The second theme of the speech of the Athenians is their claim that they exercise their rule with moderation (1.76.4: *metriazomen*). It should be recalled that Thucydides did not refer to either theme in his own summary of the speech (1.72.1). He says that the Athenians wanted to show the power (*dynamis*) of their city and from this statement one would expect a speech like the one which Pericles is said to have delivered later (1.140–144). Instead, to use the summary given by the Athenians themselves (1.73.1), they say "we want to make clear that we do not hold what we possess unreasonably, and that our city is noteworthy." Not a word about *dynamis* here! The two themes, however, are well defined, first the justification of empire, which has already been discussed, and secondly the claim that Athens is noteworthy (*axia logou*).[8]

This difference between Thucydides' own summary, in which the *dynamis* is emphasized, and the speech itself with its strong stress on the *axion* is the more striking because of the repeated statement made by Thucydides that the Spartans entered the war "because they were afraid the power of the Athenians would grow" (*epi meizon dynêthôsin*, 1.88), and that the truest cause of the war was that "the Athenians were becoming great" (1.23.6). Perhaps

7. See de Romilly, *Thucydide*, pp. 207–9.
8. De Romilly noted this contrast, ibid., pp. 224–29.

we should connect *alêthestatê prophasis* (1.23.6) and *tôn alêthôs lechthentôn* (1.22.1) and assume that what was "really" said was not necessarily actually said. Since Thucydides asserts that the "most true explanation" was "least manifest in word" (*aphanestatê logô*, 1.23.6), it is clear that the difference between *dynamis* and *axion* was consciously employed by the historian as if he wanted to say: the Athenians may have spoken of their merits and their worthiness but they really revealed their *dynamis*, and it was fear of this power which made the Spartans decide on war (1.88). This means that Thucydides expected his reader to recognize and to understand the difference between his estimate of the true intention of the Athenian speech ("to show the power of the city") and the arguments that may have been used by the Athenians ("to reveal the justice of the city"). In closing this argument, we may once more glance briefly at Plutarch's description of the motion made by Pericles which directed an Athenian embassy to proceed to Sparta (*Per.* 30). The embassy was to present a "reasonable and humane justification" of Athenian conduct, and that is exactly what the Athenians accomplished in their speech at Sparta.

Considering now more carefully the way in which the Athenians developed the second theme of their speech (1.75–77), we are struck at once by the fact that they cover the same period which Thucydides described in great detail immediately following his account of the conference at Sparta, in his famous Pentecontaetia (1.89–117). We shall therefore be first concerned with the agreement and the differences between the speech and the narrative of the historian. There is, to start with, full agreement between Thucydides (1.94–96.1) and the Athenians (1.75.1–2) concerning the manner in which Athens took over the command of the Greeks after the departure of Pausanias: *ou biasamenoi*, "not forcing" (1.75.2) corresponds to *hekontôn*, "willing" (1.96.1). The name of Pausanias is not mentioned by the Athenians although Thucydides gives as reason for the take-over "the hatred of Pausanias" (1.96.1) and tells later in detail (1.128–135) the story of the misfortune of Pausanias. The following account of the development of the command is both novel and at variance with the story told by Thucydides himself: the Athenians declare that they were forced (1.75.3) by fear, honor, advantage (*hypo deous, epeita kai timês, hysteron kai óphelias*) to increase their power. The precise Greek words which are used merit close attention because they are not easy to understand and have been misunderstood by the commentators.[9] There has been reluctance to accept the three "causes" which led to the development of Athenian power as more or less clearly defined chronological stages and to assume that it was first fear (presumably of the Persians and their possible retaliation), then the desire for honor and prestige (being at the head of a great alliance such as Greece had never seen before), and finally the economic advantage (which came from the accumulation of the tribute and other imperial income) which led the Athenians on to ever greater power and preeminence. The reluctance to accept this interpretation is derived from passages in the work of Thucydides himself. In the first place, in the very same speech, the Athenians reverse the order of the causes and assert (1.76.2) that they were overcome by honor, fear, and advantage (*timês kai deous kai óphelias*) and during the Sicilian Expedition, the Athenian Euphemus declares at Camarina (6.83.4) that the Athenians admit to holding the command because of fear (*dia deos*)—this fear surely does not apply to the Persians. It is thought, therefore, that the three causes were meant to be operative during the whole period, and this interpretation was encouraged by the disassociation of *to próton* from *epeita* and *hysteron*, but above all because the narrative of the Pentecontaetia as given by Thucydides does not contain or even suggest two internal divisions which would produce a period during which the Athenians acted out of fear of Persian counterattacks, another period during which Athens enjoyed the prestige of leadership of a great alliance, and a third period during which advantage (perhaps mutual advantage) held the alliance and the empire together. And yet, the mere mention of such periods makes it possible to identify them within the course of events described by Thucydides. The first period comes to an end with the battle at the river Eurymedon which brings the "Persian Wars" as such to a conclusion (1.100.1) and after which only the Egyptian Expedition and, not independent of it, Cimon's last campaign in Cyprus occurred (1.104; 109–110; 112.1–4), neither of which was dictated or caused by fear. The second period begins with the revolt of

9. See, however, Stahl, *Thukydides*, p. 47.

Thasos which, in contrast to the revolts of Naxos and Carystos, had nothing to do with the pursuit of the Persian Wars, and this period comes to an end with an event which Thucydides did not mention but which falls between the death of Cimon (1.112.4) and the battle of Coronea (1.113), namely the transfer of the Treasury of the League from Delos to Athens which made the empire for the first time profitable to the Athenians. It seems, therefore, reasonable to suppose that the Athenians refer in fact to three periods during which they increased and maintained their power, namely the War against Persia, the control over virtually all of Greece (except the Southern Peloponnesus), and the economic organization and centralization (if not unification) of the Aegean area (as known from the Tribute Lists and Documents). Since this is evidently not the concept which Thucydides himself presented in his account of the Pentecontaetia, it must be a view held by others, possibly including Pericles himself.

The next sentence introduces a new consideration which is so directly connected with the concept of advantage (*ôphelia*) that some editors attach it to the preceding argument. "Furthermore, it did not seem safe" say the Athenians (1.75.4), "that people hated by the majority (sc. of the allies), after some had even already revolted and had been struck down, when you were no longer friendly in the same way (as before) but suspicious and at odds (with us), that such people (namely we) should run the risk of letting them (i.e., the allies, or it, i.e., the empire) go." This clumsy but literal translation is to make clear that the Athenians do not refer here to the situation before the outbreak of the Peloponnesian War, but to an earlier moment when the question of dissolving the alliance actually must have come up. This is indicated by the imperfect *edokei*, by the reference to some revolts which had been crushed (Thasos and Euboea, 1.100–101 and 114) while relations with the Spartans were strained and the revolting allies (if permitted to secede) would turn to the Spartans. Since none of this happened during the Thirty Years Peace (as shown clearly during the revolt of Samos), it appears that the Athenians explained why they could not dissolve the alliance when it had fulfilled its original purpose: it was of advantage (*ôphelia*) to them to keep it and it was unsafe (*ouk asphales*) to give it up. The Athenians conclude that nobody can blame people who look to their own advantage when they are in great danger. It may be that Plutarch (*Per.* 17.1) refers to the same situation when he reports that before Pericles moved the Congress Decree (i.e., before the transfer of the Treasury) "the Lacedaemonians began to be offended by the increase in power of the Athenians."

The following chapter (1.76) gives the explanation and the justification of the observations which have just been discussed (1.75) and which certainly convey a note of apology: we were forced (*katênankasthêmen*) to acquire and increase our power, and it was not safe for us to give it up. Moreover, you Spartans do the same in the Peloponnesus, and you would have done the same in Greece if you had kept the command (1.76.1). Thus what we are doing is perfectly natural and in line with the universal law which affirms that the weaker is constrained by the stronger (1.76. 2). In fact, we think this to be a justified attitude and you thought so, too, until you discovered that it was advantageous to use the argument of righteousness (*tô dikaiô logô*) which has never kept anybody from making use of his power if he had any (1.76.3).

Professor Andrewes has called our attention to the fact that the doctrine here announced is characteristic of Thucydides and that the historian subscribed to it himself.[10] He pointed out, moreover, that "the Athenians' statement at Sparta goes far beyond any topical need to answer the Corinthians or advise the Spartans." Actually, this was not the intention of the Athenians nor did they identify themselves with this rather sophistic point of view which they do make their own after the Peace of Nicias and especially in the Melian Dialogue. What the Athenians here (1.76) really say is not "that might is an inescapable fact, however little we like or approve of it" (Andrewes) but that although this is so we are people worthy to be praised because while being so human as to exercise power we are more just than our power would require (*dikaioteroi ê kata tên hyparchousan dynamin*, 1.76.3). In fact, we believe that if others were to take our place they would show whether or not we are acting moderately (*metriazomen*). This argument of the Athenians reveals clearly that their claim to be

10. *Proceedings of the Cambridge Philosophical Society* 186, n.s. 6 (1960), pp. 5–6: empire as a fact of nature. See, however, Stahl, *Thukydides*, p. 50.

noteworthy (1.73.1) does not rest on the justification of their power but on the moderate use they have made of it.

Unfortunately this moderation has brought the Athenians not praise but ill repute; the one would have been deserved, the other is unfair (1.76.4). What follows is a demonstration rather than an example of this observation, as Geoffrey de Ste. Croix has shown convincingly.[11]

The area in which the Athenians chose to demonstrate their moderation is the administration of justice as a whole and not only the conduct of commercial cases, as has sometimes been thought. We would expect that political, military, economic, and financial control were issues of far greater importance than the administration of justice, but we must realize that in civilized society, then as now, the settlement of disputes of whatever kind is the mark of good government, depending on whether force (*biazesthai*) or arbitration (*dikazesthai*, 1.77.2) is employed. This means that the Athenians identify the essential issue and argue it on principle—without using any details. To be sure, both the author of the "Constitution of the Athenians" preserved among the works of Xenophon[12] and Aristophanes, especially in the *Wasps*, show clearly that the Athenian love of court trials had not gone unnoticed, and Professor Turner has commented on the meaning of *philodikein* as it occurs in the speech of the Athenians (1.77.1) and elsewhere.[13] It is, therefore, natural and justified that the Athenians should complain that they are thought to be litigious if they substitute the use of law for the use of force. "If in lowering ourselves, we arrange for trials under treaty provisions in cases against our allies and on the basis of legal equality in our own courts—we are called litigious." This translation of 1.77.1 differs from that offered by Geoffrey de Ste. Croix[14] in considering the two phrases *en tais xymbolaiais . . . dikais* and *par' hêmin . . . nomois* as parallel so that the Athenians point out that in accepting treaty provisions with the weaker allies they are lowering themselves (*elassoumenoi*) and they are in fact doing the same by treating their weaker allies according to the

11. *Classical Quarterly* 55, n.s. 11 (1961):95–100.
12. [Xenophon], *Resp. Ath.* 1.16; H. Frisch refers in his commentary (p. 223) to Thucydides 1.77.
13. *Classical Review* 60 (1946):5–7.
14. *Classical Quarterly*, p. 99.

same laws as themselves when they come to Athens. Justice, as the Athenians proclaim at Melos (5.89), is determined on the basis of equal necessity but the superior do what they can and the weak yield. If the Athenians had acted before the outbreak of the Peloponnesian War according to this principle, there would and could have been neither treaties nor legal equality (*homoioi nomoi*) in any dealings between them and their allies. But in fact the Athenians lowered themselves, they made themselves weaker in order to treat with their weaker allies on the basis of equality (*apo tou isou*, 1.77.3 and 4). Instead of being praised for this moderation, they are hated by those whom they treat justly, and they are attacked by others.

This point which is succinctly stated in one sentence (1.77.1) is then elaborated rather extensively in the following paragraph. Other people exercising power elsewhere behave less moderately towards their subjects than we do, but nobody criticizes them. For if one uses force, one does not have to administer justice, too (1.77.2). Our allies are used to just treatment and therefore they complain whenever they are dissatisfied with their position or our decisions. But, of course, they would have to admit that the weaker has to yield to the stronger (1.77.3). People are more enraged if they are treated unjustly than if violence is done to them. In the first case, an equal is thought to have taken advantage of them, in the latter a superior to have forced them (1.77.4). They suffered more under Persian rule and endured it, but our rule seems now to be harsh; rightly so, for present burdens are always heavy to bear (1.77.5). After these general observations, the Athenians turn directly to the Spartans and say (1.77.6): "If you were to put us down and to rule in our stead, you would quickly change the goodwill which you now receive because of the fear of us; just as you showed this when you for a short time held the command against the Persians—you will experience similar things also at the present time. For your legal conventions are quite different from those of others, and moreover none of you who goes abroad either adheres to these conventions or to those current in the rest of Greece."

The question forces itself upon us whether this last argument can have been made before the final defeat and before the establishment of the hated Spartan hegemony, both of which were predicted by the Athenians. Gomme feels that the open reference to Pausanias' conduct "would make the prophecy an easy one"; de Romilly[15] disagrees; I wonder whether Thucydides himself could have expressed this view already during the "Ionian War" of 412 B.C.

To sum up, the Athenians have demonstrated in their speech not only that they have a right to rule according to what we would call the "law of history" but that they exercise their rule moderately and justly in spirit; this argument is much more like that of the Funeral Oration than of the First Pericles Speech or any of the speeches made during the war. It shows Athens at her best, and it gives a true picture of Periclean Athens before the conduct of the war demoralized men, people, and policies.

The peroration (1.78) returns to the main purpose of the speech as it was stated at the beginning both by Thucydides (1.72.1: "do not decide hastily") and by the Athenians (1.73.1: "lest too easily you decide wrongly"). "Take time over your decision," say the Athenians (1.78.1), and it is to this wise counsel that the Spartan ephor Sthenelaïdas angrily replies (1.86.4): "Let nobody tell us that we should take counsel." This repeated use of the word *bouleuomai* calls to our mind the contrast between *euboulia* and *aboulia*, good counsel and bad counsel, which not only the Athenian politicians but also the poets explored, not only Sophocles in the *Antigone* but also Euripides in the *Medea*. Not satisfied with the general advice, the Athenians once more explain in detail what in their opinion should be considered by the Spartans: do not be persuaded by other people's opinions and accusations; in turn, Sthenelaïdas urges the opposite course of action (1.86), and Thucydides himself admits that to a certain extent the Lacedaemonians were persuaded by the argument made by their allies when they declared that the treaty had been broken (1.88). Secondly, the Athenians point to the unpredictability (*ho paralogos*) of war, an argument which Gomme calls "a commonplace in Thucydides." It certainly is not a view attributed by Thucydides to Pericles. Not only does Pericles not mention it in his First Speech which is a call to war, but he implicitly denies it in his last speech when he says (2.64.1) that the Plague was an event which went beyond

15. De Romilly, *Thucydide*, pp. 221–23.

what was expected and that it was the only thing which went beyond expectation. In fact, Thucydides praises the foresight (*pronoia*) of Pericles with regard to the war (2.65.6). Evidently, the Athenians in their speech at Sparta are made to emphasize the uncertainty and unpredictability of war, either because they really thought so (and thus disagreed with Pericles) or because they want the Spartans to think so and to avoid war.

Finally, the Athenians put forth the paradox of war (1.78.3): in war you act first and think afterwards when you have suffered misfortune. Therefore, the Athenians imply, think first and you won't vote for war. But we are not caught in any such mistake, conclude the Athenians (1.78.4), and when we say "we" we mean not only ourselves but, as far as we can see, you, too. And we say unto you, do not dissolve the treaty as long as we both are still free to choose good counsel (*euboulia*), do not break the oaths, but resolve differences by arbitration according to the agreement. This attitude was still maintained by Pericles in the beginning of his First Speech (1.140.2) when he says that it had been agreed that differences should be settled by arbitration and at the end when he reaffirms (1.144.2) his willingness to arbitrate according to the treaty. Pericles adds, "we shall not start the war but resist those who do" (*archomenous de amynoumetha*); the Athenians at Sparta say virtually the same thing as a parting shot. "Taking the Gods by whom we have sworn the oaths as our witnesses, we shall try to defend ourselves against you if you start the war (*amynesthai polemou archontas*), and we shall do this wherever you choose to act."[16]

The two main questions, then, are: Did the Athenians deliver a speech and what did they say? Was the speech which is attributed to them provocative and was it meant to be provocative? The first question has been answered by Kagan with disarming candor: "if we are to deny his simplest statement of fact, we must give up any hope of dealing with the history he purports to describe."[17] When it comes to the question what the Athenians ac-

16. See the remarks on this and similar "stings in the tail" by H. D. Westlake, *Greek, Roman, and Byzantine Studies* 12 (1971):500.

17. D. Kagan, *The Outbreak of the Peloponnesian War* (Ithaca, N.Y., 1969), pp. 293–300, esp. p. 293. See, however, the opposite view expressed by Schwartz, *Geschichtswerk des Thukydides*, p. 105, and by Stahl, *Thukydides*, p. 43.

tually said, we have to decide between Thucydides' summary of the speech and the speech quoted by him; the former adhered as closely as possible to what was "really" said and what was understood by the Spartans; this means that the Athenians conveyed by their speech the greatness of their power while they actually used arguments based on their virtue and moderation. Thus the speech itself contained what the Athenians actually said and what Thucydides thought the situation demanded of them to say. To answer the second question, the speech was provocative to the Spartans but it was not meant by the Athenians to be provocative, and Thucydides makes this difference clear by emphasizing in his summary that the Athenians displayed their power, in the speech itself that they emphasized their moderation and justice.

The speech of the Athenians at Sparta contains a moral justification of Athenian Democracy. A comparison of the speech of the Athenians at Sparta with the speeches of the Athenian generals at Melos and of Euphemus at Camarina shows clearly the difference between the cynicism of an Alcibiades and the idealism of a Pericles. This means that we possess in the speech of the Athenians at Sparta an authentic statement on the glory and virtue of the Athenian Empire in the days of Pericles.

THE PARTICULAR
AND THE UNIVERSAL
IN THE
SPEECHES IN THUCYDIDES

WITH SPECIAL REFERENCE
TO THAT OF HERMOCRATES
AT GELA

by N. G. L. Hammond

In using the words "particular" and "universal" I am picking up a distinction which I think Thucydides implied in announcing the program for the speeches in his *History* (1.22). "The speeches are written as in my personal judgment each set of speakers would have expressed best the essentials about the circumstances of the time, and I kept as close as possible to the general policy of what was actually said." He contrasted on the one hand the actual words and general sense of the speaker on a particular occasion, and on the other the arguments which, according to Thucydides' own judgment, would have expressed the essentials of the situation—*ta deonta*. These latter arguments, being formulated "according to Thucydides' judgment," certainly included universal statements as well as *ad hoc dicta*; for it was the universal deductions to be made from particular occasions which interested him as a historian. They were the salt of his history. Indeed the ability to draw universal deductions was a mark of the Periclean age. We see the same contrast between the particular and the universal in Sophoclean tragedy. In fact the distinction I am after has been expressed most clearly by Aristotle in the *Poetics*. He contrasted the particular and the universal, *ta kath' hekaston* and *ta katholou*,[1] and he had I think the same contrast in mind when he differentiated speeches in tragedy as being rhetorical or statesmanlike,[2] for the statesman reveals the essentials or the principles of universal application which are provided by analyzing a factual situation, while the rhetorician is concerned to persuade a particular audience at a particular moment. In what follows I wish to place less emphasis on the particular or rhetorical elements and more emphasis on the universal and statesmanlike elements.

My first example is Brasidas' speech in Lyncus (4.126). The particular elements are minimal: the dismay of the deserted Greeks, the yelling and spear-brandishing of the Illyrian savages, and the tactic Brasidas advised of standing firm under attack and of orderly withdrawal as occasion offered. The universal elements are prominent; they are what Brasidas calls *ta megista* (126.1). They are as follows. Prowess in battle is due to *aretê*, itself developed in a society which is free and is not dominated by a military clique. Any unknown opponent is alarming; to learn his true measure is advantageous if he is weaker than he seems but may be disadvantageous if he is stronger than he seems. Free range fighting permits a man to run away; but fighting in a regiment under discipline involves a sense of honor and an obligation to stand one's ground.

Let me recall the occasion of this speech. At dawn Brasidas found his allies departed and the savages about to attack; so he got his motley collection of Greeks hurriedly into battle-order and spoke on the spur of the moment. It is to me inconceivable that Brasidas had had time at dawn to draw such universal conclusions from the particular situation. Rather they are Thucydides' own

1. *Poetics* 1451 B 4–11.
2. *Poetics* 1450 B 7: *hoi men gar archaioi politikôs epoioun legontas, hoi de nun rhêtorikôs.*

contribution of *ta deonta*. That the universal elements far out-weigh the particular elements is due not only to Thucydides' preference for the universal but also to the fact that the actual words of Brasidas could hardly have been obtained by him. For any eyewitness whom Thucydides may have met after his own exile could have had only a vague recollection of what had been said months or years earlier. Thus the speech serves as a model of the extreme instance when Thucydides uses almost complete freedom of composition.

Next the Corcyraean-Corinthian *antilogia* (1.32–43). In this case Thucydides was probably present himself and, if not, he was able to obtain full information at once. Moreover, unlike Brasidas, the envoys spoke to a prepared brief. The Corcyraeans begin with reflections on isolationism which are of universal significance (32.1) and apply them to the particular situation (32.2–5). Thereafter their arguments are particular: the advantage for Athens of making an alliance at the moment (33), the fact that such an alliance is no breach of the current treaty, the reasons of equity and expediency for Athens to favor Corcyra rather than Corinth (34–35), and a summary of the arguments (36). The Corinthians begin by refuting some particular arguments: isolationism in the case of Corcyra, they say, is a cover for malpractice and disloyalty especially at Epidamnus (37–38). They then introduce a statement of universal significance about arbitration: an offer to go to arbitration is sincere if it is matched by fairminded behavior and insincere if it comes after an unscrupulous coup (39.1). This statement is applied to the particular instance at Epidamnus (39.2). Next come particular arguments: the spirit of the current treaty (40.2), the position of Athens and Corinth vis-à-vis their dependents (40.4), Corinth's claims on Athenian gratitude (40.5–41), and a summary of these points and a few minor ones (42–43). In this last part some universal statements are included in support of particular arguments: in the heat of war a state regards any ally as a friend and any opponent as an enemy, regardless of previous relations (41.3); the most expedient policy is one which runs into fewest mistakes (42.2); in dealing with one's equals in power a state is more secure if it avoids aggression than if it seizes a momentary advantage and endangers the future (42.4).

In this debate—or rather in this very concise summary of the
debate—the particular arguments predominate vastly as they doubtless did on the actual occasion. There are relatively few universal
statements. Most of these might have been included at the time
in support of the particular arguments. There is only one universal
statement which to my mind stands out as a leitmotiv. It is at the
beginning of the Corcyraean speech, and embodies the reflections
—perhaps of Thucydides—on isolationism. In my opinion, then,
the report of this debate serves as a model of the extreme instance
when Thucydides reported the general sense of what was actually
said and added relatively little of his own subjective idea of what
was essential (*ta deonta*).

With these two models in mind I turn to the Conference at Gela
in 424 B.C. (4.59–64). According to Thucydides and no doubt in
actuality the conference was concerned mainly with rival claims
(*antilogiai*: 58, 59.4, and 65.1). However, Thucydides gives none
of them; instead, he provides a speech by Hermocrates "who in
fact persuaded them most" (*hosper kai epeise malista autous*,
4.58). How and when did Thucydides obtain information about
this influential speech? No Athenian was present at the Conference in that year, 424 B.C.; the Sicilian theater went dead in effect
for some nine years; and if Thucydides ever visited Sicily in connection with the war it was presumably after the expedition of
415 B.C. to Syracuse. What would his hearers have remembered
then of Hermocrates' speech, which was only one among many?
Mighty little. But, of course, Hermocrates himself would have remembered at least the general sense of what he had said. Did Thucydides know Hermocrates? The answer is almost certainly "yes,"
for the following reasons. Thucydides gives him three long speeches
(4.59–64; 6.33–34; 6.76–80), two reported speeches (6.72.2–5 and
7.21.3–4), and a couple of anecdotes. This is a surprising enough
ration in itself, but the anecdotes are of a peculiar kind. One of
them (7.73) describes with circumstantial detail a conversation
between Hermocrates and the magistrates, and in retailing it Thucydides adds the illuminating comment on Hermocrates that "he
was saying what he really thought" (*legôn tauta ha kai autô edo-*

kei)—a comment due presumably to a remark *post eventum* by Hermocrates. Thucydides then gives the reaction of the magistrates from Hermocrates' viewpoint (73.2), and describes a trick carried out by some of Hermocrates' *hetairoi* which involved communications with the enemy. The other (8.85) describes the relations between Hermocrates and Tissaphernes and the accusations each proposed to make against the other. Now such conversations and accusations might be fictional in Xenophon, but they were vouched for by Thucydides as possessing *akribeia*. It seems well-nigh certain that Thucydides had them from Hermocrates himself. If my supposition is correct, it does not matter much whether Thucydides met Hermocrates in Sicily after September 413 B.C. or in the Aegean after 412 B.C. or as fellow-exiles later in the war. The main point is that Thucydides got the information which underlies Hermocrates' speech of 424 B.C. when ten years and more had passed; that Thucydides composed this speech late in the war and perhaps after he had written Books Six and Seven. In short this speech may be the latest that he composed.

Now the speech itself. After introducing himself Hermocrates begins with a question and an answer of universal significance: "Why do men go to war?" "Not in ignorance of what they are doing, and not in so much fear of its dangers that they will forgo the chance of gaining some advantage or avoiding some loss" (59.2). This generalization is loosely attached to the next generalization: "combatants consider proposals for any armistice only if hostilities are untimely" (59.3). The second generalization is applied to the particular occasion: for while individual states in Sicily have gone to war in the past and may wage war in the future for reasons of individual interest, it should be realized that hostilities are now untimely when Athens is on the sidelines—Athens the arch-imperialist (59.4–60).

Next comes another universal statement: "the invocation of allies should be undertaken only if a state hopes thereby to acquire new territory" (61.1). This is then applied to the particular situation of the moment; for in fact all Siceliotes stand to lose territory because they are divided and Athens is plotting against them. Thus the way to save Sicily is to become reconciled individual with individual and state with state (61.1–2). A topical argument of the day is then introduced, to the effect that racial divisions are not significant in this context because Athens is aiming to acquire the riches of all Sicily. This last point is rather awkwardly demonstrated by instancing Athens' response to the appeal from Leontini's allies who were all of the *same* racial origins as Athens (61.4).

From the mention of Athens' imperialism there arises a universal statement: that imperialism is pardonable because "it is a constant feature of human nature to dominate anyone who yields and to defend oneself against anyone who attacks" (61.5). This universal dogma is not applied. For what follows is the desirability of the Siceliotes' reacting to the common fear of Athens by making an armistice among themselves and excluding Athens, so that the fighting is ended not by fighting but disputes are ended by making peace (61.6–62.1).

Next comes a long passage which contains universal reflections on peace and war (62.2–4)—a passage which is unique, I think, in length and in content among the speeches. Peace is surely preferable to war and more favorable both to the conservation of prosperity and to recuperation after loss. War is a double-edged weapon; for success is not assured to those who have superior might, nor to those who have superior right—indeed in most cases disaster has attended them, so that those who trusted in superior might lost what they had instead of gaining more, and those who trusted in superior right were destroyed instead of gaining justice. The most decisive factor in the outcome of any war is the incalculability of the future. Realization of this can be most beneficial, if it makes us think twice before attacking one another.

In Chapter 63 we are brought back rather abruptly to the particular situation. There are three reasons for ending the present war: the uncharted fear of the unknown, the actual fear of Athens, and the frustration of our individual policies by these two things (viz., the unknowable and Athens' intervention); so let us send Athens packing and come to terms among ourselves, preserving our own independence of action and avoiding dependence on others. We must make concessions to one another, Syracuse included, and not think it humiliating to do so. Here a two-pronged generalization is introduced (64.1): it is folly to injure one's opponents at the cost of greater injury to oneself, and it is folly to suppose in a spirit of contentiousness that one is as much in control of circumstance as one is of one's own planning. This generalization is not applied to the particular case. Hermocrates continues with the policy of the moment. Let us keep Sicily for ourselves and if we are sensible we shall always combine against the outsider and we shall never invite allies or mediators into our island. By so doing we shall be rid of Athens now and maintain our freedom in the future (63–64).

In retrospect the remarkable thing about this speech, as compared with the speeches of the Corcyraeans and the Corinthians, is that the particular arguments occupy so small a part of the whole. These arguments are concerned with the need of the Siceliote states to make concessions to one another and to conclude an armistice, because Athens' presence makes further hostilities dangerous to Sicily as a whole. These particular arguments tie in with the historical narrative: that is with the claims and counterclaims of the Siceliote states (58) and with the concession of Morgantine to Camarina by Syracuse and the dismissal of the Athenians (65). The universal arguments do not tie in with the historical narrative at all. This is the more striking because Thucydides does draw a general lesson from the whole Sicilian affair in 65.4: it is that Athenian ambitions in Sicily were unrealistic, being prompted by a run of unexpected successes (*hê para logon tôn pleonôn eupragia*) which generated optimism, and that in this optimistic mood the people would not tolerate any opposition. The lesson is apposite to the year 424 B.C. and to the Archidamian War: indeed it may be said to be the theme of Book Four.

Moreover, the universal statements seem to be inapposite not only to the occasion of the speech but even to the Archidamian War. (1) "Why do men go to war?" Thucydides had devoted most of Book I to this subject. (2) "Imperialism is pardonable because it is a constant feature of human nature to dominate anyone who yields, just as it is to defend oneself against anyone who attacks." There is a good deal in Books One, Two, and Three about imperialism. But there it is the fruit of merit or of policy, or it is justified by Athens' greatness under Pericles or it is an exercise of authority, which may be a sign of "tyranny" but is dangerous to relinquish. Here the *apologia imperii* is more baldly put than for instance at 1.76.3. (3) "Peace is surely preferable to war and is more favorable to the conservation of prosperity." In the Archidamian War the argument of Pericles and others was that war, not peace, would conserve the prosperity of Athens which rested on her empire, and those arguments appeared to be justified in 424 B.C. It was only after the disaster in Sicily and the revolt of some of her subjects that this generalization about peace became applicable to Athens' prosperity. (4) "War is a double-edged weapon; for success attends neither might nor right, so that in most cases those who started with superior might have lost what they had and those who had superior right were utterly destroyed." In Books One, Two, and Three there is a strong suggestion that an intelligent statesman and an intelligent and enterprising society can predict the outcome of war: Themistocles and Pericles are the specific examples (1.138.3, 1.144.1, 2.13.2 and 9, 2.65.5–7 and 13) and Athens won and expanded her empire "by intelligence more than luck, by enterprise more than power" (*gnômê te pleoni ê tychê kai tolmê meizoni ê dynamei*, 1.144.4). Here this confidence has gone: history has revealed a new truth, that Athens which started with superior might lost even what she had—by 405 B.C. Who had had superior right? Certainly Melos; and the Melians had been utterly destroyed. (5) "The incalculability of the future is the most decisive factor in the outcome of any war." Pericles did not think so in 431 B.C., for he claimed that most things in war depend principally upon policy (*gnômê*) and capital reserves (*periousia chrêmatón*, 2.13.2). In the early books there is a general assumption by Thucydides that intelligence and courage—*gnômê* and *tolma*—play the dominant role. This belief has gone: when did it go? The Archidamian War really justified both the view of Pericles and the general assumption by Thucydides. In the end the Decelean War did not justify either; in fact at critical points it proved the opposite, that the incalculability of the future was decisive—on certain days at Syracuse and on the last day at Aegospotami. (6) "If we realized the incalculability of the future we should think twice before going to war." Perhaps even Pericles had failed to allow for this element in his confident prognosis of success; Thu-

cydides may have become conscious of this in the bitterness of
total defeat. (7) "The folly of fighting on to hurt one's enemy at
greater injury to oneself and the folly of supposing that one is in
control of circumstance (*tychē*)." The truth of this became apparent not only in the events at Syracuse but even more markedly in
the final stages of the Decelean War, when the extreme democrats
fought on and trusted mainly in luck.

The universal views which Thucydides has put in the mouth of
Hermocrates seem to me to give us an insight into Thucydides'
mind when the long war was either nearing an end or at an end.
At the start of the war he began, like Sophocles, with a belief in
man's sovereign reason and courageous enterprise. He saw that
Athens had routed the Medes, created an empire and built the
Periclean state more by reason and enterprise than by chance and
big battalions. He shared the belief of Pericles, which was itself
founded on these very qualities of reason and enterprise, that
Athens would win the greatest war of all time. Indeed, he suggested that this belief held good almost until the war did end in
defeat (2.65.13). Again, like Sophocles, Thucydides was aware of
the unexpected in war as in life, *ho paralogos*, that is, what hap-
pens contrary to one's calculations or expectations; and such unexpected turns produce *peripeteiai*, e.g., at Pylos (*es touto te pe-
riestē hē tychē*, 4.12.3). But the faith of Thucydides that man's
reason and enterprise do prevail in the end persisted for many
years. Consequently it was in that faith that he wrote a history of
the Archidamian War, and what we now have as Book One be-
longed in the main to that period of composition, as I have argued
elsewhere.[3]

Then the war entered upon its second phase. In the years that
followed Thucydides wrote up the Sicilian Expedition, continued
the main account, and revised his earlier history. During this part
of the war his beliefs began to shift. Periclean democracy had perhaps been less fine than it had seemed; there was now more to be
said in favor of the oligarchy of the 5,000 (8.97.2). Periclean faith
in reason and enterprise had perhaps been over-optimistic, even

3. *Classical Quarterly* 34 (1940):149.

illusory; for what proved to dominate the war was not reason and enterprise but the incalculability of the future, the tricks of that dame Fortune, *hê tychê*, who was raised to the position of a deity not by Sophocles but by Euripides. When the mind of Thucydides turned in that direction he began perhaps to doubt the value of the purpose for which he was writing history—the instruction of future generations in these lessons of policy which stem from reason and enterprise; for it was not they but Fortune which controlled the outcome of events. Now he felt less prepared to make logical generalizations and universal statements; so he gave up composing any more speeches. One of the last generalizations which he made may be the one we read in the speech of Hermocrates at Gela: "The incalculability of the future is the most decisive factor in the outcome of any war and if we only realized this we should think twice before attacking one another."

It is tempting to end with a speculation. When did Thucydides realize that intelligence and enterprise were not going to win the war and that Athens was doomed to defeat? In 413 B.C. prospects looked grim to the Athenians at Athens; Thucydides has described their anger, fear, and consternation (8.1.2), and he said that at the moment they despaired of saving themselves. The general expectation in Greece too was that the war would not last long and would end in the defeat of Athens (8.2.1). However, Thucydides does not make any comment of his own on this occasion; he simply lets events belie these expectations. In 411 B.C. prospects looked even grimmer. On the defeat of the Athenian fleet and the loss of Euboea consternation at Athens was even greater: "They received the greatest shock (*ekplêxis*) of all those up to then" (8.96.1). This time Thucydides made his own comments. "Were they not rightly in despair?" (*pôs ouk eikotôs êthumoun?* 8.96.2) "If the Spartans had been more enterprising (*ei tolmêroteroi êsan,* 8.96.4)," they would have brought Athens to her knees then and there. But they were not enterprising at all. The quickness of intelligence and the spirit of enterprise were entirely on the side of the Athenians: for they were *oxeis* and *epicheirêtai* (8.96.5). These comments indicate Thucydides' faith at that time in the power of these qualities to decide the outcome of war. Indeed within a few chapters, just before his history ends, he remarks that the Athenians believed that the situation was now such that victory was possible. Nor can we doubt that he shared that belief as he watched the triumphant career of Alcibiades, that embodiment of intelligence and enterprise.

It was thus only in 406 B.C., when Persia entered the war more vigorously, that fear of ultimate defeat may have stirred again. In 405 B.C. fear became certainty at Aegospotami. The answer then to my question is that only in 405 B.C. did Thucydides realize that intelligence and enterprise were not decisive in the end. It therefore seems to me to follow that it was only in or after 405 B.C. that Thucydides saw as the main determinant of war not these qualities but the incalculability of the future.

What was Thucydides doing circa 404 B.C.? Why did he not write up the events of the years after 411 B.C. and reserve his final views for that part of his history? Modern politics in Greece may remind us of the realities. Thucydides came back to a quisling junta regime and lived through the civil war of 404–403 B.C. Perhaps it was too difficult or too dangerous to write up the period of history after 410 B.C. when Alcibiades was a bone of contention. He may have preferred to turn back and use the Sicilian speech of Hermocrates for the expression of home truths.

SPEECHES AND COURSE
OF EVENTS IN
BOOKS SIX AND SEVEN
OF THUCYDIDES

by Hans-Peter Stahl

Scholarly judgments concerning the relationship of speeches and narrative in Thucydides have changed a great deal. It seems scarcely exaggerated to say that there was a time when interpreters felt that the course of events as told by Thucydides contains not more than the "naked facts," while only the speeches, more or less mouthpieces of the author, can supposedly tell us of the meaning of history, which otherwise would remain mute. Such a concept is as simple as it is false, and it does not contribute to the reputation of our guild that it was held. It disregarded—to single out only one aspect—e.g., the fact that Thucydides often presents pairs of two contradicting speeches (which then cannot both express his opinion, but may both *not* express his opinion), sometimes even up to four speeches on the same problem with as many different viewpoints.

Today, we have learned to be cautious in claiming any single speech for the author's opinion unless our claim is corroborated by a passage, mostly of the narrative, in which Thucydides expressly speaks in his own name. We do not any more, as was once done, see Thucydides as a partisan of Athens' imperial policy (we have learned to hear the voice of Athens' subjects, too, in the *History*), nor do we, as was also once done, simply declare that Pericles' speeches give us the historian's own views and convictions; rather we would carefully separate, e.g., Pericles' admirable logistical planning from his failure to distrust the general instability, physical as well as mental, of human nature. And it is only now that we begin to realize that the apparent homogeneity of style in Thucydides' speeches, which on the surface makes them seem all alike, admits of differences of characters: Alcibiades, for example, uses a more paratactic and comparatively simple way of speech, while his opponent Nicias employs hypotactic constructions to a degree of complication that he has few rivals in the whole *History*.[1]

All this, needless to say but not needless to stress, cannot mean a change on Thucydides' part of the author-reader relationship; for his text has stayed unaltered for more than two thousand years. The change is with us: *we* face a process of learning on *our*, the interpreters' side, a process which allows us to rediscover and appreciate increasingly the richness of aspects and dimensions which Thucydides consciously incorporated into his speeches. Giving up positions which were held in our discipline at an earlier time therefore in this case does not mean impoverishment, but goes together with a broadening of our own horizon.

It may, to turn from speeches to narrative, have been a bitter lesson for historians to learn that their discipline would never be able to achieve that sort of "objectivity" which scientific disciplines at one time allegedly possessed. But we have learned that mere narration of any set of historical facts already implies a subjective element (because presentation includes judgment, evaluation, selection, arrangement, in short: interpretation)—to recognize, I say, the inherent subjective character of any historical narration at the same time allows us, in this field too, to rediscover and appreciate more fully the categories which Thucydides applied for selecting and presenting events. The possible loss of allegedly objective historical knowledge is met by the gain of live aspects which the author Thucydides presents to the literary among his readers.

1. See Daniel P. Tompkins, "Stylistic Characterization in Thucydides: Nicias and Alcibiades," *Yale Classical Studies* 22 (1972):181–214.

Even more: by abandoning any simple mouthpiece-of-the-author theory about the speeches, and, instead, respecting their dramatic setting (i.e., the limited viewpoint of the speakers), we allow the author to be wiser again and less shortsighted than the speakers he created. In fact, we allow him to correct his speakers by his own presentation of the events. This evaluation of the relationship between speeches and course of events is nearly the reversal of the one I outlined at the beginning: not any more elucidation of events by speeches, but, to state it pointedly, elucidation of speeches by the narration of events seems the adequate method of reading Thucydides.

The effect is far-reaching. For example, Thucydides has often been praised for his allegedly scientific attitude towards history, mainly because his speakers often use a scientific, especially medical, approach when analyzing situations and making prognoses on future developments. If however it now turns out that not the speech, but the following narrative may contain Thucydides' last word on a prognostic method or on a speaker's way of handling such a method, then Thucydides does not appear any more a representative, but a critic of that scientific attitude towards history. He becomes for us a historian not only of the history of a war, but specifically of the intellectual history of the parties involved in that war, himself being detached from and not necessarily adhering to such reflections or theories and their applications as he records.

If it has not always been seen that the combination only of speeches and course of events gives us Thucydides' full judgment, it is, I must repeat, *our* fault for having overlooked this complex relationship, not his: *we* had to undergo a process of learning, in order to be able to appreciate Thucydides' high level of art and consciousness. (The same is true—I should like to say in parenthesis—about emotional utterances in speeches and their effects during the future course of events. For the sake of avoiding unnecessary complication, I will treat them too under the heading of intellectual history.)

If indeed it is Thucydides' intention to be, at his highest level, a historian of the *intellectual* history of the Peloponnesian War, then we are of course interested to learn in which terms he chooses to conceive of such an intellectual course of events, and also, which judgments he would like to suggest as his own and final ones to his readers. A procedure which our introductory argument recommends to us allows us to evaluate and elucidate this question in three steps of increasingly broader scope:

(1) The first step is to compare a speaker's reflections on past, present, or future developments with the foregoing or following narrative. Here we are on relatively firm ground and can often definitely show what Thucydides' judgment is of a speaker.

(2) The difficulties lie with the second step: if, on the first level, following Thucydides' leads, we trace single units of action that consist of speech (or speeches) plus events referring to the speech, then we have, for the matter of clarity, dissected the much more complicated and complex body of Thucydides' work, which consists of *many* such units and their *interplay* in action and reaction. Now, on the second level, this interplay becomes our object; here speeches themselves can become events, and the setting of a speech may reveal that the audience understands the message of the speaker in a way other than, or even opposite to what he himself wishes to be his message. The result we can expect from analyzing such a complex texture should by no means be a simple or even reapplicable technical formula of "how to handle history," but a description of the successive moods and reflections of human beings who face the contingencies of war. I have chosen Books Six and Seven for demonstration because their main content, the so-called Sicilian Expedition, offers the advantage of a limited action of relative unity rounded out and formed into a whole by the author himself.

(3) The third step would ideally consist in a comparison between war and war as described by our author. If he does not offer us the description of at least two full-scale wars, we should try to compare as large units as he himself is prepared to compose to confirm the assertion of his program (1.22.4) that he found features in history that are inevitably recurrent according to the condition of man. One of these large-scale units is the Sicilian Expedition as described in Books Six and Seven. To compare it to the other large-scale unit the historian offers us, viz., the whole Peloponnesian War, clearly exceeds the limits of my paper's title. Thus,

we shall have to confine our treatment of step three to a short
outline in the end.

I have drawn out the general part of this paper longer than I
would usually do. I would have wished to proceed inductively,
i.e., go before my listeners' or readers' eyes through all the material
which Thucydides' text offers, and after that only, present my
conclusions. However, that would exceed the limits set to this
paper. Thus I drew out the general part and shall now try to confirm its theses and illustrate its assertions by picking a few characteristic cases from the vast material.

<h2 style="text-align:center">I</h2>

Let us now turn to the first step, the comparison of the speaker's
reflections on historical developments and the actual course of
events itself. For this purpose, I have chosen the speeches of
Alcibiades and Nicias at the beginning of Book Six. A few introductory remarks as to the situation may be helpful: in Sicily, two
cities, Selinus and Segesta, are at war with each other. Selinus has
been successful in calling Syracuse to her help, and the Segestans
now, on their part, turn to Athens for support, using two key
arguments: (a) if Syracuse is allowed to help Selinus, and, further,
is not punished for having depopulated the city of Leontini, she
may soon turn her growing power even against Athens' empire in
central Greece. (b) the Segestans offer "money sufficient for the
war." It is a classic case of escalation, not dissimilar to that over
Epidamnus in Book One, which led to the outbreak of the Peloponnesian War, however, in two steps: first, Corcyra-Corinth,
then Athens-Sparta. In 416 B.C., the Athenians, who do not like to
interfere unless openly invited, are not at all unhappy about the
Segestans' request for help, because they would like to conquer
Sicily anyway. But they are at least cautious enough to send an
embassy to Segesta with orders to check whether the money they
have been offered is really there (6.6). Next spring the envoys
come back with sixty talents of uncoined silver as a month's pay
for sixty Athenian ships and a report "as attractive as it was untrue."[2] The Athenians vote to send out the sixty ships, and five
days later they hold another assembly on the subject of the expe-

2. I use the Crawley translation.

dition's further equipment. Nicias, chosen commander against his will, is concerned about his city and takes the opportunity to ask for reconsideration. Alcibiades, likewise commander of the expedition force, opposes Nicias, largely, as Thucydides himself tells us (6.15), for personal reasons: he hopes to gain personal prestige and to avoid bankruptcy by military victories in Sicily. Nicias, when asked to give his estimate of the equipment necessary, gives another speech and again tries to make the Athenians change their minds, this time by confronting them with his enormously high demands for war material.

These three speeches of the second assembly (6.8–24) supply us with ample material of the kind I have in mind. And the reader quickly realizes that Thucydides himself favors the views of Nicias, whom the Athenians did *not* follow. Nicias, like Thucydides himself in chapter 15, speaks of Alcibiades' personal motivation of prestige and wealth (12.2). Of the money allegedly waiting for them in Sicily, Nicias says: "the sums talked of as ready at Segesta are readier, you may be sure, in talk than in any other way" (22). This utterance directly echoes Thucydides' words about the "report, as attractive as it was untrue . . . in particular as to the money" (8.2). There are direct contradictions between Alcibiades and Nicias. Alcibiades: "The cities in Sicily are peopled by motley rabbles and easily change their institutions" (17.2). Nicias, on the other side: "We are going against cities that are great and are not subject to one another, or in need of change . . ." (20.2). Nicias even makes a prediction on their probable behavior (using the technical term *eikotós*). Again Alcibiades: "From a mob like this you need not look for either unanimity in council or concert in action" (17.4). He, too, ventures a prediction here on their probable (*eikos*) behavior. Nicias, however, expressly considering the possibility "if the cities should take alarm and combine . . ." (21.1) will, two years from now, turn out to be right when, in a letter from Sicily, he tells the Athenians, "a general Sicilian coalition is formed against us" (7.15.1), thus bitterly disproving Alcibiades from the later course of events. Even more ghostly in the light of later events appears Alcibiades' haughty assertion, "The faculty of staying if successful, or of returning, will be secured to us by our navy, as we shall be superior at sea to all the Sicilians put together"

(6.18.5). Nicias however in that same letter from Sicily will have to write: "the length of time we have now been in commission has rotted our ships and wasted our crews . . ." (7.12.3).

There can be no doubt, I believe: only the *combination* of speech and course of events can give us the full impact of Thucydides' judgment—or of his condemnation.

What I have done so far has been to compare two or three passages in each case. But I would like in one case at least to follow up more fully the development from speech to result, so that I can show more clearly Thucydides' method of presentation. Of Nicias' concerns I have mentioned so far Alcibiades' irresponsibility, the expedition's lack of money, a combined defense action of the Sicilian cities, the inner (and democratic!) stability of the main cities. I come now to some very solid worries, which will later turn out to be of decisive importance: besides money, Nicias several times mentions the difficulty of supplies and supply lines for a foreign army in Sicily, and, above all and over and over again, the danger that will come from the Syracusan cavalry: here he actually talks in terms of defense (*amynesthai hippikon*, 6.21.1; *pros to ekeinōn hippikon antechein*, 22.1), and not at all in terms of conquest! He demands archers and slingers against the enemies' horse and contemplates the difficulty of supplying horses for his own army in Sicily. Later, in the catalogue of the Athenian force, as it crosses from Corcyra to Southern Italy, Thucydides lists the thousands of men and the vast supplies that sail. At the end he mentions the smallest number of all: "and one horse transport carrying thirty horses" (6.43). Author's irony by "no-comment" method? Before the first full-sized battle in Sicily, Thucydides lists among the dispositions on the side of the Syracusans: "the cavalry was posted on the right, full twelve hundred strong" (6.67.2). The Athenians have, it is true, received some horses from Segesta in the meantime (6.62.3), so that the relation is not quite like twelve hundred to thirty, i.e., forty to one. But indeed, no comment could be more sobering than the naked numbers.

A similarly unwelcome justification of Nicias' speech by ensuing experience deals with *money*: before the expeditionary force leaves Corcyra for Italy and Sicily (and before Thucydides gives that summarizing catalogue of their strength which I mentioned above), the commanders send three ships ahead to gather information (6.42.2). When the bulk of the expeditionary force has arrived in Italy, the Athenians, before even considering action in Sicily, "wait for the ships sent on to come back from Segesta, in order to know whether there was really the money mentioned by the messengers at Athens" (6.44.4)—a clear reference to Thucydides' own remark (6.8.2) on the "report as attractive as it was untrue." When the three ships come and bring the news that there is only a ridiculously small sum at Segesta, Thucydides remarks, "If Nicias was prepared for the news from Segesta, his two colleagues (Alcibiades and Lamachos) were taken completely by surprise" (36.2). Nicias was "prepared": an undisputable justification of his statement in 6.22 that the money was readier in talk than in any other way. And by thus honoring Nicias Thucydides implicitly exposes Alcibiades (and those who voted for his plan). The immense Athenian force, instead of capturing Syracuse, now moves along the northern coast of Sicily to Segesta to fetch that small sum of money (30 talents in all) and on the way captures Hykkara, in order to sell the inhabitants as slaves (6.62). Cash amount: 120 talents. War begins to show its true face.

I return from money to the question of horses. The summer is gone, and so is the element of surprise. In the winter of 415 to 414, the Athenians are constantly insulted by the Syracusan horsemen, who ride up to their camp at Catana and ask whether the Athenians have come for a settlement or a military success (6.63.3). The Athenian generals *have* to react, and *do* react, by luring the Syracusans and their horse away from Syracuse to the north, and by sailing themselves at nighttime (at nighttime!) around to capture a place (the Olympieion) for a camp south of Syracuse (65). The Syracusans, coming back home, accept a battle and are defeated except—in accordance with Nicias' warning before fighting starts (68.3)—for their cavalry, which restrains the Athenians from completing their victory by pursuing the Syracusan troops (70.3). The day after the battle the Athenians even leave the scene and sail back to Catana: "it was now winter; and it did not seem possible for the moment to carry on the war before Syracuse, until *horse* should have been sent for from Athens and levied among the allies in Sicily—to do away with their utter inferiority in cavalry—and *money* should have been collected in the country and received from Athens . . . and corn and all other necessaries provided for a campaign in the spring against Syracuse" (71.2). And again (74.2): "meanwhile they sent a galley to Athens for *money* and *cavalry* to join them in the spring." *Money, horse, supplies*: what a sad triumph for Nicias to find the analysis he gave at Athens so thoroughly justified by the later course of events, even to the point which he had hoped to avoid, viz., that he would have to ask for reinforcements. But it becomes worse still before spring. Not only do the Syracusans build new fortifications to their city, but they even march to Catana and "set fire to the tents and encampment of the Athenians" (75.2), while the Athenians themselves had left their camp and retired into winter quarters. Clearly, the Syracusan *attack* on the Athenian camp indicates a change in the power situation in Sicily: the large Athenian force, superior in the beginning of the summer, is now reduced to a power equal to that of Syracuse, and this change is largely due to the Athenians' lack of money and horses.

The change from initial superiority of Athens and initial inferiority of Syracuse to equality and balance of power between the two indicates a new phase of the Sicilian War. Thucydides marks this moment of indecision, when the pendulum might swing to either side, by an assembly in Camarina (75–88) and a pair of speeches by the Syracusan politician Hermocrates and the Athenian envoy Euphemus: both speakers want to upset the equilibrium, by winning over Camarina as an ally, and both, lacking at present the power of forcing Camarina, take recourse to skillful argumentation. Both lie, of course, according to their respective expediency. But both may also tell the truth, where the truth seems useful to their intentions. But the meeting at Camarina clearly is part of the intellectual history of the Sicilian war and should, if at all, be treated in the next section of my paper. I will end for now my observations on Nicias' speeches and the ensuing facts with just a few remarks.

We all know how devastating the effect of the Syracusan cavalry is in the later stages of the war, when the encircled Athenian soldiers cannot even go and get water without being attacked by the horsemen, or in the final stage when they try to get away from

Syracuse by marching on land, and we also know the decisive role the lack of supplies plays for the Athenians all the time. The horsemen arriving from Athens in the spring of 414 upon Nicias' request are no more than 250, and they come without horses (6.94.4). The highest number Thucydides ever gives for the Athenian cavalry is 650 in all (6.98.1), as compared with 1200 Syracusan horses, as we heard earlier. No wonder, therefore, that the relief is transient only and not of any durable effect, so that it could alter decisively some of the other factors involved.

II

In the second step of my argument, I said earlier, I would try to show how Thucydides writes a sort of intellectual (and emotional) history of the parties involved in the Sicilian War. Facts, whether they come expected (as for Nicias the financial plight in Sicily) or unexpected (as the same plight for Nicias' colleagues) are reflected in human minds, often as if in a sort of mirror, and often also distorted. We can, without being dogmatic, distinguish three sections of the Sicilian War: (a) the initial stage when both sides are still at the peak of their strength or are even still increasing it. Correspondingly both sides have great (not to say: wild) hopes for victory. (b) The middle period, marked by a certain balance of power (for example, when both sides woo Camarina), but by no means stable: changes may occur, e.g., according to the arrival of reinforcements on either side, like that of the Athenian Demosthenes and his fresh troops in the summer of 413 (7.42), or of the Spartan Gylippus at Syracuse (7.2). The corresponding feeling usually is that things have gone out of control and that one must, instead of pursuing the initial program of victory, adapt one's actions to the facts of the day. (c) The final stage, when the dice are really cast and, as the outcome shows, decisive changes no longer occur. This would be after Nicias' decision to comply with the soothsayers and delay the final departure from Sicily for twenty-seven days (7.50.4), or, at the latest, after the final naval victory of the Syracusans in their Great Harbor (7.52-54).

As I have tried to show in this survey and as we all know, there tends to be a correspondence between the state of affairs and the

state of mind of the parties involved. What I wish to bring out into
the open now is Thucydides' technique of making large parts
of the material he presents—facts stated (as we met them in section
I of this paper), events recorded, speeches held—serve the idea of
describing attitudes and ways of thought of the human mind.

Let me start out with a very factual, even dry, passage: the
"digression" as it is sometimes called, at the beginning of Book Six
(6.2–5) on Sicily, its geographical size, its vast population, cities,
history of settlements and colonization, and so on: an impressive
and often admired document of Thucydidean research. But we
understand only part of Thucydides' intentions if we do not regard the setting of the alleged digression: in the sentence immediately before it he introduces to us the Athenians' intention of
conquering *all* of Sicily, adding: "most of them being ignorant of
its size and the number of its inhabitants, Hellenic and barbarian,
and of the fact that they were undertaking a war not much inferior
to that against the Peloponnesians. For," etc. With "for" he introduces the digression, logically speaking: in the chapters on Sicily
he justifies and elaborates on the predicate "ignorant," which he
used for "most of the Athenians" (Nicias, of course, excepted).

Characterizing ignorance by supplying the facts not known
seems to be his method, and not here only. He uses the same device elsewhere: the so-called digression, *Exkurs*, on the alleged
tyrant-killers Harmodius and Aristogeiton (6.54–59) likewise
serves to correct wrong beliefs and explain historical ignorance,
led by which the whole city of Athens was driven into a state of
unjustified frenzy. Similarly, the *pentecontaetia* (1.89–118) serves
to make plausible Sparta's fear of Athens' rising power. Both these
digressions, too, are introduced by *gar*, "for." This is also true of
the catalogue of all the troops involved in the last battle before
Syracuse (7.57–59): certainly a set of facts worth recording for later
generations. But also, it is designed to prove (the introductory
gar serves this purpose) that the Syracusans' present hopes for
everlasting fame are well reasoned, if one considers the size and
variety of the armies participating. Even more: at the same time,
Thucydides throughout the catalogue expressly lists the participants' motives for helping one side or the other, thereby finding
further confirmation of his thesis of 3.82, that violent schoolmaster

War teaches men's minds new concepts. The motives for taking sides before Syracuse are not the traditional ones of right and kinship, by no means, but advantage or force throughout. On this level, a catalogue, being by no means a digression, becomes a summarizing contribution to the intellectual history of the war.

I return to the beginning of Book Six. The Athenians' ignorance about Sicily is grotesque. Thucydides, when writing, of course knew from autopsy about Syracuse's key position in the Mediterranean and the potential of Sicilian cities. (Still today, the archaeological sites of Siracusa or of Agrigento can well rival the size of ancient Athens.) The Athenians could too, if they listened to Herodotus, who (in an important passage in Book Seven) credits Gelo of Syracuse with the power to defeat even Xerxes. But Thucydides has to end his report by stressing again the unknown size: "Such is the list of the peoples, Hellenic and barbarian, inhabiting Sicily, and such the magnitude of the island which the Athenians were now bent upon invading; being ambitious in real truth of conquering *the whole*, although they had also the specious design of succoring their kindred and other allies in the island" (6.6.1, referring to 6.1.1). The setting proves it: ignorance (combined with desire for conquest) is the keynote for understanding the following process of decision-making in Athens (chapters 8–24). Only a few are excepted from that ignorance, among them, of course, Nicias, who (to quote Thucydides' own words) "thought that the state was not well advised, but upon a slight and specious pretext was aspiring to the whole of Sicily, a great matter to achieve" (8.4). Nicias' thoughts here participate in the same wording in which Thucydides expressed his own judgment at the beginning of Book Six. We may say that Thucydides himself felt offended by the Athenians' refusal to follow Nicias. The atmosphere at the time of the decision, however, is not one of sound judgment, but of heat and of calumny: Nicias himself, before speaking against the general enthusiasm, feels the embarrassing compulsion to prove his own honesty first (9.2) and to implore his own contemporaries to display courage: "I ... summon any of the older men ... not to let himself be shamed down, for fear of being thought a coward if he do not vote for war ..." (13.1: he even speaks of "the mad dream of conquest," as Crawley translates *dyserôtas einai tôn apontôn*). In short, Nicias very much uses the same language which the Athenians use in the Melian Dialogue when they warn the Melians, while Alcibiades' speech has much in common with the irrational desires and hopes of the Melians. (In this respect I have corrected my position of former years[3]). We may say that facts and true information do not count, but if we say so our statement implies a new fact: when the unfounded view, that of Alcibiades (I need not repeat again his main arguments, but note that he does not even mention cavalry) prevails, then the *unreal* becomes *real,* because people are going to act out their hopes and desires, and the *real,* like the facts Nicias tells his audience, becomes, at least for some time, *unreal,* because it is simply overlooked. (The great surprise, however, is that the irrational desires might even have been realized successfully: in 6.47–50 Thucydides makes it quite clear that an attack on Syracuse immediately upon the Athenians' arrival in Sicily would give a very real chance for victory, bcause the Syracusans were then shocked by surprise and inadequately prepared. Of course it was a chance, no more. Demosthenes, when bringing the reinforcements for Nicias in 413, tries to correct his predecessors by taking just this chance of surprise. He is defeated, although for other reasons.)

I return to Athens: we may say that the speech of Alcibiades (and of some unnamed others) creates new facts, a new course of events, so overwhelmingly, that existent facts are reinterpreted by his followers. Nicias' large-scale demands for equipment, designed to have a deterring effect, are now taken as supporting Alcibiades' view, namely as a guarantee for safe return, or, psychologically speaking, as silencing any doubts that might still exist unpronounced in the Athenians' hearts (24.1: this chapter alludes five times to the idea of safety). From now on, Thucydides will continuously characterize the Athenians' moods through the language of irrational hope and ignorance as they derive from Alcibiades' arguments; but slowly step by step he will reintroduce the facts of Nicias' speech and confront the Athenians' with them, and each time he will list the Athenians' surprised reaction. In other words, running parallel with the increasing justification of Nicias which

3. See H.-P. Stahl, *Thukydides. Die Stellung des Menschen im geschichtlichen Prozess* (Zetemeta 40, Munich, 1966), p. 160.

I outlined in part one of my paper, we see a process on the side of the blind Athenians of waking up again from mad dream to reality. I can pick out only a few passages for confirmation beginning with stage (a), the initial period of the war.

1. 6.24. The initial mood at the time of decision-making: Nicias' second speech makes the Athenians "more eager than ever." (In passing, I would like to remark that Nicias himself from here on is very much a figure like Cassandra, meeting his fate open-eyed: he knows it, we the onlookers know it, but those with him do not know: three levels of information, and another proof of how intensively Thucydides may speak through devices which he took from tragedy.) The Athenians "fell in love" (*erôs*, recalling Nicias' *dyserôtas einai*) with the enterprise on different levels: the older, the younger, the common soldiery, each having special motives. But "the few that liked it not, feared to be unpatriotic by holding up their hands against it, and so kept quiet"—in spite of Nicias' appeal to show courage. (Let me just hint at a parallel: the open vote plays an important part in Sparta's decision of 432 to begin the Peloponnesian War [1.83.2]. Then, too, the warning of the wise and moderate—*xynetos kai sôphrôn*—as Thucydides describes King Archidamus' reputation, was useless.)

2. 6.31–32: The departure of the expeditionary force from Athens. This scene of splendor doomed to be destroyed has often been admired. The moment of saying goodbye to kindred, sons, friends (all listed) is a very short glance at the truth: "at this moment the danger came more home to them than when they voted for the expedition; although the strength of the armament . . . was a sight that could not but comfort them" (the eyes are closed again quickly). Now follows a "digression" (introduced by *gar*, of course), giving the reason of this confidence: the catalogue of the departing force. However, it is not, as one has sometimes thought, that Thucydides himself admires their strength. He describes much more the money value, the outside appearance, the impression on other Greek cities, even the emotional side: prayers together—not singly, singing of the hymn, sailing out in column, racing to Aegina. But when he compares it to Hagnon's and Pericles' expedition, he mentions, also, their three hundred horse, but cannot mention any horse for the present expedition: comment

through silence? To the attentive reader the realities of Sicily as outlined in Nicias' speeches are present throughout.

3. 6.46, a passage we know already, but not in this dimension: Upon arrival in Sicily the Athenians learn that the money offered them by Segesta does not exist. Except for Nicias, the generals are surprised (they find the facts *alogôtera!*), and—first encounter with reality!—are "not a little disheartened at being thus disappointed at the outset." And it is only now that Thucydides tells us how the Athenian embassy to Segesta had been tricked into believing in the money's existence. To tell the fact of deceit to the reader at the same time he tells of the Athenians' discovery of it helps explain the disappointment, and is another example of the same technique of using facts to characterize human moods and attitudes. "The dupes in question—who had persuaded the rest— were much blamed by the soldiers."

So much from stage (a), the initial period. I leave out here section (b), the middle period of undecided, but often changing warfare, and proceed to give three examples picked from what I would call the final period (c).

First, 7.55. The situation: Demosthenes and the reinforcements he brought from Athens have not only failed when trying a surprise attack on Syracuse, but the whole Athenian navy, attacked by the Syracusan coalition, has lost a decisive battle. The text: "deep, in consequence, was the despondency of the Athenians, and great their disappointment (*ho paralogos*), and greater still their regret (*metamelos*) for having come on the expedition." Here we have the reverse mood from that of 6.24, which led to the decision to go to war. Erôs then is now answered by regret (*metamelos*)— the same happened twice after the chance victory of Pylos ten years earlier—twice elation, twice regret;[4] ignorance is answered by *paralogos* for the participants (for Thucydides, Nicias, the reader, there is no *paralogos*). Clearly Thucydides now complements the intellectual and emotional attitude of the initial phase by describing the mood of the Athenians facing the results of their irrational decision. But he not only complements, he nearly quotes Nicias' words of 6.20 now in 7.55: "these were the only cities that they had yet encountered similar to their own in character (*homoiotropoi—*

4. See ibid., pp. 140 ff., 150 f.

Nicias had used the form *homoiotropôs*), under democracies like themselves, which had ships and horses, and were of considerable magnitude": *hippoi, megethê* (it was *megalai* in 6.20)—the whole outline of Nicias' second speech appears again, even the word *metabolê* is in both places: they had to face the fact that the cities in Sicily could not be weakened by bringing about inner changes —as Nicias had predicted.

There is no doubt at all: Thucydides now measures the Athenian failure by the bushel of Nicias' speech. But Alcibiades' speech, too, is recalled, and his belief in safe return through the navy: "They . . . had now been defeated at sea, where defeat could never have been expected, and were thus plunged deeper in embarrassment than ever" (7.55 end). Thucydides' kind of architecture becomes visible, reaching from speeches at the beginning of Book Six over to near quotation of the same speeches in the face of the events in Book Seven. The speeches are elucidated by the course of events rather than vice versa, as I tried to say earlier.

2. 7.75: The final naval battle has been lost, and the Athenians try to march away from Syracuse on foot. This chapter shows them leaving the camp, their wounded and dead, their lost hopes. Again we find verbal correspondences to another departure, namely that from Athens in 6.31–32 which then too was to be measured against Thucydides' own statements on ignorance and inadequate equipment. One short quotation may suffice: "their disgrace and . . . the universality of their sufferings were . . . felt at the moment a heavy burden, especially when they contrasted the splendor and glory of their setting-out with the humiliation in which it had ended." Splendor versus humiliation, ignorance first versus experience later, irrational desire (*erôs*) versus inescapable suffering, beginning versus ending, dream versus awakening, *speeches versus course of events:* the reader is invited to compare, to follow through the history of human enterprise, to see whether Thucydides' categories are adequate in describing the intellectual history of the war.

One last remark: although ignorance and greediness rule from the beginning, there is no word of moralizing or even triumph because the sober judgment is justified in the end, or something similar. On the contrary, Thucydides follows the Athenian soldiers through even more suffering and torture: he even offers his own voice to make their sorrows known. This is important for understanding him: his outlook is not of the simple kind that the wicked must be punished or the ignorant be taught. In spite of seeing blindness ruling from the beginning, and in spite of not agreeing with the attitude that leads to the expedition, he does not fail to pay tribute to the last terrible situation in which all men are alike. Why? Because, I propose, the Athenians' blindness is not an isolated phenomenon, but indicates a universal (if regrettable) fact about human condition.

3. I have said already that their regret, *metamelos*, is a repetition of a former regret. Similarly, their readiness to close their eyes is repeated when the news of the Sicilian disaster arrives in Athens. Their first reaction: "The truth is not true": they don't believe, even *tois saphôs angellousi* (8.1.1.). But upon recognition (*epeidê de egnôsan*), they turn against the orators who had advocated the expedition, "as if they had not voted for it themselves" (*hôsper ouk autoi psêphisamenoi*). Now they give up hope (*anelpistoi sôthêsesthai*, 8.1.2) as easily as they had grasped it (*euelpides sôthêsesthai*, 6.24.3). The reversal of moods is complete.

III

The third part of my argument, I said, should consist in comparing war and war, as described by Thucydides. I do believe that such a comparison is what he expects from his reader, and that when he calls the Sicilian enterprise a war not much inferior to the war in central Greece, he suggests that we look for recurrent features in both wars. The Sicilian War might even serve to indicate what the end of the Peloponnesian War would have been like had Thucydides described it. Considering the fear and suffering in Athens and Sicily in 413, we might believe that Xenophon, although with inadequate literary means, was not quite off the track when he described Athens' fall in 404 in so passionate terms and, at the same time, made the Athenians think of Athens' former evil deeds (*Hell.* 2.2.3–19). Certainly, Thucydides' presentation of Sparta's final victory and of Athens' fall would have reflected the various analyses and predictions given by the speakers in Books

One and Two. I cannot carry out that proposed large-scale comparison here, because it lies beyond the scope of this paper. But I can indicate how it may confirm the results we gained from Books Six and Seven, thereby taking up hints I gave before. In Book Six the discussion at Athens is nearly duplicated at Syracuse: Nicias' counterpart is Hermocrates, who—we have to imagine the Athenian army to be at sea already at the time of his speech—vainly tries to make the truth known (*legein peri tou epiploy tês alêtheias*, 6.33.1: [a] that they are coming, [b] that they are coming against *all* of Sicily). He is even ridiculed by part of his audience, experiencing a Cassandra situation similar to that of Nicias. His successful opponent argues that an Athenian expedition against Sicily would not be a sensible enterprise, and therefore one which the Athenians cannot in all probability (*eikos*), be credited with. Thus, the truth is untrue, the real is not real—again. Of course, crediting the Athenians with common sense, means, in Thucydides' eyes, a cynical judgment on their irrational vote for the expedition.

The other parallel: when in 432 B.C. the escalation originating from far away Epidamnus finally triggers Sparta's decision for war, the warning speech of the Athenian envoys is outweighed by the Corinthian harangue, and cautious King Archidamus, appealing—like Nicias—to the older generation and their experience of the negative aspects of war, is parodied and mocked at by fiery Sthenelaïdas, who asks his audience to vote by getting up and walking to two different spots: here, too, nobody likes—in Nicias' words—to "be shamed down, for fear of being thought a coward if he do not vote for war." The result: Sparta votes for the Peloponnesian War, and is soon in for surprise, encountering realities which King Archidamus had analyzed to them before. I leave out here the parallels of Pericles and the Athenian side.

If these are the kind of recurrences Thucydides had in mind when he wrote (in 1.22) of things "such and similar to happen again in the future according to the condition of man, *kata to anthrôpinon*,"[5] we can only, with great modesty and embarrassment, say that he has proved to be right, for, by now, more than twenty-three centuries.

5. For the meaning of this phrase, see ibid., pp. 33 ff.

THE "NON-SPEECHES" OF PISANDER IN THUCYDIDES, BOOK EIGHT

by W. James McCoy

It is impossible to discuss the set speeches in Book Eight of Thucydides; there are none. At the same time it would be somewhat frivolous to argue the question of whether or not Thucydides would have included set speeches here or there had he finished his *History*. However appropriate *oratio recta* might seem in a given situation, the fact remains that Thucydides, for whatever reason, did not utilize this technique in Book Eight. Instead, on occasions where speeches were obviously delivered, he resorted to simple narrative or summaries in *oratio obliqua*. Thucydides presumably reports the substance of what a speaker (or speakers) actually said but without extensive elaboration. Among this group of what we might call "non-speeches" are those which Pisander addressed to the Athenian *ecclesia* prior to the establishment of the Four Hundred (specifically, 8.53 and 8.67). It is the purpose of this paper to examine these "non-speeches" in context and setting and in particular to comment on certain underlying political implications derived therefrom which, to my mind, the brevity of Thucydides' account tends to obscure.

First a few comments on Pisander and the beginnings of the conspiracy of the Four Hundred.

Pisander was a leading participant in the conspiratorial movement which engineered the "great Athenian constitution robbery" of 411 B.C. He functioned as the conspirators' "public relations man" (especially before the Athenian *ecclesia*) and played his role with consummate skill. Judging from references in the comic poets,[1] his public career probably dates from the early 420s, and, in spite of the dearth of evidence, he seems to have enjoyed continued prominence until the fall of the Four Hundred. Perhaps he can be identified with the son of Glaucetes of Acharnae; this Pisander was a superintendent of statuary for the Hephaisteon in 421/20[2]— a position which might have depended upon census classification.[3] In any case, Pisander must have possessed at least moderate means since he was surely eligible for inclusion in the so-called Five Thousand.[4] In 415 he was appointed to the board of commissioners (*zētētai*) to investigate the mutilation of the Herms and uncover what was thought to be a subversive plot against the democracy.[5] He next appears with the Athenian fleet at Samos in 412, perhaps as a trierarch.[6]

The fact that Pisander plotted with oligarchs in 411 need not taint his earlier career. On the contrary, he had proven himself a loyal and trusted supporter of the radical democracy—an association which would be most useful for his role in the coup. Perhaps like Hyperbolus and Androcles he had once aspired to be the successor to Cleon as leader of the radical element. If so, his ambitions were crushed when Alcibiades flamboyantly usurped this position. Whatever their relationship in former years, Pisander and Alcibiades went their separate ways as a result of the Herms-Mysteries affair.[7] Alcibiades was openly bitter towards the radical democracy

1. E.g., Hermippus, fr. 9; Eupolis, frs. 31, 181; Aristophanes, fr. 81 in J. M. Edmonds, *Fragments of Attic Comedy* I (Leiden, 1957).

2. *Inscriptiones Graecae* I^2 370.

3. A. G. Woodhead, "Peisander," *American Journal of Philology* 75 (1954):133. In general, I am much indebted to this article.

4. Lysias (7.4) mentions the confiscated property of Pisander. Aristotle (*Ath. Pol.* 32) says that Pisander was a man of good birth (*andrón kai gegenēmenón eu* . . .) which suggests zeugite census if not higher.

5. Andocides 1.36.

6. Woodhead, "Peisander," p. 140; Reincke, s.v. "Peisandros," in Pauly-Wissowa-Kroll, *Real-Encyclopädie der klassischen Altertumswissenschaft* 19, pt. 1 (1937):142. Cf. Nepos (*Alcibiades* 5) who says that Pisander was a general.

7. See D. MacDowell, *Andokides on the Mysteries* (Oxford, 1962), p. 193. Cf. Woodhead, "Peisander," pp. 136 ff.

which condemned him and was not likely to forget the *zététai*, especially Pisander who proposed rewards for incriminating evidence during the course of the inquiry.[8]

We do not know what stand Pisander took on the Sicilian issue, but apparently he was not adversely affected by the disastrous outcome of this campaign. Perhaps, like other Athenians, he then began to question the effectiveness of the radical democracy and to doubt its ability to guide Athens in her current crisis. He might even have recognized the wisdom in the appointment of the board of *probouloi*; then again he might have opted for more stringent limitations. This, of course, is speculative, but it does provide a possible explanation for Pisander's sudden *volte-face* during the winter of 412.

At this time Alcibiades began to communicate with the "most influential men" (*tous dynatôtatous*) among the Athenians stationed at Samos. He said that he wanted to return to Athens and bring with him the friendship of the Persian satrap Tissaphernes if the radical democracy which had banished him was supplanted by an oligarchy. These "influential" men as well as the trierarchs (who together were already contemplating a dissolution of the existing government) quickly took advantage of this unexpected opportunity and sent representatives to confer in person with Alcibiades.[9] Upon their return they formed a conspiracy (*xynômosia*) of "suitable" persons which met in private to examine Alcibiades' proposals more carefully. Despite the objections of the general Phrynichus, the conspirators voted to send Pisander and other ambassadors to Athens to negotiate the return of Alcibiades and the overthrow of the democracy (8.47–49).

Pisander's role in this delicate mission appears to be part of a well-designed plan. His former attachment to the radical democracy coupled with his animosity towards Alcibiades made him the perfect choice (as ironic as it may seem) to send before the Athenian *ecclesia*. It stands to reason that the *ecclesia* would be more

8. Andocides 1.27. K. Dover (Gomme, Andrewes, and Dover, *A Historical Commentary on Thucydides* 4 [Oxford, 1970]:284) comments that Pisander was a zealous *zététés*.

9. G. Busolt, *Griechische Geschichte*[2] 3, pt. 2 (Gotha, 1904):1467, says that Pisander was evidently ("offenbar") a member of this embassy; I disagree.

easily persuaded by someone they believed to be an ardent proponent of the existing government than by an avowed oligarch or someone suspected of oligarchic sympathies. In addition, since the initial success of the conspiracy depended upon Athens' readiness to recall Alcibiades, what better instrument of persuasion than a known antagonist of Alcibiades? If Pisander could convince the Athenians that he was willing to concede a private grudge for a public good, perhaps other opponents of Alcibiades would follow his example.

Pisander's complicity in the conspiracy at this point, however, should not be construed as a deliberate act of treason. Thucydides emphasizes the fact that the conspirators on Samos were resolved to continue the war against Sparta; there was no talk of an immediate end to hostilities either by treaty or surrender.[10] Nevertheless, they were convinced that the war effort would be better accomplished by a change in the Athenian government, and the present possibility of financial aid and alliance with Persia strengthened their convictions. To be sure, Pisander's switch in allegiance was an "opportunistic" move, but it was not yet an unpatriotic one.

Pisander's embassy to Athens is the setting for the first of his "non-speeches" (8.53). The *demos* was called to assembly, but Thucydides implies that Pisander did not at first take part in the proceedings. Instead his fellow envoys made statements in which they summarized many arguments (e.g., no doubt, the present numerical equality of the Peloponnesian navy, the balance of allied states in Sparta's favor, and the bankruptcy of the Athenian treasury),[11] especially the possibility of obtaining an alliance with the Great King and prevailing over the Peloponnesians if Alcibiades were recalled and the radical democracy changed (*mê ton auton tropon dêmokratoumenois*, 8.53.1). Initial reaction was negative, and the enemies of Alcibiades were most vociferous in their opposition.

It was at this point in the meeting that Pisander made his presence felt. He took the objectors aside one by one and spelled

10. This was especially true even after the collapse of the subsequent negotiations with Tissaphernes and Alcibiades (see Th. 8.63.4).

11. Pisander himself mentioned these items when talking privately with objectors (see Th. 8.53.2).

out the reality of the crisis using all the talents of a shrewd lobby-
ist. He forced them to admit that the most important issue at stake
was the security of Athens and that Alcibiades was indispensable
towards this end. He concluded his private conversations by assur-
ing each objector that the price of Alcibiades' assistance was not
all that costly—merely the establishment of a wiser (*sôphrones-
teron*) and more limited (*es oligous mallon*) government in
Athens (8.53.3)—a change which need not be a permanent one if
it was not to the Athenians' liking. Pisander seems to have repeated this line of argument before the entire *ecclesia*. The Athenians, who were in desperate straits, finally yielded but did so con-
ditionally with the expectation of reverting to radical democracy at
a later time (8.54.1).

The tactics of the conspirators were very clever. There was
never a direct public reference to "oligarchy" but rather to a
"change in the democracy." (The same stratagem was employed
at Samos to win over the soldiers and sailors there.[12]) Even Pisander in his *tête à tête* maneuvering made only a guarded reference to "oligarchy" when he urged the temporary substitution of a
modified government in which state offices were entrusted to a
more select group. Yet he was very careful not to say that the
ecclesia, the *dicasteria*, and the *boule*—the bulwarks and foundation
stones of Athenian radical democracy—would cease to function
on a regular basis under this new arrangement.

Thucydides confuses this picture somewhat. He says that the
demos was at first greatly disturbed at the mention of "oligarchy"
(8.54.1), but this opinion was surely based on a complete understanding of the situation and what was to follow. It is clear, however, from Thucydides' own account that the Athenian *demos*
had no such "clear understanding." Neither the envoys nor Pisander told the Athenians that they must set up an "oligarchy" in
order to win the support of the Great King. Instead they carefully
camouflaged their plan in vague and ambiguous terms. The conspirators could not afford an open break with the *demos* at this
time; they had to try to effect a change of government through
legal means.

There was also another reason for using this method of approach.

12. Th. 8.48.2: *kai mê dêmokratoumenôn*. . . .

The reforms alluded to by Pisander were bound to attract the moderates,[13] a faction which was leaderless after the death of Nicias but whose influence seems to have been paramount in the creation of the board of *probouloi* in 413. The moderates, in general, were likely to support limitations on the democracy, and their cooperation at this point was deemed necessary for a successful and peaceful revolution.[14] It was left to silence the noble Eumolpidae and Ceryces (who objected to Alcibiades' return on religious grounds) as well as the leaders of the radicals. This was not too difficult. No Athenian, least of all the radicals, could overlook the fact that Alcibiades was the means of gaining Persian support against Sparta. By playing on their patriotism, Pisander gained a vote approving formal negotiations with Alcibiades and Tissaphernes.

The *ecclesia*, besides agreeing to a temporary change of government, dispatched Pisander and ten others to the court of Tissaphernes at Magnesia in Asia Minor. We are not told who the ten representatives were, nor can we be certain whether they included any or all of the envoys who accompanied Pisander from Samos. We can readily assume, however, that they were acceptable to Pisander and that they were probably men of an "opportunistic" or oligarchic bent because of their later participation in the revolution. Pisander's influence was at its peak; he had gained the public trust. Not only was he instrumental in causing the dismissal of Phrynichus and Scironides as generals of the fleet, but he and his fellow ambassadors were empowered to conduct the negotiations in whatever way seemed best to them.[15]

With the "public" part of his mission accomplished, Pisander, before departing for Magnesia, made private contact with the various oligarchic clubs in Athens (8.54.4). In this quarter he did not need to employ specious arguments, and the true nature of

13. On the role of the moderates in Athenian politics from 413–403 B.C., see my "Theramenes, Thrasybulus and the Athenian Moderates" (Ph.D. diss., Yale University, 1970).

14. W. S. Ferguson, *Cambridge Ancient History* 5 (Cambridge, 1935):323; C. Hignett, *A History of the Athenian Constitution* (Oxford, 1952), p. 272.

15. Th. 8.54.2–3. Busolt, *Griechische Geschichte* 3, pt. 2, p. 1471, n. 1, comments: "Peisandros operierte so geschickt, dass die Uneingeweihten ihn noch für einen Demokraten hielten."

the intrigue must have been openly discussed. The result was a conspiratorial partnership designed to operate on two fronts to effect the overthrow of the Athenian democracy.

The next "non-speech" of Pisander probably occurs in 8.67.1. The setting is the first of two meetings of the *ecclesia* which led directly to the establishment of the Four Hundred. Pisander and five of his fellow ambassadors have just returned from Magnesia, and we might expect them to have made some official report of their embassy. Thucydides, however, mentions no such report and tells us only of a joint resolution (proposed, no doubt, by Pisander himself) calling for the selection of ten plenipotentiary commissioners to draft the laws and to submit to the assembly on an appointed day their recommendations for the best administration of the state. The resolution passed without opposition, and the meeting was presumably adjourned. Thucydides' perfunctory account on this occasion is disappointing and fails to provide sufficient insight into the unusual nature of these proceedings. Pisander, to be sure, was deliberately acting out a legal charade designed to set the stage for the subsequent assembly at Colonus, but the intent of his resolution was more subtle than Thucydides leads us to believe. Some interpolation is necessary. It might be helpful to begin by reviewing the circumstances which prompted Pisander's present tack.

Pisander's embassy to Magnesia had ended in failure. The conference was sabotaged from the start by Alcibiades, and any hope for an Athenian-Persian alliance had to be abandoned, at least temporarily. Logically the ambassadors should have set out at once for Athens; instead they went first to Samos (8.56). Pisander, for one, must have recognized the urgency of the situation. Without Alcibiades, the coup, as planned, was in jeopardy. It was of the utmost importance, therefore, that he and his fellow conspirators on Samos reexamine the matter. If they lost heart, the entire project was surely doomed, and they themselves ran the risk of discovery. If they decided to go ahead with their plans, ultimate success depended upon calculated deception and swift action. Actually the conspirators had little choice except to take a positive stand and devote themselves to the revolution. To this end they sent Pisander and five of his fellow envoys back to Athens to make the final arrangements (8.63.3–64.1).

Pisander must have been somewhat apprehensive when he arrived in Athens. He knew that the *demos* would be inquisitive about his embassy and expect an official report, but to make such a report before consulting with the oligarchs in the city would be foolhardy, especially since he had no idea what had taken place there during his absence. Besides, a public admission of his failure would be detrimental to the coup. Consequently Pisander must have made contact with his fellow conspirators before the assembly in question was convened. Only by a mutual exchange of information and a revised plan of strategy could things have developed the way they did.

Thucydides is silent about the private reflections of the conspirators at this point, but their machinations proved ingenious. So long as they could continue to disguise their true intentions, nothing seemed to stand in the way of a legal and peaceful coup. Even though the matter of the Athenian-Persian alliance was now a dead public issue, they had every reason to proceed with confidence. This was due primarily to the meticulous preparations of the oligarchs in Athens. The demagogue Androcles, the most prominent leader of the radicals, had been secretly murdered (8.65.2). Public propaganda had been circulated which hinted that a government of "not more than five thousand" would replace the existing democracy (8.65.3)—a spurious ploy to assuage moderates, bewilder radicals, and add confusion about the actual number and identity of the conspirators. The Athenians had been deprived of legislative initiative and uninhibited speech since all meetings of the *ecclesia* and the *boule* were strictly supervised by the conspirators and outspoken objectors were liable to immediate assassination (8.66.1–2). This atmosphere of suspicion and fear must have been further enhanced when Pisander arrived in Athens accompanied by foreign hoplites (8.65.1). If all went according to plan, the Athenian coup would be the culmination of a general oligarchic movement which had already been set in motion by Pisander and others in several Athenian subject cities and was even now in progress against the Samian democracy (8.63.4–65.1).

Since the conspirators controlled the assembly Pisander and his fellow envoys could forego any mention of their embassy to Magnesia and concentrate on matters relevant to the coup. They could, in effect, use the *ecclesia* with impunity as the vehicle of legal revolution. The Athenians were now sufficiently "conditioned" not to object or interfere with speakers or agenda at meetings of the *ecclesia* and the *boule*. They might be suspicious of a conspiracy, but they did not know when, how, or if it would take place. Since the conspirators wanted to prolong this state of uncertainty until they were ready to play their hand, they took every precaution against an abortive coup. This seems very apparent when Pisander and his colleagues finally convened the *ecclesia*. As public spokesmen of the conspirators they (or Pisander) proposed only a clever resolution touching upon a matter of common interest to all Athenians, namely, a revision of the constitution. A commission of ten was appointed with full powers to draft the laws and make an official report to the assembly on a fixed day. As mentioned above, this was a device to set up the Colonus meeting, but at the same time it was a "red herring" to keep the *demos* off guard. Thucydides' brief description of this particular assembly fails to emphasize this latter point. Because of his general silence, any reconstruction must be regarded as speculative, but there is no way to appreciate the subtlety of Pisander's resolution simply by following the narrative of Thucydides. I suggest that the crucial explanation is found in Aristotle's *Constitution of Athens* 29.

Aristotle here records a *psephisma* of a certain Pythodorus which provided for the creation of a special board of thirty commissioners (including the ten *probouloi*) for the purpose of framing a new constitution for Athens. It was further stipulated that any Athenian could offer his own suggestions. The committee itself proposed that all measures which they deemed "in the interests of public safety" were to be submitted to the *prytaneis*, who, in turn, "should be" compelled to put them to a vote. The committee's final recommendations (*Ath. Pol.* 29.5), therefore, must have been duly presented to the *prytaneis*, and it is more than likely that they referred them to a special assembly. If this is true, the Athenians must have reached some tentative agreement on a provisional constitution calling for a moderate government of "not less than

5000" to exist in Athens for the duration of the war. There was no mention of a council of 400.

This particular passage of Aristotle has been a source of controversy. Some scholars[16] maintain that Aristotle is here describing the same commission which Thucydides mentions briefly in 8.67.1. They explain away one factual discrepancy in the two accounts by admitting that Thucydides is in error about the number of commissioners (that there were thirty and not ten), but otherwise they debunk Aristotle's information as generally untrustworthy and make no effort to find an independent historical setting for *Ath. Pol.* 29.2–5. To be sure, Aristotle's account of the events leading up to and during the oligarchy of the Four Hundred tends to be confusing and ambiguous, but it is certainly possible in this instance (as other scholars have correctly pointed out[17]) that Aristotle and Thucydides are talking about two different commissions and furthermore that Aristotle's commission is chronologically first.

The activity suggested by *Ath. Pol.* 29 could have taken place soon after Pisander left for Magnesia.[18] It is unlikely that once the Athenians had voted to alter their government they would delay the appointment of a constitutional committee until Pisander returned. It would take time to make a suitable and acceptable revision of a constitution which had been basically the same for a hundred years. Also, if an alliance with Persia materialized, the Athenians would want to be ready to fulfill their part of the agreement. Possibly the Athenians drafted the provisional constitution as

16. E.g., E. Meyer, *Forschungen zur alten Geschichte* 2 (Halle, 1899):416 ff; Hignett, *History of Athenian Constitution*, p. 356. M. Jameson, "Sophocles and the Four Hundred," *Historia* 20 (1971):562–63, is less dogmatic but prefers this interpretation.

17. Especially M. Lang, "The Revolution of the 400," *American Journal of Philology* 69 (1948):272–81. See also Lang, "Revolution of the 400: Chronology and Constitutions," *American Journal of Philology* 87 (1967):176–87; M. O. B. Caspari, "The Revolution of the Four Hundred at Athens," *Journal of Hellenic Studies* 33 (1913):1–5; M. Cary, "Notes on the Revolution of the Four Hundred at Athens," *Journal of Hellenic Studies* 72 (1952):56. I am greatly indebted to Miss Lang for what follows, particularly her discussion of the *two* boards of *syngrapheis*.

18. Miss Lang (*American Journal of Philology* 69 [1948]:275–76) even suggests that the decree of Pythodorus (Aristotle, *Ath. Pol.* 29.2–3) was passed by the same *ecclesia* which Thucydides describes in 8.57.

described by Aristotle and were only waiting for confirmation of
the Athenian-Persian alliance to put it into effect. Perhaps Pisander
told the Athenians that the constitution which they had prepared
was still too democratic to satisfy the Great King. When he moved
the selection of the board of ten commissioners,[19] therefore, perhaps he was proposing a new commission to reexamine the work
of the previous commission of thirty and produce a more restric-
tive constitutional draft. This seems to fit in logically, and if true
it adds a new dimension to the abbreviated account of Thucydides.

The last "non-speech" of Pisander also occurs in 8.67. The setting
is again a meeting of the *ecclesia*, but one unique in Athenian history. It met not on the Pnyx but on the hill of Colonus over a mile
outside Athens. Overawed by the threat of force presented by the
conspirators, the *ecclesia* ratified, without a dissenting vote, a proposal of Pisander which formally established the government of
the Four Hundred. For the first time since Solon, Athens was
ruled by an oligarchy.

The assembly at Colonus, like the previous assembly, was convened by Pisander and five of his colleagues from the Magnesian
embassy. An armed guard of the conspirators was present for the
ostensible purpose of protecting those in attendance from the
Spartans at Decelea but really to inspire fear and intimidation. If
the ten commissioners were prepared to present a constitutional
draft to this assembly, they did not do so. Instead they proposed
the suspension of the *graphê paranomôn* which was exactly what
the conspirators wanted. Pisander immediately stood up and without concealment proceeded to rob the Athenians of their cherished
constitution (8.68.1). They had no means to resist.

Ratification by the *ecclesia* confirmed the Four Hundred as a
legal body, but the new government was only vaguely defined.
Pisander, in the context of his resolution, spoke of the "Five Thousand" as if they already existed (8.67.3), but it was by means of

19. Jameson ("Sophocles and the Four Hundred") argues that this board of ten
(if it was independent of the board of thirty) would have consisted of the ten
probouloi. He bases his statement on passages in Aristotle's *Rhetoric* (especially
3.18.6, where Sophocles admits that *probouloi* as a group voted for the establishment of the Four Hundred). But the *probouloi* could still be considered as having
voted for the Four Hundred at Colonus whether or not they themselves constituted
this board of ten commissioners; Pisander's motion at Colonus passed unopposed.

this deception that the conspirators hoped to de-emphasize and even conceal the narrow and autocratic nature of the oligarchy. This is also a reason why they were prepared to include certain moderates in their number.[20] But no formal constitution was introduced or voted upon at Colonus; the conspirators wanted to delay any such document as long as possible.

At the Colonus assembly, Pisander performed his last act as the conspirators' "public relations man." Despite his former convictions he soon cast his lot with those extreme oligarchs among the Four Hundred who wanted to come to terms with Sparta even at the cost of betraying Athens (8.90.1). When the Four Hundred finally fell, Pisander escaped to Decelea (8.98.1) and is not heard of again. He was probably condemned *in absentia*,[21] and his property and possessions were confiscated.[22] There can be no doubt however, that Pisander played the most critical public role in the revolution of 411. His actions and words—*erga* and *logoi*—(as indicated by these "non-speeches" in Thucydides) temporarily changed the course of Athenian political history.[23]

20. See Th. 8.89.
21. See Lycurgus, *Leocrates* 121.
22. Lysias 7.4.
23. I would like to thank my colleague Professor Henry C. Boren for his helpful suggestions and criticisms during the preliminary stages of this paper.

THE SETTINGS OF
THUCYDIDEAN SPEECHES

by H. D. Westlake

When Thucydides planned his *History* and began to put his plans
into operation, he was, like any other author of a major historical
work, confronted with a whole series of practical problems. It
must not be assumed because the results have impressed posterity
that he found the solution of these problems an easy task. There
is indeed good reason to believe that he did not. In the famous
chapter explaining his methods and aims (1.22) he shows himself
to be fully conscious of some difficulties which the collection and
presentation of historical material entails, though the passage is
not intended to be exhaustive and may be thought to be insuffi-
ciently explicit. A basic point made in this chapter is that *logoi* and
erga are expressly differentiated, and the method to be adopted in
dealing with each of them is separately defined. As soon as Thucydides decided to include speeches in his *History* (this must surely
have been at an early stage, though he did not necessarily write
any speeches till much later), he had to consider how to find a solution to the problem of welding into a coherent whole the two
essential components of his work, narrative and speeches. One
way of approaching the subject would be to consider why Thucydides has chosen to include *oratio recta* versions of some speeches
but not of others which might be deemed to have been no less
significant. I feel, however, that the results of such an investigation would necessarily be speculative and subjective. Accordingly

I shall confine myself to examining a somewhat more tangible aspect of the subject, which must now be defined. Whenever Thucydides reports a political debate and includes a speech or speeches in *oratio recta*, he begins with a passage explaining the circumstances leading to the debate and ends with a passage recording the outcome. To denote the passage at the beginning I shall use the term "preamble," to denote the passage at the end the term "postscript." (The more obvious terms "prologue" and "epilogue" do not seem to me to be appropriate in this context because they are often used of the speeches themselves.) Where Thucydides includes two or more speeches delivered in the same debate, the passages between the speeches normally serve as a preamble to the next speech and do not require a separate definition. The intention of this paper is to study the preambles and postscripts and to consider what may be learned from them, especially the extent to which they follow a uniform pattern and also their relation to the substance of the speeches themselves. My investigation will be confined to political debates in public assemblies or large gatherings of delegates. Exhortations by generals to their troops before battles belong to a different category and are differently handled by Thucydides. He makes use of both military and political speeches largely for the enlightenment of his readers, but clearly military speeches, however inspiring they may have been, can hardly ever have influenced the outcome of battles as decisively as many political speeches influenced the outcome of debates. The investigation will also exclude the epideictic Funeral Speech and the juridical antilogy between the Plataeans and Thebans after the surrender of Plataea.

The most prominent feature of these preambles and postscripts is that they are normally brief, straightforward, and factual, in striking contrast to the complexity of the speeches, where the influence of sophistic thought and rhetoric is frequently so pronounced. Nor does Thucydides normally choose to exploit the dramatic possibilities of the situations before or after each debate was held. Most preambles supply only such information as is necessary to explain why the debate took place. In a considerable number of instances the aims of the speaker are not defined in advance and emerge only from the substance of the speech. Examples are the speeches of Archidamus (1.79.2) and Sthenelaïdas (1.85.3) at the first congress at Sparta, of Pericles immediately before the outbreak of war (1.139.4), and of Hermocrates at Gela (4.58). Sometimes, it is true, no definition of aims is needed because they are easily deducible from the preceding narrative, as in each case where the two successive congresses at Sparta are addressed by Corinthian spokesmen (1.67.5; 1.119). Occasionally the aim of the speaker is stated in a short and not at all informative phrase, as, for example, when Hermocrates makes a speech in the Syracusan assembly "because he thought that he was accurately informed about the situation" (6.32.3). There are, however, some preambles in which Thucydides provides more abundant and more specific information about the aims of the speaker, and some of these will be discussed at a later stage.

The postscripts are somewhat fuller and more complex than the preambles, as might be expected, but few of them are at all detailed. At the conclusion of almost every major debate a vote is taken—the meeting of the Syracusan assembly addressed by Hermocrates and Athenagoras is an exception (6.41.4)—and in all such cases Thucydides reports the majority decision, but often very little else. He may include some comment on the reaction of the audience to the speech, or speeches, and on the division of opinion. He may mention that other speeches were delivered (statements on this point occur also in some preambles). A more important feature of these postscripts is that some of them give reasons for the majority decision, occasionally in detail, whereas others do not. In some cases where no reason is given, Thucydides may have been handicapped by the incompleteness or untrustworthiness of his evidence and may accordingly have been unwilling to commit himself. It is, however, possible to trace a more or less regular pattern governing the inclusion or exclusion of the reasons why the assembly or meeting of delegates reached its decision. Where there is only one speech in *oratio recta* and the proposals of the speaker are accepted, apparently with little or no opposition, the reasons for acceptance are not normally stated. The reader is evidently expected to assume that the case presented by the speaker was considered to be convincing by a substantial majority of the audience. Examples are the reports on the second congress at Sparta addressed by a Corinthian spokesman (1.125.1), on the meeting of delegates at Olympia addressed by one of the envoys from Mytilene (3.15.1), and on the congress at Gela addressed by Hermocrates (4.65.1). Occasionally in cases where a single speech is included the reasons for the acceptance of its recommendations are stated in a few words which do not leave the reader appreciably the wiser. When Pericles advocated the rejection of the Spartan ultimatum shortly before the outbreak of war, the Athenians voted their support of his policy "because they thought that he was giving them the best advice" (1.145). After Alcibiades had delivered his speech at Sparta, the Spartans became much more earnest in their intention to take action to relieve the pressure on Syracuse "because they believed that they had been listening to the man who was most accurately informed" (6.93.1). A more specific explanation is provided of the reasons why the people of Acanthus, after hearing a speech by Brasidas, voted by a majority, which was apparently slender, to revolt from Athens. They are stated to have been influenced partly by the persuasiveness of his arguments (a very unusual reference to the technical quality of a speech) and partly by fears that he would destroy their harvest if they rejected his overtures (4.88.1). Here Thucydides seems to be at pains to make clear that Brasidas did not achieve the first success of his mission through diplomacy alone, despite his diplomatic skill, but also through the presence of armed forces, which, as he threatens in a passage of his speech (4.87.2), might have been used to plunder Acanthian territory.

Where Thucydides provides more elaborate reports on debates which include two or more speeches in *oratio recta* involving conflicts between opposing points of view (*antilogiai*), his postscripts tend to be somewhat more complex. The upshot of such debates was almost invariably that the overall recommendations of one speaker were accepted and those of another were rejected, the only obvious exception being the debate at Camarina where the assembly refused to be won over either by Hermocrates or by the Athenian Euphemus (6.88.2). Where Thucydides gives a full account of the case presented by each of two opposing speakers, he evidently feels himself to be under some obligation to his readers to point to factors which led to the ultimate choice between two very different courses of action. No specific reason is given why the Athenians voted to reject the advice of Cleon and to accept that of Diodotus on the punishment of the Mytileneans (3.49.1), but every other postscript to a report including more than one speech in *oratio recta* offers some explanation of the majority decision. Even in these instances, however, the explanation tends to be quite short. At the end of the lengthy and complex report on the first congress at Sparta, though the postscript is fuller than most, as will be noted later, the reasons why the Spartans decided that the peace had been broken are reported in a few words. Thucydides states that they reached this decision "not so much because they were persuaded by the arguments of their allies as because they were afraid that the Athenians might grow even stronger, seeing that most of Greece was already subject to them" (1.88). This statement sums up his highly personal and original thesis on the causes of the war, which he then seeks to substantiate by his lengthy excursus on the Pentecontaetia (1.89–118). Nevertheless he might have been expected to have analyzed in some detail the immediate reactions of the Spartans to a long and wide-ranging debate, and such an analysis would have been very valuable.

In another case, that of the debate at Athens in 433 on the question whether the Athenians should conclude an alliance with Corcyra, Thucydides explains in greater detail why the Athenians voted as they did (1.44.2–3); but here there were exceptional circumstances which called for a fuller postscript. One unusual feature is that, in order to avoid a flagrant violation of the Thirty Years Peace, the Athenians agreed to conclude with Corcyra not an offensive and defensive alliance (*xymmachia*), as the Corcyreans wished, but only a defensive alliance (*epimachia*). A feature more important to the present investigation is that the Athenian assembly did not vote as soon as it had heard the speeches of the Corcyrean and Corinthian envoys, which Thucydides reports in *oratio recta*; the debate continued for two days, and speeches were made by Athenians which he might also have reported in *oratio recta* but has chosen not to report at all, not even in *oratio obliqua* summaries. Accordingly there is a greater need than usual to explain why the assembly reached its fateful decision to conclude a defensive alliance with Corcyra, though the three factors to which he attributes this decision might indeed be legitimately inferred from the epilogue to his version of the speech by the Corcyrean envoy (1.36.1–3).

Another fairly detailed analysis of popular reaction to speeches by rival ambassadors occurs at the end of the report on the debate at Camarina, which I have already mentioned, where Hermocrates solicits support for Syracuse, Euphemus for Athens (6.88.1–2). The Camarineans are swayed this way and that by conflicting feelings. They are evidently uncertain which side is likely to win, and they are terrified of suffering reprisals if they offend the ultimate victors. In their dilemma they decide to give the same answer to both sides, namely that, because they are allied to two powers at war with each other, they believe the best way of keeping their oaths to be for the present to assist neither. Their state of indecision and anxiety, which causes them to sit so uncomfortably on the fence, is most subtly depicted. The passage provides an instructive illustration of a general trend, since others were at the same time sitting on similar fences elsewhere in Sicily.

This preliminary survey of preambles and postscripts has, I hope, established the general principle that Thucydides normally includes in them only such information and comment as he believes to be essential. There is perhaps some affinity between the factual tone of these passages and that of his reports on minor military operations, in which he seems to be deliberately casting himself in the role of a mere annalist. One reason, though not, I think, the principal reason, may be that he wishes the attention of his readers, when studying his reports on debates, to be concentrated upon the speeches themselves, from which they are expected to derive almost all the instruction that these reports are designed to convey. He might indeed be accused of somewhat unrealistic oversimplification arising from his desire to isolate the basic issues in a debate and to make them as intelligible as possible to his readers. Accounts of deliberations in the fifth and eighth books, where there are no *oratio recta* versions of speeches but only summaries in *oratio obliqua*, suggest that the process whereby decisions were reached on important questions could be very involved, even confused, and that the issues themselves were seldom absolutely clear cut. Reports on two meetings of the military assembly at Samos when the Four Hundred were in control of Athens may be cited as examples (8.76.2–77; 8.81.2–83.2).

I shall now examine in more detail a few reports on debates, mainly because they are not entirely compatible with the principle which I have tried to establish, so that some consideration of their incompatibility seems to be required. First, however, I wish to study one report which does conform to my principle and provides an excellent illustration of it. At the beginning of the Lesbian revolt an embassy is sent from Mytilene to Sparta to appeal for Peloponnesian support (3.4.5–6). The envoys are instructed to present their case at a meeting of delegates held at Olympia after the conclusion of the festival (3.8.1). A spokesman of the embassy then delivers his speech. It is a speech of major importance, which is relevant outside its context because it throws more light than any other on the relations between the Athenians and their allies as envisaged from the allied point of view. The Mytilenean proposals are then accepted, apparently without demur; the Lesbian cities in revolt are admitted to the Spartan alliance; orders are issued for the immediate mobilization of the Peloponnesian League army at the Isthmus, which is to invade Attica and is to be supported by a fleet (3.15.1). This plan eventually miscarries, largely through the aversion of Peloponnesian farmers to military service far from home during the late summer harvest (3.15.2–16.2); but the episode is historically of some significance, not least because it ends in fiasco. Nevertheless Thucydides confines his preamble and postscript to bare essentials, evidently wishing to focus attention upon the speech. One somewhat unusual feature may be noted. When the disillusioned Spartans finally abandon their project, they are stated to have concluded that "what the Lesbians had said was not true" (3.16.2), clearly a reference to a prediction in the speech of the Mytilenean envoy which had proved to be over-optimistic (3.13.3–4). It is not often, as will be seen later, that the narrative of Thucydides refers to a specific passage of a speech.

Among debates presented in an exceptional manner that on the punishment of the Mytileneans may be considered first. Here the most striking difference of presentation is not that the preamble (3.36) and postscript (3.49) are unusually detailed, though the former is considerably fuller than most. In order to try to establish my view on the account of this debate I shall have to summarize it, familiar though it is. I shall be as brief as possible. Thucydides begins with the arrival at Athens of the captives sent by Paches and the decision of the Athenians to execute the entire adult male population of Mytilene. He mentions two factors leading to their decision but supplies no other information about this first meeting of the assembly. A trireme is at once sent to Paches with orders to carry out the sentence, but next day there is a change of feeling, and efforts are made, supported by a majority of the citizens, to have the debate reopened. A second meeting of the assembly is held at which the speeches of Cleon (3.37–40) and Diodotus (3.42–48) reported by Thucydides in his *oratio recta* versions are delivered. The assembly then votes by a narrow majority to accept the recommendation of Diodotus and to rescind the decree condemning all the adult Mytileneans. A second trireme is sent to Paches, and measures are taken, which are described with a wealth of graphic detail, to try to secure that it shall arrive in time to prevent the mass execution. It reaches Mytilene shortly after the arrival of the first trireme when Paches has read his orders but has not yet carried them out. *Para tosouton men hê Mytilênê êlthe kindynou* (3.49.4).

This summary has, I hope, demonstrated that here Thucydides exploits fully and effectively the opportunity for dramatic treatment afforded by the setting of the debate. It is this feature that sharply differentiates his report from others in which he seems deliberately to play down any dramatic element. The tone of the preamble and postscript also contrasts with that of the speeches, which is intellectual, even sophistic, to an extent that might be considered unrealistic, at least so far as that of Cleon is concerned. Consequently the speeches are not in complete harmony with their context.

Another exceptional case, though it is exceptional in a totally different way, is that of the debate at Athens when the Spartans, after concluding a local truce at Pylos, send an embassy to negotiate a general peace and to secure the speedy recovery of their troops cut off on Sphacteria (4.16.3–22). The speech by one of the envoys, which is reported in *oratio recta* (4.17–20), has puzzled modern scholars, but its problems lie mainly outside the scope of this paper. The postscript (4.21–22) begins with a statement that the Spartans, because the Athenians have earlier wished to make peace, expect them to accept the present proposals gladly and to hand over the marooned troops. The Athenians, however, confident that they are in a position to extract very substantial concessions, are incited by Cleon to make demands which, if accepted, will cause the Spartans to sacrifice the interests of their allies. The envoys respond by suggesting that the terms be considered in private session between themselves and Athenian representatives. Cleon then violently denounces them, choosing to interpret their unwillingness to negotiate in public as conclusive evidence of dishonesty. The envoys fear that they may lose face by making concessions in public at the expense of their allies and yet fail to conclude a settlement with the Athenians, who are not disposed to agree to their proposals on reasonable terms. They therefore abandon their mission and return home.

One unusual feature of this postscript is that Thucydides defines in some detail the feelings and motives of the parties involved in the negotiations, especially those of the envoys. He may have chosen to include this information in regard to the envoys because, while he had somehow learned of it from a trustworthy source, it was not at all widely known. Their wholly mistaken forecast that their overtures would be welcomed is not likely to have become common knowledge, and certainly their sentiments on the risk of alienating their allies cannot have been publicly disclosed either at the time or soon afterwards. In neither case is the information easily deducible from the Thucydidean version of the speech by their spokesman, which conceals rather than reveals their real feelings.

A more striking abnormality of this report is that it contains no version in *oratio recta* of what Cleon said, though he evidently spoke twice (4.21.3; 4.22.2) and is seen to have exerted a decisive influence upon the course and outcome of the negotiations. Some scholars have maintained that no report in *oratio recta* on his speech, or speeches, is included because Thucydides disapproved of his policy but shared the views expressed by the Spartan spokesman. It was, however, not the normal practice of Thucydides virtually to suppress opinions which seemed to him to be wrongheaded, or worse, by refraining from including versions in *oratio recta* of speeches in which they were expressed: for example, he reports very fully the speech of Athenagoras at Syracuse and that of Cleon in the debate on the punishment of Mytilene, although it is obvious that he was totally out of sympathy with almost all the views of each speaker. Nor, in my opinion (which cannot be elaborated here), is there any reason to believe that he subscribed to the general principles outlined by the Spartan envoy, much less that they are largely *ta deonta* provided by himself. The Spartan case with its vague offers of lasting friendship has a thoroughly authentic ring and is consistent with the embarrassingly weak position in which the Spartans found themselves. The reason why no speech by Cleon is included here is not at all obvious. Thucydides may have felt that the series of moves and countermoves culminating in the breakdown of the negotiations was more significant than the details of the case presented by Cleon. He may also have thought that the standpoint of Athenian demagogues at this period, which was in his opinion consistently aggressive and not at all subtle, was adequately represented by the speech of Cleon in the report of the debate on the punishmnt of Mytilene. In the account of the second debate on the situation at Pylos (4.27–28) there is again no speech in *oratio recta* by Cleon, although he played the leading part in it. These explanations are, however, admittedly guesses. I often find myself tempted to try to penetrate the mind of Thucydides, but it is a most hazardous undertaking, and if I were wiser, I would doubtless resist the temptation.

Less important than either of the two cases which I have just discussed is a peculiarity which occurs in the postscript to the report on the first congress at Sparta (1.87.1–3). It is, however, sufficiently strange to call for some consideration here. When the ephor Sthenelaïdas has concluded his forthright speech urging the Spartans to go to war, he first puts the issue to the assembly by the customary method, namely acclamation. He then declares that he is unable to judge whether his supporters or his opponents have shouted the louder. He therefore orders the assembly to divide into two groups, the one consisting of those who believe that the peace has been broken, the other of those who believe that it has not. The former group proves to be by far the larger. The intention of the ephor in insisting upon this abnormal procedure, according to Thucydides, is "to make the Spartans more eager to go to war by a clear demonstration of opinion" (1.87.2). Sthenelaïdas evidently calculated that many waverers, and even some favoring the delaying tactics of Archidamus, would lack the courage to allow themselves to be seen voting against the predictably predominant view that the peace had been broken. If he won by a substantial majority, which in fact he did, his case for going to war at once would be much strengthened. Presumably Thucydides has chosen to give a full account of this seemingly rather trivial incident in order to suggest that, since the ephor is seen to have been capable of demagogic subterfuge, the blunt forthrightness of his speech is to be interpreted as a mere pose, adopted because it was the most effective method of securing his object. Thucydides may also have been influenced by the interest which he shared with many other Greeks in the operation of Spartan institutions. At all events, it is surprising that he devotes more attention to the procedure whereby the Spartan decision was reached than to the reason for it, which, as has already been pointed out, he states in a few words.

I shall now turn to an examination of the question whether the preambles and postscripts are closely integrated with the speeches. There seems to me to be some evidence, partly positive and partly negative, that the links between these two elements are somewhat tenuous, as I shall endeavor to show. In some instances a certain lack of harmony is discernible, one of these being the report on the meeting of the Athenian assembly at which Pericles delivers the last of his three speeches reproduced in *oratio recta* by Thucydides (2.59–65). The preamble describes how the Athenians, distressed by the plague and the devastation of Attica, blame Pericles for having persuaded them to go to war and hold him responsible for their sufferings. He calls a meeting and addresses them. His aim is carefully defined (2.59.3): "he wished to hearten them and by diverting their angry feelings to bring them into a gentler and less apprehensive state of mind." A similar definition of his aim is found (most exceptionally) at the beginning of the postscript (2.65.1): "he was trying to relieve the Athenians of their anger against himself and to divert their minds from their present sufferings." It is true that the speech of Pericles in its Thucydidean form consists mainly of exhortation and that various arguments are used to encourage the Athenians to adopt a more resolute attitude towards their misfortunes. On the other hand, the sentences quoted from the preamble and the postscript create a somewhat misleading impression in regard to the reaction of Pericles to the widespread criticisms of himself. Who would infer from these sentences that in his speech he makes no effort to conciliate the Athenians but actually defies them; that he criticizes his critics, arguing that their resentment against him is unjustified, their attitude to the present crisis illogical, whereas his convictions are sound and have not changed (2.60.1–61.3; 2.64.1)?

The speech of the Athenians at the first congress at Sparta (1.73–78) raises many problems which lie outside the scope of the present investigation. My only concern with it here is to suggest that the relationship between the preamble and the speech itself is strange and indicates some lack of coordination. The preamble explains in some detail the purpose of the Athenians in making their speech (1.72). They do not intend to defend themselves against the accusations directed against them but to point out that the general issue is one on which the Spartans ought not to take a hasty decision but ought to ponder further. They also wish to impress upon their hearers, old and young, how powerful Athens is. They believe that they will thereby incline Sparta towards keeping the peace rather than going to war. It is not surprising that this preamble, which I have shortened in my paraphrase, is longer than most, since the Athenians are stated to have come to Sparta on other business and to have felt impelled to ask for permission to speak only when they heard Athens accused. What is surprising is that, when the Athenians in the prologue of the speech explain their aims in addressing the assembly, these are more or less identical with those already stated in the preamble (1.73.1). Possibly Thucydides may wish to convey to his readers that the explanation given by the Athenians in the speech is an entirely sincere explanation of their purpose and is not designed to hoodwink the audience in any way. If, however, such was his object, he could, one must feel, have found a less clumsily repetitive method of achieving it. It may also be thought that, although the function of preambles is not primarily to provide an indication of what is to follow, this unusually full preamble fails to foreshadow at all adequately the very wide-ranging character of the Athenian speech.

I have already mentioned that the tone of the speeches by Cleon and Diodotus on the punishment of the Mytileneans is not wholly in accord with that of the context in which they are framed. A further discrepancy may be noted here. As scholars have observed, there are indications in the preamble (3.36.4) and the postscript (3.49.4) that it was because many Athenians considered the decision to execute the adult male Mytileneans to be inhuman, when they had had time for reflection, that misgivings became so widespread. These humanitarian feelings may well have been more influential in producing the narrow majority in favor of rescinding the decree than the arguments of Diodotus, who expressly denies that he is appealing to sentiments of this kind (3.48.1), whatever his personal opinion may have been. Thucydides states only that "the view of Diodotus won the day," without giving any reason for the ultimate outcome of the deliberations. This omission is most unusual, as has been noted earlier. It could be intentional, since Thucydides may have wished to render the disharmony between narrative and speeches as inconspicuous as possible. At all events, even though this disharmony may be thought insignificant where the narrative is so dramatic and the speeches so instructive, it does nevertheless exist.

Another method of testing the extent to which speeches and their settings are fully integrated is to consider whether many of the preambles or postscripts contain specific references to identifiable passages in the speeches. A passage in the speech of Brasidas at Acanthus mentions an oath sworn by the Spartan government to grant autonomy to any states won over by him (4.86.1); the postscript refers to this oath in very similar language (4.88). In the account of the first debate at Athens on the situation at Pylos the phrase *tou pleonos oregesthai* occurs both in the speech of the Spartan envoy (4.17.4) and in the postscript (4.21.2); but the same phrase is found elsewhere in a totally different context (4.92.2), and variations of it are not uncommon (cf. 4.41.4; 6.10.5; 6.83.1). In the postscript to the speech of Pericles urging the rejection of the Spartan ultimatum issued shortly before the outbreak of war, the Athenians are stated to have accepted his advice and to have framed their answer accordingly (1.145). There are some links, as is natural, between the summary of their answer and passages in his speech (1.140.2; 1.144.2), but they are not at all explicit. Attention has already been drawn to a passage which follows the report on the meeting at Olympia when envoys from Mytilene addressed the Spartans and their allies. This passage (3.16.2), in which the Spartans are stated to have concluded that the envoys had been untruthful, records a reaction to the speech which developed some weeks after the meeting at Olympia; it does not belong strictly to the postscript, as the term has been interpreted in my paper. Unfortunately this test has only a limited value. Because, as has been shown, preambles and postscripts are normally short and confined to essentials, the number of specific references in them to points made in the speeches would not in any event be expected to be very large. Nevertheless the extreme scarcity of such references has some significance and strengthens somewhat the case for believing that narrative and speeches tend to be imperfectly integrated.

I must now try to show that my investigations throw some light on the working methods of Thucydides, lending some support to conclusions by scholars which have won some acceptance on other grounds. The subject of his working methods is highly controversial, and whoever ventures to voice opinions about them is likely to incur charges of indulging in speculative hypotheses. One point concerning the composition of the *History* on which there has been some measure of agreement is that the patent inferiority of the fifth (5.25–116) and eighth books to the rest of the work is due largely to less complete revision. Since neither book contains speeches in *oratio recta* (apart from the highly abnormal Melian Dialogue), the inclusion of such speeches may be deemed to belong to the final stage of composition. If the fifth and eighth books represent the penultimate stage of composition, substantial parts of the rest of the *History* are likely to have existed at various different times in much the same condition as the fifth and eighth books, without speeches in *oratio recta*. At this penultimate stage summaries of speeches in *oratio obliqua* were doubtless included (there are plenty of examples in the fifth and eighth books) together with brief preambles and postscripts at each end. When Thucydides embarked upon the final stage, he evidently left many of these *oratio obliqua* summaries as they were, and he may well have shortened or even omitted others. *Oratio obliqua* summaries are not uncommon in the most fully finished parts of the *History*. A typical example is the summary of a speech by Hermocrates after the first Athenian victory at Syracuse (6.72.2–5): it has a short preamble and postscript, the latter stating only that the Syracusans took the action recommended by Hermocrates.

The principal step, so far as speeches were concerned, in the final stage of composition seems to have been that, in certain cases which Thucydides believed to be especially important or instructive, he expanded his *oratio obliqua* summary into a much longer *oratio recta* version. Doubtless he selected some of these in advance, but in other cases he is likely to have deferred his choice till the final stage of composition, when he would be in a better position to make his decision. It may be partly for this reason that preambles and postscripts tend to be brief and factual: when they were written, he had not yet decided, in at least some cases, where to include speeches in *oratio recta* or, almost more important, which elements in his *oratio obliqua* summary he might choose to develop most fully by the addition of *ta deonta*. The imperfect coordination between the speeches and their settings which has been noted in some instances suggests that he did not always write both at the same time. When he reached the final stage of composition, he could have expanded his preambles and postscripts somewhat and have modified them in order to obviate any disharmony with the *oratio recta* speeches, and he may well have done both in certain instances, though minor tinkering with an existing text was a difficult and often unsatisfactory operation.

Even though there seems to have been some interval between the composition of the preambles and postscripts and that of the speeches in *oratio recta*, this interval was not necessarily a long one. The view once widely accepted that whole speeches (or large parts of speeches) were added after the end of the war to a work composed many years earlier has little to recommend it. The passages of the *History* demonstrably written near or after the end of the war are few and mostly quite short. If, however, Thucydides wished his *oratio recta* speeches to make their maximum impact and serve as landmarks in his work, as he evidently did, one method of achieving this aim would be to write a substantial section, perhaps covering several war years, without including such speeches and to add them only when he could survey his own account of a considerable period and could assess the issues which it raised. If I may adapt an observation of A. W. Gomme on a different topic, I believe that the speeches and their settings "were not written at the same time, in the same breath as it were, both in the mind of the writer all the time." There is, however, a noteworthy exception, in my opinion, and I shall conclude this paper by drawing attention to it.

It may have been observed that no reference has hitherto been made to the report at the beginning of the sixth book on the debate in the Athenian assembly concerning the project to send an expedition to Sicily, which had already been authorized at an earlier meeting (6.8–26). I have postponed consideration of this report till now because it seems to me to differ substantially from other reports and to be outstanding in achieving effective coordination between speeches and their setting. The preambles and the postscript supply an abundance of information about the motives and feelings of the principal speakers, especially Nicias. These motives and feelings, though most of them are deducible from the speeches, need to be defined at the outset, since Thucydides evidently believed the development of the situation to have been deeply influenced by the personalities of Nicias and Alcibiades and by their personal rivalry. There is no inkling of disharmony with the content of the speeches. The preamble to the speech of Alcibiades concludes with a passage discussing the attitude of the Athenians towards him throughout his career (6.15.3–4). This quite substantial discussion may be felt to cause some imbalance in its context, a factor strengthening somewhat the case for believing the passage to be a late addition, which for different and much stronger reasons seems to me to be overwhelming. The preamble to the second speech of Nicias is most remarkable, though it is confined to a single sentence (6.19.2). It attributes to him motives which are deliberately concealed in his speech. He adopts a stratagem designed to secure the abandonment of the expedition by insisting that it demands the use of military resources on a much increased scale. The postscript reiterates this motive but adds an alternative, namely that "if forced to go on the expedition, he would thus sail with the greatest degree of security" (6.24.1). Thucydides seems to have no doubt that he is right in believing that the primary aim of Nicias was to hoodwink the assembly. Neither in the preamble nor in the postscript does he use any of the qualifying formulae, such as *legetai* or *hôs elegeto*, which occur not infrequently where he evidently feels somewhat distrustful of his evidence. Since he is well-informed about the plans, motives, and feelings of Nicias, many of them undisclosed, throughout the campaign in Sicily, he is probably in this instance relying upon information derived from a person, or persons, closely associated with Nicias. His assurance on this point is characteristic of his entire report on the debate. Although he cannot have attended it himself, he is confident that he is in possession of complete and trustworthy evidence on every aspect of the situation. Whether justifiable or not, his confidence, especially on the personal feelings and aims of the leading characters, undoubtedly contributes to the effectiveness of his account.

Another striking feature is the masterly presentation of popular reaction to the speeches. It is true that the first speech of Nicias and the speech of Alcibiades are followed only by brief and conventional notes, such as are often found elsewhere: namely that other speeches are delivered by Athenians and by envoys from Sicily; that opinion hardens in favor of undertaking the expedition (6.15.1; 19.1). The second speech of Nicias is, however, followed by a most illuminating passage (6.24.2–4) which includes the celebrated sentence *erôs enepese tois pasin homoiôs ekpleusai* ("a passion to sail came upon them all alike"). The speech produces (almost ludicrously) an effect which is the opposite of what was intended: his plea for a larger expedition is welcomed on the ground that an increase in its size will render it less vulnerable. Thucydides then analyzes the mood of the assembly, explaining why each group is enthusiastically in favor of the expedition. This analysis is notable for its psychological insight, though it may be thought to be prejudiced since he adopts the somewhat contemptuous tone which is perceptible in almost all his references to mass opinion. An un-named Athenian impatiently calls upon Nicias to make specific proposals regarding the size of the expedition; his reluctant reply giving his personal assessment is summarized in a sentence of *oratio obliqua;* the assembly then grants the generals full powers to act as they think fit (6.25.1–26.1). The reasons for the final vote are not defined: they have already been made abundantly clear.

This debate in the Athenian assembly was long and complex, and Thucydides has written a long and complex account of it, influenced no doubt by the importance of the occasion. So far as can be judged, he makes no attempt to simplify his account in order to make it more intelligible to his readers. His report in the first book on the first congress at Sparta is equally long and complex (it includes a larger number of speeches in *oratio recta*), and the issue under discussion was no less important. Yet these two reports are fundamentally different. As has been pointed out, there is inap-propriate duplication between the preamble to one of the speeches at the congress at Sparta and the beginning of the speech itself; and the postscript is concerned largely with a side issue, namely the unusual method of reaching a decision which was adopted on this occasion. Attention is concentrated upon the speeches, which, apart from that of Sthenelaïdas, cover a wide range of topics evoked by the dispute with Athens and the prospect of war. Accounts of many other debates are similar in character, but the account of the debate on the Sicilian expedition is not one of them.

The speeches of Nicias and Alcibiades, though they contain generalizations of the kind found in all Thucydidean speeches, are almost exclusively concerned with the practical problems of the situation as it existed on the day of the debate. References to the more or less distant past, which are elsewhere often used as the basis of arguments about the present, are in this case very few, though Alcibiades does allude to the period when the Athenians won their empire (6.17.7) and also to their reputation for energy and enterprise (6.18.2–3 and 7). Neither speaker considers whether an expedition designed to deprive others of their autonomy is morally justifiable, but only whether it would benefit Athens. It may be that Nicias and Alcibiades did in fact confine themselves to the issues under discussion more strictly than was the normal practice of speakers in public assemblies at the time, on which unfortunately no reliable evidence survives. It is, however, at least arguable that the Thucydidean versions of their speeches do follow contemporary practice more closely than most other speeches in the *History*, in which the discussion of general principles relevant outside the context may be attributable in many cases to *ta deonta* supplied by Thucydides himself. In other words, these speeches of Nicias and Alcibiades may be nearer to what may be termed "live reporting" than almost any other Thucydidean versions of speeches delivered in public assemblies.

This impression, and it is only an impression, is perhaps strengthened somewhat by the unusually close coordination in this case, to which attention has been drawn, between the speeches on the one hand and the preambles and postscript on the other. Thucydides may be deemed to have thought out and written down his entire report on this debate continuously at the same time, adopting a largely new technique designed to create a more realistic effect. Traces of this technique may also be observed in other speeches in the sixth book, those of Hermocrates and Athenagoras at Syracuse (6.32.3–41) and of Alcibiades at Sparta (6.88.9–93.3). Thucydides did not, however, abandon his former methods, which are as conspicuous as ever in his treatment of the debate at Camarina with its speeches by Hermocrates and Euphemus (6.75.4–88.2). I would like to think that the modification of his methods which I have suggested is connected with his increased preoccupation in the second half of the *History* with the personality of leading characters, a thesis which I have endeavored to establish in my *Individuals in Thucydides*.

THUCYDIDEAN ORATORS
IN PLUTARCH

by Philip A. Stadter

The impact of Thucydides' *History* on our view of the late fifth century is of course far-reaching, but by that very token difficult to measure. Its effect on ancient writers is perhaps more accessible. Since after Thucydides Plutarch's *Lives* are our best sources for this period, I would like to consider how Thucydides' *History*, especially the speeches, influenced Plutarch, and how much Plutarch was able to profit from, or free himself from, the presentation of the master. I hope that an account of these problems may provide a different perspective on Thucydides' *History*, how it was read in ancient times, and Plutarch's own interpretation of his protagonists.

There is no doubt that Plutarch knew Thucydides well and used him heavily in the appropriate lives—*Themistocles, Pericles, Nicias, Alcibiades*—and elsewhere. The radical view expressed by Eduard Meyer[1] and others, that Plutarch never used Thucydides, has died a natural death.[2] Plutarch cites by name specific passages from Thucydides some 23 times in the *Lives*, 30 times in the *Essays*, not including general references or negative statements such as "Thucydides does not mention this." In the 23 citations

---

1. *Forschungen zur alten Geschichte* (Halle, 1899), 2:67.
2. Cf. A. W. Gomme, *A Historical Commentary on Thucydides* (1956), 1:75, 81–84; C. Theander, "Plutarch und die Geschichte," *Bulletin de la Société Royale des Lettres de Lund* (1950–51), pp. 48–50; K. Ziegler, s.v. "Plutarchos 2," in Pauly-Wissowa-Kroll, *Real-Encyclopädie der klassischen Altertumswissenschaft* 21, pt. 1 (1951):912.

in the *Lives*, only once does he criticize a statement of Thucydides (at *Lycurgus* 27, on the question of *xenêlasia* at Sparta, referring to the Funeral Oration, 2.39.1). He regularly prefers Thucydides to other conflicting sources. A detailed study of the *Pericles*, *Nicias*, and *Alcibiades* reveals that the narrative of Thucydides has been systematically mined for material relevant to the protagonists.[3]

Let me give two brief examples of his technique. In chapter 6 of the *Nicias*, Plutarch brings together in one place notices of the conquest of Cythera, victories in Thrace, an expedition against Megara and Minoa,[4] an attack on Corinthian territory, and the capture of Thyrea taken from scattered passages in Thucydides Books Three and Four (4.53–54, 4.129–131, 3.51, 4.42–45, and 4.56–57). That is, he has gathered together every mention of Nicias in Thucydides down to the Peace of Nicias except the debate with Cleon on Pylos, which he reserves for fuller treatment in chapter 7, and the attack on Melos, which however is mentioned in the *Comparison of Nicias and Crassus*, 3.5.

In the case of the *Pericles*, matters are much more complicated, since Plutarch has so much more information about his protagonist and Thucydides mentions him only briefly before the outbreak of the war. Nevertheless, we find that every reference to Pericles in Book One of Thucydides has been picked up by Plutarch and used in its proper place. The expedition in the Corinthian gulf (Th. 1.111.2 = *Per.* 19.2), the Euboean expeditions (1.114.1 = *Per.* 22.1; 1.114.3 = *Per.* 23.3), the Samian War (1.116–117 = *Per.* 24.1, 25–26, 27.1, 28.1), the Alcmaeonid curse (1.127.1 = *Per.* 33.1, an explicit citation), and finally, the debate on the Megarian decree (1.139.4–1.145 = *Per.* 29.8) are all brought into the *Life*.

This technique is less apparent in the case of Alcibiades, since Thucydides introduces him for the first time at 5.43.2, and from then on he is one of the leading figures of his history. Plutarch, of course, was very familiar with Thucydides' portrait of Alcibiades, as will become apparent.

Thucydides rarely makes general comments on or evaluations of

3. See most simply the testimonia in Ziegler's Teubner edition of the *Lives*, and the introduction and notes by Flacelière to the Budé edition.

4. For a discussion of Plutarch's misinterpretation of Thucydides' account of this venture, see W. E. Thompson, *Classical Quarterly* n.s. 19 (1969):160–62.

historical figures, but when he does they are treasured by Plutarch. The evaluation of Pericles in 2.65 is quoted twice explicitly in the *Pericles* (9.1 and 15.3), as well as once in the essays (802 C); the comment on Nicias' religiosity at 7.50.4 is praised as equitable in *On Herodotus' Malice* 855 C and is cited at *Nicias* 4.1; and the sketch of Alcibiades' character at 6.15 is quoted at *Alcibiades* 6.3. Even the two-word evaluation of Hyperbolus, *mochthêron anthrôpon*, a rascally fellow, at 8.73.3, is cited at *Alcibiades* 13.4 and *On Herodotus' Malice* 855 C, and referred to in *Nicias* 11.5 (*tên mochthêrian*).

Granted then that Plutarch knew Thucydides well, and used him, what use could he make of the speeches? Unlike most historians, Thucydides did not regularly use speeches to introduce personal touches, draw character, or otherwise make the speaker more human and accessible to our understanding. Still less does he speak of personal motivations behind political acts. The speeches most frequently are statements of position, or analyses of possibilities, present or future, on the most general terms. Yet it was exactly the element of character and private influences on action which attracted Plutarch. He wished to bring out the man behind the act, and show that he was a real figure, influenced by human concerns, virtues, and weaknesses.

The biographer, therefore, has a tendency to use the speeches in the historian, even those attributed to his protagonist, as he had the narrative: as a mine for useful detail. He ransacks the speeches for factual or character-revealing material.[5] Let us look at his practice in the *Pericles*. Thucydides attributes three direct speeches and one indirect to the statesman. The first speech is summarized by Plutarch at 29.8, in discussing the Megarian decree as the cause of the war: "Pericles opposed the repeal and urged the people to persist in their hostility towards the Megarians." Shortly thereafter (31.1), he considers the motives which led Pericles to do this. All writers agreed, Plutarch tells us, that he was responsible for the war, but some said it was from aggressive arrogance, others (the worst but most popular charge) that he wanted to turn attention

5. D. A. Russell has shown how under quite different circumstances Plutarch used the speeches in Dionysius of Halicarnassus in the same way for the Coriolanus: "Plutarch's Life of Coriolanus," *Journal of Roman Studies* 53 (1963):21–28.

away from the charges against him and his friends, and yet others
that he did it for a nobler reason, and with good sense. This last
judgment, the one given first by Plutarch and the one he approves
most,[6] states "that his firm stand on this point was based on the
highest motives combined with a shrewd appreciation of where
Athens' best interests lay, since he believed that the demand for
repeal had been made to test the city's resistance, and that to comply with it would be regarded as an admission of weakness." This
argument is taken directly from the speech of Pericles in Thucydides (1.140.5), where the same words *apischurizomai, peira,
xynchôreô* appear as in Plutarch's paraphrase. This speech in
Thucydides has been made to contribute a statement as to the
moral position of Pericles at the outbreak of the war.

In chapter 33, Plutarch recalls the tricks by which the Spartans
hoped to weaken Pericles' position. First he refers to the Alcmaeonid curse, citing Thucydides (1.127), and then to the possibility
that Archidamus might spare Pericles' estates. This possibility,
and Pericles' response, offering his properties to the state, are drawn
from Thucydides 2.13. The historian mentions Pericles' suspicions
that Archidamus might spare his land for personal or political
reasons, and reports a speech in which Pericles promises to give
his lands to the people if they are spared. Plutarch gives the same
arguments reported by Thucydides, though in slightly different
words. H. D. Westlake comments on this passage in Thucydides
"it is only here that Thucydides refers to the private interests of
Pericles, and they are mentioned because the incident was politically
of some importance."[7] It is noteworthy, therefore, that Plutarch
has exploited this very section to portray Pericles' character and the
methods by which he kept his ascendancy over the Athenians.
Pericles' willingness to take such a step was an important element
of his leadership. Plutarch certainly has in mind the case of Fabius
Maximus, the hero placed parallel to Pericles in his *Lives*, whose
position was seriously weakened when Hannibal spared his lands
while ravaging those of his neighbors (*Fabius* 7.4–5). In Thucydides, Pericles' action would seem to be an example of his fore-

6. Cf. his comment against the accusations of the comic poets, *De Malignitate
Herodoti* 856 A.
7. H. D. Westlake, *Individuals in Thucydides* (Cambridge, 1968), p. 31.

sight. In Plutarch it is evidence of his ability to hold monarchical power in a democracy.

Plutarch refers only once more to a Thucydidean speech by Pericles, at 35.4, where he says that the statesman attempted to calm and encourage the Athenians, referring to the last speech of Pericles (2.60–64), and to the phrase with which Thucydides introduces it: "he wanted to restore their confidence and lead them from their angry feelings to a calmer and less fearful state of mind."[8] Here again the emphasis on controlling his opposition brings out one of the chief characteristics Plutarch saw in Pericles, his *praotês*, or refusal to become excited, and with it his ability to hold out against the unreasonableness of his opponents, a quality he shared with Fabius Maximus (*Per.* 2.5).

If we turn instead to the *Nicias* we find that the selections from the Thucydidean speeches attributed to Nicias serve to bring out the basic timidity and weakness of the protagonist, the fault of *deilia* mentioned at *Nic.* 3.5. The debate between Cleon and Nicias on Pylos in Thucydides (4.27–28) furnished the material for Plutarch's account in *Nic.* 7: there are many verbal reminiscences although no direct quotes.[9] Plutarch sees Nicias' action of surrendering the campaign of Pylos to Cleon as a serious mistake, revealing his timidity and undermining his reputation. This interpretation of the debate is brought out in *Nic.* 8, with the help of material and quotations from Theopompus, Aristotle, and Aristophanes.

The two great encounters between Nicias and Alcibiades in Thucydides are used in the same way. In the case of the Spartan embassy (Th. 5.45–46), Plutarch shows clearly the trickery of Alcibiades and the futility, albeit noble futility, of Nicias. He does not find it necessary to quote Nicias' speech, but merely refers to it (*Nic.* 5.7). A fine but weak man is outdone by the unscrupulous brilliance of Alcibiades. Similarly in drawing upon the debate on the Sicilian Expedition (Th. 6.9–26) Plutarch speaks of Nicias' efforts to block the action, even to making personal attacks on Al-

8. Dionysius of Halicarnassus notes that the speech itself is not conciliatory, as we might expect in such a situation (*On Thucydides* 44). Rather it is an example of the triumph of *gnômê* over *orgê*, as Thucydides says.

9. Note especially *Nic.* 7.3–5 and Thuc. 4.28.1–2.

cibiades in his speech (*Nic.* 12.4 = Th. 6.12.2), but makes clear that once again his caution is futile.

Plutarch's account of the Sicilian Expedition is, as he himself says (*Nic.* 1.5), heavily dependent on Thucydides. He finds the utterances attributed to Nicias by Thucydides especially useful in delineating the weaknesses from which he thought Nicias suffered. Thus Nicias' opinion at the generals' council (6.47) is repeated at *Nicias* 14.3, using the same basic phrases as Thucydides: *epideixasthai ta hopla* and *apoplein Athênaze*, "to show their force" and "to sail to Athens." Plutarch goes further than Thucydides, however, and explicitly criticizes Nicias for not facing up to the problem at hand and for causing the demoralization of his troops. The biographer mentions the letter of Nicias from Sicily, written after the arrival of Gylippus (Th. 7.11–15) only briefly (19.10), but the sense of discouragement which permeates the letter is clearly brought out by Plutarch. The particular arguments ascribed to Nicias in the letter are used in the next chapter to describe the actual situation of Nicias and the Athenians at this time (*Nic.* 20.3–4).

The Council of Nicias and Demosthenes after the attack on Epipolae (Th. 7.47–49) is reported by Plutarch in chapter 22. Thucydides ascribed two opinions on that occasion to Nicias, his private views (introduced by *enomize*) on the need for care in talking about retreating, the difficulties of the Syracusan position, and the information he had received from Athenian partisans in Syracuse, and his public statement (*emphanês logos*) on the disgrace and danger of death involved in returning to a hostile Athens, and on the weakness of the Syracusan position. Plutarch chooses to report only the *emphanês logos*, and only that part dealing with Nicias' fears. The statement that he preferred to die by the hands of his enemies rather than of his fellow citizens (Th. 7.48.4 = *Nic.* 22.3) is especially stressed, both by the closeness of his paraphrase of Thucydides, and by contrasting it with a statement of Leon of Byzantium. Nicias once more is made to appear weak, and afraid to do his true duty. As so often, the Thucydidean analysis of power is omitted. The possibility that Nicias possessed information from a pro-Athenian group at Syracuse is however suggested at *Nic.* 22.4.

Nicias' final pathetic exhortation of the army (Th. 7.77) is not directly quoted, but is referred to and exploited in drawing the picture of the last efforts of Nicias, sick and weak, to save the army. Thucydides uses the pathetic phrase *tais para tên axian nun kakopathiais*, "our present undeserved sufferings" (7.77.1), and shortly later talks of *xymphorai ou kat' axian*, "undeserved disasters" (7.77.3); Plutarch picks this up in the *par' axian* of *Nic.* 26.4 and the whole tenor of 26.4–6.

We have seen, then, that in the *Nicias* as in the *Pericles*, Plutarch has drawn from the speeches facts and those elements of character interpretation which fit his conception of his protagonist. The speeches of Nicias proved much more fruitful than those of Pericles in this regard. Already in Thucydides, it seems, the debate with Cleon, the two duels with Alcibiades, and even Nicias' opinions as general are more filled with a sense of personality than the speeches of Pericles. The latter seem in large part to belong to an ideal, timeless world, whereas those of Nicias are tied to human feeling, political struggle, and weakness.[10]

Alcibiades' first appearance as a speaker in Thucydides is in the famous deception of the Spartan ambassadors, already considered in connection with Nicias. As might be expected, the biographer presents the material somewhat differently in the *Life of Alcibiades*. For dramatic effect he changes Alcibiades' advice to the Spartans to direct discourse, and lengthens it (14.8–9, contrast Th. 5.45.2). Later when the Spartan ambassadors appear before the assembly, Plutarch elaborates Thucydides' statement that "Alcibiades shouted more loudly than ever against the Spartans" (5.35.4). In the biography, in fact, we find: "At once Alcibiades assailed them with angry shouts as though *he* were the injured party, not they, calling them faithless and fickle men, who were come on no sound errand whatever." As might be expected, in this episode full light is thrown by the biographer on the persuasiveness and unscrupulousness of Alcibiades in attempting to be first in the city. Despite the modifications, the episode is clearly taken from Thucydides, as is confirmed by the citation of the historian in this regard in the *Comparison of Coriolanus and Alcibiades* 2.2. Thucydides himself in this passage has focused attention in a most unusual fashion on Alcibiades' personality and private ambitions.

10. Cf. the conclusions of Westlake, *Individuals*, p. 308.

We are surprised to discover that Plutarch passes over rather rapidly the debate on Sicily, especially the speech of Alcibiades (6.16–18), which has been defined "largely a study of character."[11] The accent in Plutarch's account (*Alc.* 17–18) is on the greatness of the enterprise: Nicias' speech is reported because it stresses the difficulties to be expected, but Alcibiades' appears only as "Alcibiades countered his arguments and carried all before him." Yet in fact Plutarch is very aware of the speech, and the character traits it presents. However, he chooses to distribute material from this speech throughout his life, wherever it best fits his design. The item on Alcibiades' chariot victories at the Olympic games (6.16.2) appears at *Alc.* 11.2, where the evidence of Thucydides is compared with that from a song by Euripides. His liberality in liturgies (6.16.3) is mentioned at *Alc.* 16.4. Of course, his yearning to be first, so clearly stated in this speech (6.16.4–6), is seen by Plutarch to be his chief quality, as is pointed out frequently. Note especially his first reference to *to philonikon ... kai to philoprôton* in chapter 2, and the final comment in the *Comparison of Alcibiades and Coriolanus*, 5.1: "Alcibiades never denied that he loved being praised and hated being overlooked." Finally, Plutarch's interpretation of the Argive alliance and the battle of Mantinea (*Alc.* 15.1–2, 41.3) is taken from Alcibiades' words in this speech (6.16.6).

Alcibiades' speech on his arrival at Sparta is again used selectively. Plutarch chooses to report only the three chief strategic recommendations for action—to send Gylippus to Syracuse, to push the war against Athens, and to occupy Decelea (*Alc.* 23.2). The designs for the conquest of Sicily, Carthage, Italy, and the Peloponnese outlined here by Alcibiades had already been mentioned in connection with the Sicilian Expedition (*Alc.* 17.3).[12] The rest of the speech is passed over as irrelevant. The few speeches of Alcibiades in the eighth book are either omitted or referred to very generally by Plutarch, and need not be considered here.

Whether because of a change in Thucydides' attitude toward history, or because Pericles' political style actually was impersonal and rational, while Alcibiades' was personal and flamboyant, the speeches of Alcibiades appear much more lively and close to the

11. Ibid., p. 220.
12. Cf. also *Nic.* 12.2.

man than those of Pericles. Plutarch clearly takes advantage of the fact, yet somehow not as much as we might expect, mainly because he possessed so much material on Alcibiades from other sources, contemporary or near-contemporary.

A word is perhaps in order on the speeches or sections of speeches which Plutarch has omitted. His principles are perhaps most clearly seen in the *Pericles*. From the great statesman's first two speeches he has omitted the analyses of power and strategy which for the historian are their chief value (1.141–144, 2.13.2–8) and concentrated on questions concerning character. The biographer chooses to avoid discussion in his life of the calculations which might prove Pericles correct: he is concerned with the decision and its immediate consequences. It is worth noting in passing that Plutarch is not ignorant of financial matters brought up in these speeches or of the ultimate correctness of Pericles' decision. In the *Life of Aristides* 24.4 he quotes the speech in indirect discourse (Th. 2.13.3) for the figure of 600 talents income from tribute, and he quotes from the same speech (2.13.5) in *On Not Borrowing* 828 B for the emergency use of the gold on the statue of Athena. The wisdom of Pericles' plans is mentioned in the *Comparison of Pericles and Fabius* and elsewhere. The most famous of Thucydides speeches, the Funeral Oration, is passed over completely, for reasons I hope to make clear shortly. Yet Plutarch knows it well, for he cites it in his other works more frequently than any other passage. There are direct quotes in *On False Modesty* 533 A and *Whether an Old Man Should Participate in Government* 783 F, free citations at *Lycurgus* 27.6 and in *Female Bravery* 242 E, and a verbal reminiscence in the *Comparison of Aristophanes and Menander* 854 A.

The Thucydidean analysis of the true nature of Athens' position found in the last oration of Pericles was also deleted by the biographer, although this too was well-known to Plutarch, and is cited four times in other works (direct quotes in *On Self-praise* 540 C and *How to Tell a Flatterer from a Friend* 73 A; a loose quotation in *On Self-praise* 535 E; a general reference to the speech —"the one after the plague"—in *Rules for Governing* 803 B).

The same sort of material is deleted in the *Nicias* and the *Alcibiades*: the searching considerations of power and principles of

action, of prognostication and interpretation. A particular class is
the general's speech before battle, which so regularly serves to clari-
fy the elements of the battle. Although Nicias delivers four of these
in Thucydides (6.68.1–4, 7.61–64, 7.69.2, 7.77), only 7.77 is drawn
upon, and this for its pathos.[13]

I have gone into some detail to demonstrate one way in which
Plutarch used the speeches in Thucydides as sources for material.
And yet, Plutarch seldom gives any hint that he considers these
speeches to be something more: a record of the thoughts and words
of his protagonist at a certain time. The question arises, to what
extent does Plutarch consider the speeches to be authentic?

In chapter 8 of the *Pericles*, Plutarch considers the statesman's
gifts as a speaker, gifts which gave him preeminence in Athens.
He speaks of the influence of Anaxagoras, quotes Plato and Aristophanes, relates various anecdotes. But after all this, he has to
conclude, "He has left nothing written except his decrees" (*en-
graphon men oun ouden apoleloipe plēn tōn psēphismatōn*).[14]
Only a few expressions were remembered, he goes on to say, and
quotes some of them. We can add a few others from Aristotle's
Rhetoric. These, with another quoted by Plutarch in chapter 33,
make a total of eight fragments. Apart from Thucydides, our
knowledge of Pericles' speeches is meager indeed.[15] The opinion
of Plutarch is clear: if he knows only phrases by Pericles, then
Thucydides' speeches cannot be taken as representative of Pericles'
oratory. In fact, none of the memorable expressions which were
preserved are found in Thucydides, not even in loose paraphrase.
The preserved fragments do not even appear to refer to occasions
at which Thucydides reported that Pericles spoke.[16]

13. The speeches of Alcibiades and Nicias were less famous than those of Pericles
and do not seem to be referred to by Plutarch other than in these lives.

14. The notion that Pericles left nothing written is also stated firmly by Quintilian 12.2.22, 12.10.49, and 3.1.12. The last expressly rejects Cicero's statement in
Brutus 27, that some speeches of Pericles survived. Cicero is thinking of those in
Thucydides: see A. E. Douglas, *M. Tulli Ciceronis Brutus* (Oxford, 1966), pp.
xlv–xlvi.

15. There are also various traditions of critical comment on Pericles, one of
which W. R. Connor succeeds in tracing back to Theopompus: "*Vim quandam in-
credibilem*—A Tradition Concerning the Oratory of Pericles," *Classica et Mediae-
valia* 23 (1962):23–33.

16. Of the eight fragments, two are from the Samian funeral oration: Arist.

The most interesting case is that of the Funeral Oration, undoubtedly the finest speech in Thucydides. This speech, the historian tells us, or something like it (*toiade*), was delivered by Pericles at the end of the first year of the Peloponnesian War. Strangely enough, however, in view of its brilliance, Thucydides is our only evidence for the oration.

On the other hand, we know that Pericles delivered another funeral speech, for the dead of the Samian War. A phrase from it was quoted by Stesimbrotos and repeated from him by Plutarch (*Per.* 8.9), and refers to Pericles' praise from the platform of those who died on Samos. The same phrase, on the immortality of the dead, appears to be imitated in the funeral speech ascribed to Demosthenes (60.34). Are there then two noteworthy funeral orations by Pericles? We may wonder, for Aristotle (*Rhet.* 1.7.34) quotes another passage, saying "As Pericles says in the funeral speech" (*hoion Periklês ton epitaphion legôn*). *The* funeral speech: the expression may only mean "The customary Athenian funeral speech," but I rather think that it means "Pericles' famous funeral speech." The fragment he quotes, comparing the youth of a country to the spring of the year is not reflected in Thucydides' Funeral Speech, but seems to have influenced Herodotus 7.162.1. It would appear that *the* funeral speech of Pericles was not delivered in 431, but for the Samian war dead some years earlier.[17]

Which oration, then, does Plato refer to in the *Menexenus*, in which Socrates states that Aspasia had once taught him a funeral oration composed of fragments left over from the funeral oration composed by herself but spoken by Pericles (*ton epitaphion logon hon Periklês eipen, Menex.* 236 B). Once more only one funeral oration of Pericles—but composed by Aspasia! Plato in this dialogue is especially ironic, and can hardly be trusted for accurate historical information—suffice it to say that Socrates, who died in 399, is made to refer to the peace of Antalcidas of 386 (*Menex.* 245 E).

Rhet. 3.10.7 and 1.7.34, Plut. *Per.* 8.9; the rest from other unidentified orations: *Rhet.* 3.10.7, 3.4.3, 3.18.1; Plut. *Per.* 8.7, 33.5.

17. Cf. P. Treves, "Herodotus, Gelon and Pericles," *Classical Philology* 36 (1941):321–45, esp. 322–26. For speculation on the content of this oration and possible parallels to it, see Leo Weber, "Perikles samische Leichenrede," *Hermes* 57 (1922):375–95. The passage in Aristotle is interpreted differently by C. W. Fornara, *Herodotus, An Interpretative Essay* (Oxford, 1971), pp. 83–84.

However, the various echoes of the Funeral Oration in Thucydides suggest that Plato had that particular speech in mind, while the complete absence of references to the Athenian empire or the glories of the Peloponnesian War argues that Plato strongly opposes the imperialistic attitudes expressed in that speech. Is Plato referring to the Periclean original of Thucydides' speech? I rather tend to agree with the view expressed in a recent article by Charles Kahn,[18] that the oration that Plato had in mind is that of Thucydides, which probably had only recently been published. Plato takes exception not to a Periclean speech of almost fifty years before, but to the contemporary interpretation of a view of empire and democracy which Plato found intolerable.

It appears reasonable to conclude with Plutarch that the famous funeral oration is essentially Thucydidean, not Periclean, and if Pericles did climb the *bema* in 431, as someone must have done every year throughout the war, he said nothing so memorable.[19]

Since Plutarch does not accept the speeches in Thucydides as evidence for Pericles' style, it follows that his judgments on Pericles' oratory are not based on them. Rather he quotes a variety of sources—Plato, Theopompus, the comedians, Thucydides himself—to document the effectiveness of his rhetoric (see especially chapters 8 and 15). The same is true of Alcibiades, for whose oratory he quotes Demosthenes and Theophrastus (*Alc.* 10.4), but not the Thucydidean speeches.

I believe the point is especially important in view of the fact that Plutarch makes a practice of using authentic speeches or other written material as sources in his *Lives*. We have only to recall the *Lives of Demosthenes* and *Cicero*: in each frequent citations are made from the works of the protagonist. We might cite as well—the list is not complete—the use of Solon's poems, the letters of Alexander, the *Memoirs* of Aratus and Sulla, and the *Commentaries* of Caesar in the respective *Lives*. Plutarch was eager to use genuine material by his protagonists as a source, but he could not accept Thucydides' orations as genuine.

18. "Plato's Funeral Oration: The Motive of the *Menexenus*," *Classical Philology* 58 (1963):220–34.

19. The view is shared by Dionysius of Halicarnassus, *On Thucydides* 18. Dionysius' criticism of Thucydides' orations as public speeches, cc. 49–50, is not merely theoretical, but is shared by Cicero *Orator* 30–32, *Brutus* 287–288.

The phrase of Plutarch from which I began this inquiry, however, contributes something else to the discussion: "he left nothing in writing except the decrees." The decrees, then, were preserved, Plutarch thought. In fact, the biographer cites a number of decrees by Pericles: decrees recalling Cimon (10.4), calling a panhellenic congress (17.1), sending an expedition against Samos (24.1 and 25.1) and sending the herald Anthemocritus to the Megarians and Spartans (30.2–3). (It is uncertain whether the citizenship law, 37.3 and 5, should be included in this group.) Presumably Plutarch found these in the collection of Craterus which he cites elsewhere.[20]

These decrees, as authentic expressions of Pericles' views at certain moments, are given some prominence by Plutarch. His use of the Congress decree is particularly interesting. He devotes all of chapter 17 to it, describing the occasion of its passage and summarizing its content. Yet nothing came of the decree, and Plutarch feels he must justify in some special way his extensive reference to it (17.4). "I have included this item," he affirms, "to show Pericles' spirit (*phronêma*) and highmindedness (*megalophrosynên*)." The decree, with its call for united action by all the Greeks, is an example of leadership in the grand style, of the greatmindedness which Pericles both practiced himself and urged upon the Athenians, as Plutarch stresses in introducing this decree: "he encouraged the people to cherish high ambitions and to believe themselves capable of great achievements" (*epairôn ho Periklês ton dêmon eti mallon mega phronein kai megalôn hauton axioun pragmatôn*, 17.1). The funeral oration in Thucydides certainly is another study of the *megalophrosynê* of Pericles, and of Athens, and one more frequently cited for the force and beauty of its expression. Yet the biographer here chose to rest his case not on the eloquence of Thucydides, excellent though it be, but on the authentic proposal of his protagonist. Thucydides' Funeral Oration represented for him the thoughts not of Pericles but of Thucydides, and he preferred the less expressive yet more genuine decree.

This respect Plutarch had for contemporary decrees undoubtedly influenced his presentation of the outbreak of the Peloponnesian

20. On Craterus, see F. Jacoby, *Fragmente der griechischen Historiker* 342 and the bibliography there cited. His regular use by Plutarch in the Pericles is argued by E. Meinhardt, *Perikles bei Plutarch* (Frankfurt am Main, 1957).

War, for besides Thucydides, Ephorus, and the comic poets, certain pertinent decrees seem to have been available. Plutarch refers especially to the reasonableness and goodwill shown by Pericles' decree sending Anthemocritus to Megara, and to the hostility of the Charinus decree which followed it. The passage on the attacks on Phidias and Aspasia (31–32) also seems to be drawn from decrees and indictments such as Craterus would have published:[21] the decree of Glaucon granting *ateleia* to Menon the accuser of Phidias (31.5), the decree of Diopeithes against holders of unorthodox religious opinions (32.2), and the decree of Dracontides on Pericles' accounts, with the amendment of Hagnon (32.3–4).

Decrees seem to play less of a role in the *Nicias* and the *Alcibiades*, despite Plutarch's promise in the preface of the Nicias (1.5) to supplement Thucydides' and Philistus' accounts with dedications, decrees, and other materials. But he may know the final decree on the Sicilian Expedition, which he ascribes to Demostratus, who is not named by Thucydides (*Nic.* 12.6; *Alc.* 18.3),[22] and he is able to quote verbatim the indictment against Alcibiades by Thessalus son of Cimon (*Alc.* 22.4, cf. 19.2–3).

Recent studies have borne out, I think, the integrated relationship of narrative and speeches in Thucydides. This investigation of Plutarch's treatment of the speeches shows that he also considered them an integrated whole, the work of the historian, from which he could draw material for his *Lives*. The speeches are given no special treatment as authentic representations of the speaker, though they are prized for the historical facts or insights into the protagonist's character and motives which Thucydides had written into them. Throughout, Plutarch in his biographies avoids the more intellectual analysis beloved by Thucydides. This is especially true of his handling of Pericles' speeches, in which this element is most prominent. In the case of Nicias and Alcibiades, the historian's method is closer to that of the biographer, and so he provides more abundant material for him. The case of Alcibiades' deception of the Spartan ambassadors is especially useful for the bi-

21. Cf. Plutarch *Aristides* 26.4 (*FGrHist* 342 F 12), "Craterus furnishes for this no written evidence, either lawsuit or decree (*oute dikēn oute psēphisma*), although he is accustomed to write out such material and add those who report it."

22. Perhaps not from a decree, but deducing the fact from Aristophanes *Lysistrata* 387–398.

ographer. Plutarch supplemented the lack of authentic speeches in Thucydides by using decrees which he believed were authentic and gave him a true, if pedestrian, statement of Pericles' *megalophrosynê*.

Finally, we cannot help but marvel at the effectiveness with which Thucydides in only a few pages (basically from 1.139 to 2.65) was able to shape a portrait of Pericles which was the fundamental influence on Plutarch, despite the wealth of additional material available to him, and which still remains fundamental for us today.

A BIBLIOGRAPHY
OF SCHOLARSHIP
ON THE
SPEECHES IN THUCYDIDES
1873-1970

by William C. West III

The investigation of scholarship on the speeches in Thucydides poses initially a problem of limitation.[1] Study of the speeches is represented in nearly all approaches to Thucydides and cannot be neatly segregated. The chronological scope of such a survey must be restricted in terms which allow an effective presentation, and as soon as one turns from reading the literature to reading the text, it becomes evident that the concept of speech itself has to be defined. There are the obvious orations in direct discourse and those in indirect speech which are clearly indicated as such, often by some kind of ring composition, a preceding *eipen hoti* . . . and a

1. This bibliography conforms in format to the style followed in *L'Année Philologique*. In the case of books each entry is followed by a list of reviews in the order journal, volume, pages, reviewer. The abbreviations of journals are the standard ones used in *L'Année Philologique*. In accordance with usual American practice, however, AJP, CP, and HSCP are used for AJPh, CPh, and HSPh.

concluding *tosauta eipôn*. . . . But this formula is frequently varied and is not always apparent in casual reading. How should one categorize, moreover, short monologues, brief remarks, dialogues, letters, treaties, and the like? Answers to these questions were required, if only for the practical need of arranging the material in an economical manner. The compiler knows that the arrangement produced suggests an order which is at once only apparent and superficial. His decisions will not satisfy everyone. In brief, the bibliography covers a period of about a century. The material is listed chronologically under various topics which show the range of approaches adopted toward the speeches and conclude with a list of them.

During the century under survey the problem of composition is at first in the forefront of Thucydidean scholarship. It exercised an influence upon Thucydidean studies for nearly a century, from the middle of the nineteenth century until just before the Second World War. Mme de Romilly, in her study of Thucydides and Athenian imperialism (65), felt obliged to discuss it at length, to show that the results of developmental approaches to Thucydides were inconclusive, and to justify investigation of the thought of the author from a new perspective.

For students of the composition of the work the speeches had to be explained, either as historically faithful reproductions of those actually delivered or as free compositions. Thucydides' own statement on method, 1.22, made this approach imperative, but it has imposed an undue emphasis on the direct orations as speech proper and tended to cause neglect of speeches in indirect discourse. This bias in favor of direct speech can be observed in the lists compiled by Blass (4) and Jebb (1). Both exclude indirect discourse, although the latter remarks on the presence of speeches in *oratio obliqua* in some instances. The prevailing tendency, however, was to regard indirect discourse as simply a form of narrative.

In terms of one's understanding of the factors which influenced the composition of the work, the question arises as to the degree of historical accuracy in the speeches. "Separatists" held the view that Thucydides wrote the first and second halves of his work at widely different times over a period of two decades or more, with perhaps occasional revision of early work in the later stages of writing. It might be judged that he reported his speakers more or less faithfully and that the speeches reflect this difference in the time of composition. But if, to adopt the "unitarian" approach, the history was the product of only a few years, after the conclusion of the war, it was easier to think of them as distinct compositions.

In either case it was desirable to investigate the degree to which the speeches reflected the actual rhetoric of the last thirty years or so of the fifth century. Hence one encounters, in the early part of our period of survey, studies of Thucydides and the sophists (cf. 88, 89) and comparison of his diction with that of Antiphon and other orators. Even if the speeches were judged to be free compositions, they could still be shown to be open to the influence of the rhetoric of the period, in the use of commonplaces, technical vocabulary, and the arrangement of words and ideas for maximum effect upon the issue involved. For the most part, however, students of the composition of the work adopted attitudes toward the speeches in harmony with their views of this problem, but recognition of them as free compositions led naturally to study of the speeches on an independent basis.

With the coming of a new era in the study of Thucydides, an era in which the problem of composition is less compelling, speeches, too, have had to be studied on a new basis, although the grounds for this had already been established in the willingness to understand them as free compositions. They could still be shown to reflect the milieu of the sophistic culture of Athens from which they arose. Finley's work is an admirable example of this approach, especially "Euripides and Thucydides" (cf. 97) and the chapter on style in his book on Thucydides (17). Mme de Romilly shows the fruitfulness of another avenue of investigation in interpreting the speeches in the context of Thucydides' thought as a historian and his understanding of the forces which shaped the events he described. The thoroughgoing restudy of the Athenian tribute lists, moreover, and numerous associated documents stimulated historical studies and investigation of the background of Thucydides. In this area, study of the speeches could contribute distinctly to the examination of the political constellations of cities and internal factions, to evaluation of the degree of effectiveness of groups and of individuals and their impact upon events. It would seem that the speeches can now be approached in terms of the broad categories of literature, history, and rhetoric.

The limits of this bibliography have been chosen largely for convenience. The years 1873–1970 constitute a period sufficient for the observation of the trends noted above; Bursian's *Jahresberichte über die Fortschritte der klassischen Altertumswissenschaft* began publication in 1873 and its bibliographical supplement, *Bibliotheca Philologica Classica*, appears annually from 1874. Bibliography on Thucydides is available in yearly lists, during our period, in the *Bibliotheca*, S. Lambrino's *Bibliographie classique des années 1896 à 1914*, *Dix années de bibliographie classique*, and *L'année philologique*. These can be supplemented by the detailed articles on Thucydidean scholarship in Bursian up to the period before the Second World War. Thereafter one can be guided by the discussions of work on Thucydides in *Classical World* (by Wassermann and Chambers); *Fifty Years of Classical Scholarship* (by Griffith), reprinted in *Fifty Years (and Twelve) of Classical Scholarship*, with an appendix on bibliography; Schmid-Stählin; Luschnat's recent article on Thucydides in supplement 12 of Pauly-Wissowa; and important books and monographs of the last several years. One can never feel confident that he has found everything, but I hope that most omissions of a serious nature have been avoided. In order to produce a catalogue of reasonable length, I have excluded texts, translations, and commentaries, with the exception of Gomme's.

Although for these mechanical reasons 1873 was a convenient year for starting the bibliography, it plunges the survey in medias res, at a time when study of the speeches is dominated by the problem of the composition of the work. This problem continues to exert an influence on their study for several decades, but interest in the speeches as distinct compositions can be observed as an increasing trend, which is particularly noticeable since the 1930s. Similarly, the terminal limit of the bibliography, 1970, constitutes in no sense the end of an era of scholarship. It is marked by a fortunate coincidence, the publication in the same year of Luschnat's article on Thucydides in Pauly-Wissowa and of volume four of Gomme's commentary (by Andrewes and Dover).

GENERAL

This section embraces those studies which investigate broadly the role of speeches in Thucydides' history and Thucydidean speeches in the history of Greek oratory and prose of the fifth century B.C. Among recent works Luschnat's article on Thucydides in *RE* (37) and von Fritz' monograph on Greek historiography (34) merit special mention as introductions to the current state of Thucydidean studies in general, apart from valuable discussions of the speeches and their function in the work. If there is any value in setting them within an established tradition in Thucydidean scholarship, they may be ranked with the works of Schmid (21) and Finley (17). The new conception of Thucydides which emerged after the First World War, resulting from Schwartz' brilliant study of the problem of the composition of the work (50), is surveyed by Wasserman (12) and Pohlenz (14), and these may serve as a transition between the periods when study of the speeches is dominated by *Entstehungsgeschichte* and that during which they are studied as distinct compositions.

For general estimates of Thucydidean speeches in the development of Greek oratory and prose, our period is served by Jebb's essay (1), the extensive works of Blass (4) and Norden (9), and, recently, that of Kennedy (29). Similarly, the historian's viewpoint is represented by Busolt (5), Bury (7), Adcock's essay (28), and Gomme's commentary (19, 25, 36), which has been appearing over the last three decades, a period very nearly equal in itself to the recent era in Thucydidean studies. Regenbogen's selection and translation of the political orations has been included because it contains an excellent introduction to the general topic of speeches in Thucydides (22). Herter's collection in the Wissenschaftliche Buchgesellschaft's *Wege der Forschung* series (35) provides a representative selection of important work since 1930. Lists of speeches in direct discourse may be found in Jebb (1), Cammerer (3, p. 3), Blass[2] (4, pp. 232–233; cf. Blass[1] [1868], pp. 227–239) and Taeger (11, p. 206 f.). These lists are expanded by Luschnat (37, cols. 1163–1166), who also includes many of the speeches in indirect discourse.

1. Jebb R., "The speeches of Thucydides," *Hellenica. A collection on Greek poetry, philosophy, history, and religion*, ed. by Abbott E. (London Rivingtons 1880 viii & 492 p.) 266–323.

2. Bászel A., *Thukydides beszédei* (The speeches of Thucydides) Budapest 1881 vii & 211 p.

JAW LVIII 1889 86–92 Müller.

3. Cammerer C., *Quaestiones Thucydideae. De orationibus directis operi Thucydideo insertis*: Programma Burghausen 1881 20 p.

JAW LVIII 1889 76–77 Müller.

4. Blass F., *Die attische Beredsamkeit*, I: *Von Gorgias bis zu Lysias*, 2. Aufl. (Leipzig Teubner 1887 vi & 648 p.) 231–244.

5. Busolt G., *Griechische Geschichte bis zur Schlacht von Chaeroneia*, III, 2: *Der Peloponnesische Krieg*, 2. Anfl. (Gotha Perthes 1904 xxxv & 1049 p.) 671–676.

JHS XXIV 1904 76; RC XVIII 1904 339–341 Cavaignac; RSA VIII 1904 587–590 Tropea; REG XVIII 1905 386 Reinach; NPhR 1906 100–106 Swoboda.

6. Harrison J. E., "Thucydides' mode of presenting his speeches," PCPS LXXIX–LXXXI 1908 10–13.

7. Bury J. B., *The ancient Greek historians*: New York Macmillan 1909 x & 281 p. (appendix on Thucydides and his use of speeches, 261–265).

EHR XIV 1909 542–546 Walker; Cultura XXX 1911 242–245 Fesca.

8. Uzun F., *De orationum in Thucydidea historia sententiis et causis*: Diss. Wien 1909 78 p.

9. Norden E., *Die antike Kunstprosa. Vom VI. Jahrhundert v. Chr. bis in die Zeit der Renaissance*, I (5. Aufl. Stuttgart Teubner 1958 xx & 450, 22 p.; Nachdruck & Wiedergabe, 2. Aufl. Berlin 1909 & Nachträge, 3. Aufl. Berlin 1915) 95–101.

10. Howald E., "Ionische Geschichtsschreibung," Hermes LVIII 1923 113–146 (int. al., on Thucydides' methods in composing speeches).

11. Taeger F., *Thukydides*: Stuttgart Kohlhammer 1925 viii & 300 p.

DLZ XLVII 1926 654–662 Jacoby; JAW CCVIII 1926 158 Widmann; PhW XLVI 1926 116–117 Rossbach.

12. Wassermann F., "Das neue Thukydidesbild," NJW VII 1931 248–258.

13. Deffner A., *Die Rede bei Herodot und ihre Weiterbildung bei Thukydides*: Diss. München 1933 118 p.
PhW LIV 1934 995–997 Fries.

14. Pohlenz M., "Die thukydideische Frage im Lichte der neueren Forschung," GGA CXCVIII 1936 281–300.

15. Gomme A. W., *Essays in Greek history and literature*: Oxford Blackwell 1937 viii & 298 p.
CW XXXI 1937 5–6 Wallace; CR LI 1937 234–235 Giles; G&R VII 1937 60; NRS 1937 456–458 Treves; AJP LIX 1938 240–241 Calhoun; JHS LVIII 1938 117 Hammond; MPh XLV 1938 124 Thiel; PhW LVIII 1938 970–973 Lenschau; REA XL 1938 76–77 Legrand; RPh XII 1938 284–285 Hatzfeld; BFC XLV 1938–1939 172–176 Corradi; CP XXXIV 1939 150–157 Dow; DLZ LX 1939 1271–1274 Lesky; MC 1939 29 Corradi; REG LII 1939 207 Roussel.

16. Meyer E., *Erkennen und Wollen bei Thukydides*: Diss. Göttingen 1939.

17. Finley J. H., *Thucydides*: Cambridge Harvard Univ. Pr. 1942 344 p.
CW XXXVI 1943 281–282 Lord; AJP LXV 1944 181–185 McGregor; CP XXXIX 1944 57–59 Cochrane; CJ XL 1945 432–435 Schoder; LEC XIV 1946 302 Vanneste; Lychnos 1946–1947 382–383 Rudberg; CR LXI 1947 15–17 Gomme; EHR LXII 1947 239–240 Heichelheim.

18. Howald E., *Vom Geist antiker Geschichtsschreibung. Sieben monographien*: München Oldenbourg 1944 233 p. (int. al., chapter on Thucydides, dealing with speeches).

19. Gomme A. W., *A historical commentary on Thucydides*, I: *Introduction and commentary on book I*: Oxford Clarendon Pr. 1945 xii & 479 p.
AHR LI 1946 492–493 Swain; AJA L 1946 497–499 MacKendrick; AJP LXVII 1946 268–275 McGregor; CR LX 1946 27–29 Cary; EHR LXI 1946 270–271 Heichelheim; CP XLIV 1949 258–262 Larsen; JHS LXIX 1949 83–85 Wade-Gery; TG LXII 1949 121 Thiel.

20. Jaeger W., "Thucydides, political philosopher," *Paideia. The*

ideals of Greek culture, transl. by Highet G., I, 2nd ed. (New York Oxford Univ. Pr. 1945) book II, chapt. 6, 382–411 (1st ed. 1939). CJ XXXV 1940 362–364 Duncan; CW XXXIII 1940 177–178 Morgan; Isis XXXII 1940 375–376 Diller; CP XXXVII 1942 197–206 Hack; AJP LXVIII 1947 200–215 Grube.

21. Müller I. von, *Handbuch der Altertumswissenschaft*, fortgef. von Otto W., VII,1,5: Schmid W. & Stählin O., *Geschichte der griechischen Literatur*, 1: *Die klassische Periode*, 4; *Die griechische Literatur zur Zeit der attischen Hegemonie nach dem Eingreifen der Sophistik*, 2,2: München Beck 1948 377 p. (161–181 on speeches).

Athenaeum XXVII 1949 302–306 Castiglioni; LEC XVII 1949 415–416 Walbrecq; AAHG III 1950 96–99 Lesky; AC XIX 1950 476–477 Severyns; Aegyptus XXX 1950 106 Calderini; Helmantica I 1950 393 Fantini; AJP LXXII 1951 451 McGregor; RFIC XXIX 1951 351–353 Luppino; RPh XXV 1951 249–250 Chantraine; JHS LXXII 1952 124–125 Dover; REA LIV 1952 120–122 Mugler.

22. *Thukydides. Politische Reden*, ausgewählt & übers. von Regenbogen O.: Leipzig Koehler & Amelang 1949 290 p. (includes introduction on Thucydidean speeches in general).

DLZ LXXI 1950 244–248 Luschnat; Lychnos 1950–1951 333 Rudberg; CW XLIV 1951 122 Wassermann; AAHG VI 1953 107 Lesky.

23. Erbse H., "Ueber eine Eigenheit der thukydideischer Geschichtsbetrachtung," RhM XCVI 1953 38–62 (argues that the speeches are a kind of digression, giving significance to events).

24. Gomme A. W., *The Greek attitude to poetry and history*: Sather Class. Lect. XXVII Berkeley & Los Angeles Univ. of California Pr. 1954 viii & 190 p. (on speeches in Thucydides, 141–142).

CB XXXI 1954 23 Costelloe; CW XLVII 1954 187–188 Oates; RFIC XXXII 1954 410–411 Rostagni; AJP LXXVI 1955 329–330 McGregor; HibJ LIII 1954–1955 201 Armstrong; CR V 1955 254–256 Tate; G&R II 1955 41 Sewter; Hermathena LXXXV 1955 70–72 Stanford; RPh XXIX 1955 252–253 de Romilly.

25. Gomme A. W., *A historical commentary on Thucydides*, II: *The ten years' war (books II–III)*; III: *The ten years' war*

(*books IV–V 24*): Oxford Clarendon Pr. 1956 xi, ix & pp. 1–436
& 437–747 map.

G&R III 1956 165 Sewter; Emerita XXV 1957 221 Adrados;
Mnemosyne X 1957 351–353 Aalders; TG LXX 1957 98 Thiel;
AJP LXXIX 1958 416–423 McGregor; CP LIII 1958 122–125
Larsen; CR VIII 1958 30–33 Hammond; EHR LXXIII 1958
700–701 Heichelheim; Historia VII 1958 251–254 Ehrenberg;
History XLIII 1958 43 Kells; RFIC XXXVI 1958 189–198 Maddalena; Hellenica XVI 1958–1959 389–392 Kyriakidis.
   26. Griffith G. T., "Some habits of Thucydides when introducing persons," PCPS VII 1961 21–33.
   27. Gomme A. W., *More essays in Greek history and literature*,
ed. by Campbell D. A.: Oxford Blackwell 1962 x & 229 p.

CJ LIX 1963 32–33 Guthrie; CP LVIII 1963 251–253 Burnett;
CR XIII 1963 319–321 Westlake; CW LVI 1963 176 Eliot;
Gnomon XXXV 1963 325–334 von Fritz; Phoenix XVII 1963
310–311 McGregor; JCS XII 1964 132–136 Aisaka; JHS LXXXIV
1964 201–202 Walbank; REG LXXVII 1964 324–325 Weil; TG
LXXVII 1964 72–74 Thiel; SicGymn XVIII 1965 295–299 Cataudella; AJP LXXXVII 1966 115–118 Immerwahr.
   28. Adcock F. E., *Thucydides and his history*: Cambridge
Univ. Pr. 1963 viii & 146 p.

AHR LXIX 1963–1964 725–726 McGregor; Lychnos 1963–1964
336–340 Palm; AC XXXIII 1964 161 Mossé; AUMLA No. 21
1964 94–95 Weaver; CF XVIII 1964 70–73 Marique; CW LVII
1964 190 Oost; Gnomon XXXVI 1964 650–654 Sieveking; History XLIX 1964 48 Walbank; LEC XXXII 1964 74 Degueldre;
RBPh XLII 1964 1448–1449 Peremans; REA LXVI 1964 411–
412 Payrau; AJP LXXXVI 1965 326–328 McGregor; CJ LX
1965 328 Lenardon; CP LX 1965 207–208 Chambers; DLZ
LXXXVI 1965 37–40 von Fritz; Hermathena C 1965 84–85
Parke; JCS XIII 1965 165–167 Fujinawa; P&I VII 1965 293–294
Colombi; REG LXXVIII 1965 398–400 Weil; SicGymn XVIII
1965 309–311 Cataudella; TG LXXVIII 1965 77–78 Aalders;
Athenaeum XLIV 1966 391–394 Treves; Mnemosyne XIX 1966
185–186 van Dijck; Phoenix XX 1966 91–92 Eliot.
   29. Kennedy G., *The art of persuasion in Greece*: Princeton
Univ. Pr. 1963 xi & 350 p.

CW LVI 1963 218 Bateman; REG LXXVI 1963 469–470 Clavaud; AJP LXXXV 1964 315–316 Hubbell; CP LIX 1964 302–304 Johnson; Eos LIV 1964 206–207 Chodorowski; Helmantica XV 1964 284–285 Oroz Reta; RPh XXXVIII 1964 304–305 Weil; CR XV 1965 200–202 Hudson-Williams; Gnomon XXXVII 1965 6–10 Schindel; JCS XIII 1965 185–188 Iio; Mnemosyne XVIII 1965 404–405 Schenkeveld; RF LVI 1965 358–361 Viano; JHS LXXXVI 1966 189–190 Healy.

30. Syme R, "Thucydides," PBA XLVIII 1963 39–56 (separately publ. Oxford Univ. Pr. 1963).

AC XXXIII 1964 462–463 Mossé.

31. Barth K. L., *Individuelle Züge in den Reden des Thukydides*: Diss. Innsbruck 1965 334 p.

32. Bowersock G. W., "The personality of Thucydides," AntR XXV 1965 135–146.

33. Finley J. H., *Three essays on Thucydides*: Loeb Class. Monogr. Cambridge Harvard Univ. Pr. 1967 xv & 194 p.

CB XLIV 1967 14–15 Horner; CP LXIII 1968 221 Evans; CR XVIII 1968 285–286 Westlake; G&R XV 1968 203 Sewter; Hermathena CVI 1968 77 Hinds; REG LXXXI 1968 282–283 Weil.

34. Fritz K. von, *Die griechische Geschichtsschreibung*, I; *Von den Anfängen bis Thukydides*: Berlin de Gruyter 1967 Textbd. xii & 823 p. Anmerkungsbd. iv & 423 p. 4 indices.

AHR LXXIII 1968 1485–1486 Brown; BVAB XLIII 1968 197–200 den Boer; CW LXI 1968 402 Ostwald; Helmantica XIX 1968 181 Campos; LEC XXXVI 1968 191–192 van Ooteghem; SZG XVIII 1968 540–543 Meyer; TG LXXXI 1968 224–227 Aalders; AJP XC 1969 347–352 Pearson; Aevum XLIII 1969 331–337 Garzetti; CJ LXV 1969 28–29 Wassermann; CR XIX 1969 198–201 Brunt; Mnemosyne XXII 1969 310–315 Breebaart; RBPh XLVII 1969 982–985 Peremans; RH XCIII 1969 201–204 Will; StudClas XI 1969 357–363 Pippidi.

35. *Thukydides*, hrsg. von Herter H.: Wege der Forschung XCVIII Darmstadt Wissenschaftliche Buchgesellschaft 1968 vi & 716 p.

36. Gomme A. W., Andrewes A. & Dover K. J., *A historical commentary on Thucydides*, IV: *Books V 25–VII*: Oxford Clarendon Pr. 1970 xv & 502 p. 6 pl. maps.

TLS LXIX 1970 873.

37. Luschnat O., "Thukydides," *Paulys Realencyclopädie der classischen Altertumswissenschaft*, neue Bearb. begonnen von Wissowa G. fortgef. von Kroll W. & Mittelhaus K., unter Mitwirkung zahlreicher Fachgenossen, hrsg. von Ziegler K.: Suppl. XII: *Abdigildus bis Thukydides* (Stuttgart Druckenmüller Verl. 1970 ii & 1711 cols.) cols. 1085–1354 (1146–1183 on speeches).

38. Turska C. M., "Caractère des discours dans les Helléniques de Xénophon," Meander XXV 1970 428–443 (comparison with speeches of Herodotus and Thucydides; in Polish, with a summary in Latin).

SPEECHES AND THE PROBLEM OF COMPOSITION

The problem of the composition of the work stems from F. W. Ullrich's *Beiträge zur Erklärung des Thukydides* (Hamburg 1846). It has had enormous influence upon Thucydidean studies, and although most of the works listed under this rubric antedate the Second World War, this should by no means imply that the problem is no longer important. Its influence can still be seen in the items listed under the following rubric (Thought and Objectives of Thucydides), which are inclined to investigate the work as we possess it and recognize the subjectivity involved in a genetic approach.

Briefly stated, Ullrich's theory postulated that the history was composed in two stages: after the Peace of Nicias in 421 and after the defeat of Athens in 404. The second stage of composition was marked by the new prooemium in 5.26. In the years following the Peace of Nicias Thucydides thought of the war as a ten years' war. After 404 he revised his earlier text in view of new insights and added certain references to later events. The theory may be seen to arise from certain ideas about Thucydides' biography and became influential some twenty years after its publication, with the widespread interest in historicism in German universities. In the period under survey Meyer (46), Schwartz (50), Pohlenz (51), and Schadewaldt (53) are landmarks in the study of the problem from a historical-biographical approach. Schadewaldt, Grosskinsky (54), and Patzer (57) emphasize the importance of 1.22.

39. Junghan E. A., "Die Reden bei Thukydides," NJPhP CXI 1875 657–682.

40. Drefke O., *De orationibus quae in priore parte historiae Thucydideae insunt et directis et indirectis*: Diss. Halis Sax. 1877 56 p.

JAW LVIII 1889 74–76 Müller; JAW LXXIX 1894 198 Meyer.

41. Junghan E. A., "Nochmals die Reden bei Thukydides," NJPhP CXVII 1878 691–694.

42. Sörgel J., "Die Reden bei Thukydides," NJPhP CXVII 1878 331–364 & 849–851.

JAW LVIII 1889 77–79 Müller.

43. Fellner T., *Forschung und Darstellungsweise des Thukydides, gezeigt an ein Kritik des 8. Buches*: Wien Konegen 1880 76 p.

44. Junghan E. A., *Studien zu Thukydides. Neue Folge. Historisch-Kritisches, Exegetisches, Polemisches*: Berlin Calvary 1886 95 p.

JAW LVIII 1889 79 Müller.

45. Friedrich G., "Die Entstehung des thukydideischen Geschichtswerkes," NJP CLV 1897 175–188 & 243–256.

46. Meyer E., *Forschungen zur alten Geschichte*, II: *Zur Geschichte des fünften Jahrhunderts v. Chr.* (Halle Niemeyer 1899 viii & 554 p.) 269–436.

47. Wilamowitz-Moellendorff U. von, "Lesefrüchte, LXVII," Hermes XXXV 1900 533–561 (int. al., on Thucydides' sources of information for the Plataean episodes).

48. Bodin L., "Thucydide. Genèse de son oeuvre," REA XIV 1912 1–38.

49. Meyer E., *Thukydides und die Entstehung des wissenschaftlichen Geschichtsschreibung*: Mitt. der Wiener Vereinigung der Freunde des humanistischen Gymnasiums XIV Wien Fromme 1913 26 p.

MHL XLIV 1916 9 Geyer; JAW CLXXVIII 1919 208 Widmann.

50. Schwartz E., *Das Geschichtswerk des Thukydides*: Bonn Cohen 1919 365 p.

BPhW XL 1920 1–6 & 25–34 Münscher; LZB LXXI 1920 451–453 Geyer; MPh XXVIII 1921 5–6 Vürtheim; JAW CXCV 1923 193–210 Widmann.

51. Pohlenz M., "Thukydidesstudien," NGG 1919 95–138 & 1920 56–82.

52. Wilamowitz-Moellendorff U. von, "Gerippe einer Thukydidesbiographie, soweit sie sich geben lässt," *Platon*, II: *Beiträge und Textkritik* (Berlin Weidmann 1920 445 p.) 12–16.

53. Schadewaldt W., *Die Geschichtsschreibung des Thukydides. Ein Versuch*: Berlin Weidmann 1929 vi & 100 p.

BAGB (SC) II 1930 74–81; BBG LXVI 1930 101–105 Rupprecht; DLZ LI 1930 543–548 Dornseiff; Gnomon VI 1930 76–100 Kapp; HZ CXLII 1930 324–328 Jacoby; JAW CCXXV 1930 116–118 Widmann; LZB LXXXI 1930 247; Litt VII 1930 98–105 Momigliano; MPh XXXVII 1930 83 Leyds; PhW L 1930 193–201 Ziegler; Aevum VI 1932 666–667 Cessi.

54. Grosskinsky A., *Das Programm des Thukydides*: Neue Dt. Forsch., Abt. Klass. Phil. III Berlin Junker & Dünnhaupt 1936 108 p.

CR L 1936 174–175 Powell; GGA CXCVIII 1936 281–300 Pohlenz; BAGB (SC) IX 1937 41–47; CW XXX 1937 208 Larsen; PhW LVII 1937 1025–1029 Oetzmann.

55. Harrison A. R. W., "Thucydides I 22," CR LI 1937 6–7.

56. Laqueur R., "Forschungen zu Thukydides," RhM LXXXVI 1937 316–357.

57. Patzer H., *Das Problem der Geschichtsschreibung des Thukydides und die thukydideische Frage*: Neue Dt. Forsch., Abt. Klass. Phil. VI Berlin Junker & Dünnhaupt 1937 118 p.

CR LI 1937 173–174 Powell; RFIC XV 1937 284–287 Momigliano; BAGB (SC) X 1938 28–34; REG LI 1938 191–192 David; AJP LX 1939 108–111 Finley; RPh XIII 1939 364–365 Mathieu.

58. Longo Rubbi C., *Un nuovo aspetto della questione tucididea. I discorsi e l'evoluzione del metodo*: Quad. di Orpheus Catania Centro di studi sull' antico cristianesimo 1963 43 p.

THOUGHT AND OBJECTIVES OF THUCYDIDES

Although the history was left in an unfinished state, investigation of the thought of the author as a historian and literary artist must consider the entire work as it is preserved. As most of the studies listed here were written during the past 25 years, this may signify recognition of the need to develop an approach to Thucydides which is relatively independent of, and distinct from, formal solutions to the problem of the genesis of the work. Mme de Romilly's study of Thucydides and Athenian imperialism is a brilliant example of such an approach (65), which departs initially from the problem of composition and takes it in a new direction. In providing an intellectual background against which events, individual motives, and political movements may be interpreted, the speeches are especially open to investigation in this line of inquiry. Studies of Thucydides' thought may be investigations of ideas in the work expressed by key words, phrases, and concepts (68, 73, 74, 76, 77, 78) or examinations of the author's attitude toward contemporary issues and intellectual trends (59, 60, 62, 63, 64, 65, 67, 69, 70, 72, 75).

59. Beardslee J. W., *The use of physis in fifth-century Greek literature*: Diss. Chicago Univ. of Chicago Pr. 1918 v & 126 p.

JHS XXXVIII 1918 205–206 J. H. S.; PhW XLIII 1923 79 Nestle.

60. Menzel A., *Kallikles. Eine Studie zur Geschichte der Lehre vom Rechte des Stärkeren*: Wien & Leipzig Deuticke 1922 101 p. (int. al., on Thucydides and the sophists).

PhW XLIII 1923 193–200 Seeliger.

61. Aly W., "Form und Stoff des Thukydides," RhM LXXVII 1928 361–383.

61a. Regenbogen O., "Thukydides als politischer Denker," HG XLIV 1933 2–25.

62. Bender G. F., *Der Begriff des Staatsmannes bei Thukydides*: Würzburg Triltsch 1938 iv & 115 p.

AC VIII 1939 441–442 Crahay; CR LIII 1939 61–62 Gomme; LEC VIII 1939 126 Charlier; RBPh XVIII 1939 806–807 Peremans.

63. Gundert H., "Athen und Sparta in den Reden des Thukydides," Antike XVI 1940 98–114.

63a. Herter H., "Freiheit und Gebundenheit des Staatsmannes bei Thukydides," RhM XCIII 1950 133–153.

64. Grene D., *Man in his pride. A study in the political philosophy of Thucydides and Plato*: Univ. of Chicago Pr. 1950 xiii & 231 p.

Hermathena LXXVII 1951 81–83; REA LIII 1951 352–353 Mo-

reau; REG LXIV 1951 364 de Romilly; CP XLVII 1952 35–38
Ehrenberg; CR II 1952 73–75 Gomme; CW XLVI 1952 40 Raubitschek; PhR LXI 1952 121 Robinson; RPh XXVI 1952 91–92
Louis; AJP LXXIX 1953 179–183 McGregor; JHS LXXIII
1953 155 Russell; RPhilos CXLIII 1953 452–453 Leroy.

65. Romilly J. de, *Thucydide et l'impérialisme athénien. La
pensée de l'historien et la genèse de l'oeuvre*, 2me ed.: Coll. d'études
anciennes Paris Les Belles Lettres 1951 326 p. (1st ed. 1947).

JHS LXVI 1946 136–137 Ehrenberg: REG LIX–LX 1946–1947
467–474 Aymard; MPh LII 1947 273–276 Vliet; AUP XVIII
1948 133–135; Emerita XVI 1948 313–318 Adrados; LEC XVI
1948 50–51 van Ooteghem; RBPh XXVI 1948 203–210 Cloché;
REA L 1948 145–152 Audiat; RU LVII 1948 218–219 Bequignon;
AJP LXX 1949 105–107 McGregor; CR LXIII 1949 16–18
Gomme; Gnomon XXI 1949 169–171 Taeger; RPh XXIII 1949
69–70 Chantraine; CW XLVI 1953 123 Wassermann; G&R XXII
1953 27–32 Gregor.

66. Strasburger H., "Die Entdeckung der politischen Geschichte
durch Thukydides," Saeculum V 1954 395–428.

67. Wassermann F., "Thucydides and the disintegration of the
polis," TAPA LXXXV 1954 46–54.

68. Romilly J. de, "La crainte dans l'oeuvre de Thucydide,"
C&M XVII 1956 119–127.

69. Romilly J. de, *Histoire et raison chez Thucydide*: Coll.
d'études anciennes Paris Les Belles Lettres 1956 314 p.

GIF IX 1956 370 Scivoletto; AC XXVI 1957 189–191 Labarbe;
BAClLg V 1957 22–24 Henry; CJ LIII 1957 143 Wassermann;
LEC XXV 1957 128 Vanneste; Mnemosyne X 1957 74–77 Kamer-
beek; REG LXX 1957 540–542 Moulinier; Lychnos 1957–1958
373–375 Zilliacus; A&R III 1958 170–173 Alberti; DLZ LXXIX
1958 611–615 Ebener; Gnomon XXX 1958 15–19 Gomme; MPh
LXIII 1958 272–275 den Boer; REA LXI 1959 453–459 Audiat;
HZ CXCVI 1963 383–385 Treu.

70. Parry A., *Logos and ergon in Thucydides*: Diss. Harvard
Univ. 1957. Cf. summary in HSCP LXIII 1958 522–523.

71. Romilly J. de, *Thucydides and Athenian imperialism*, transl.
by Thody P.: Oxford Blackwell 1963 xi & 400 p.

CW LVII 1964 321 Oost; REG LXXVII 1964 341–343 Pouilloux; CR XV 1965 115 Brunt.

72. Stahl H.-P., *Thukydides. Die Stellung des Menschen im geschichtlichen Prozess*: Zetemata XL München Beck 1966 viii & 188 p.

Athenaeum XLIV 1966 381 Levi; CW LX 1966 120 Rose; Erasmus XVIII 1966 555–556 Lasserre; CR XVII 1967 278–280 Brunt; DLZ LXXXVIII 1967 1074–1077 Popp; FL VIII 1967 65–67 Kamerbeek; LEC XXXV 1967 200–201 Delaunois; MH XXIV 1967 241 Wehrli; Lychnos 1967–1968 311–312 Palm; CJ LXIII 1968 230–232 Wassermann; CP LXIII 1968 225–227 Donini; Gnomon XL 1968 232–236 de Romilly; Mnemosyne XXI 1968 307–309 van Dijck; RBPh XLVI 1968 624–626 Janssens; REG LXXXI 1968 283–284 Will; RPh XLII 1968 329–331 Weil; RFIC XCVII 1969 84–90 Donini.

73. Gardiner T., *Terms for power in Thucydides*: Diss. Harvard Univ. 1968. Cf. summary in HSCP LXXIII 1969 312–314.

74. Huart P., *Le vocabulaire de l'analyse psychologique dans l'oeuvre de Thucydide*: Études & Commentaires LXIX Paris Klincksieck 1968 545 p. index.

BBF XIV 1969 *980–*981 Ernst; Platon XXI 1969 357–370 Oikonomakos; BIEH IV 1970 57–58 Corominas; CR XX 1970 307–309 Westlake; Emerita XXXVIII 1970 470–472 Gangutia; Gnomon XLII 1970 529–534 Schneider; JCS XVIII 1970 137–140 Kubo; REA LXXII 1970 161–163 Levet; RPh XLIV 1970 316–319 Weil; StudClas XII 1970 337–339 Barbu.

75. Klinz A., "Demokratie und Machtgedanke im Geschichtswerk des Thukydides," AU XI 1968,5 19–28 (int. al., on Pericles' funeral oration and the Melian dialogue).

76. Gardiner T., "Terms for thalassocracy in Thucydides," RhM CXII 1969 16–22 (int. al., on 2.62.2, 5.97.1, 5.109.5, 6.18.5, 7.48.2).

77. Tanaka M., "*Dikaios logos* and *aléthés prophasis*," JCS XVIII 1970 1–18 (in Japanese, with a summary in English).

78. Woodhead A. G., *Thucydides on the nature of power*: Martin Class. Lect. XXIV Cambridge Harvard Univ. Pr. 1970 xii & 222 p.

CW LXIV 1970 21 Raubitschek; LEC XXXVIII 1970 381 Duhoux; TLS LXIX 1970 1465–1466.

RHETORIC AND ORATORY

This section includes studies which examine Thucydidean speeches for evidence of oratorical technique and the influence of rhetoric (79, 81, 86, 92, 93, 99, 100, 103) or explore the relation of Thucydides to other literary figures, especially orators (80, 85, 90, 96, 98), and contemporary forces in intellectual perception (82, 83, 87, 94, 97). In the latter category fall studies of Thucydides and the sophists (88, 89, 101). Although interest in rhetoric and oratory may be seen to run throughout the years covered in this survey, studies of a literary-historical nature are more popular in the early part of the period. Studies of individual speeches which are relevant to this topic are listed under the respective speeches, below. One should note especially Kakridis on Pericles' funeral oration (251) and Moraux on the Mytilene debate (279) in this regard.

79. Kleist H., *Ueber den Bau und die Technik der thukydideischen Reden*, I: Programma Dramburg 1876 23 p.

80. Lehmann J., *Thucydidem in orationibus suis vere habitas minus respicere demonstratur et genus dicendi, quo historicus in illis usus est, cum Antiphontis dictione comparatur*: Programma Putbus 1876 19 p.

81. Stein F., *De figurarum apud Thucydidem usu*: Programma Friedrich Wilhelm Gymnasii Köln 1881 19 p.
JAW LVIII 1889 94–97 Müller.

82. Rockel C. J., *De allocutionis usu qualis sit apud Thucydidem, Xenophontem, oratores Atticos, Dionem, Aristidem*: Diss. Königsberg 1884 56 p.
WKPh IV 1887 559–561 Keil; JAW LVIII 1889 92 Müller.

83. Zeitschel (*sic*), *De Thucydidis inventione cum usu oratorum congruente*: Programma Realgymnasii Nordhausen 1884 13 p.
JAW LVIII 1889 97 Müller; LZB 1884 1435.

84. Altinger J., *De rhetoricis in orationes Thucydideas scholiis*: Programma Gymnasii Guilelmini Monacensis München 1885 66 p.
JAW LVIII 1889 73–74 Müller.

85. Nieschke A., *De Thucydide Antiphontis discipulo et Homeri imitatore*: Programma Progymnasii Münden 1885 73 p.
JAW LVIII 1889 98 Müller; JAW LXXIX 1894 155–156 Meyer.

86. Kleist H., *Ueber den Bau und die Technik der thukydideischen Reden*, II: *Die Argumentation*: Programma Dramburg 1887 19 p.

WKPh IV 1887 1395-1396 Widmann; Gymnasium VI Paderborn 1888 273; JAW LVIII 1889 84-86 Müller.

87. Radford R. S., *Personification and the use of abstract ideas in the Attic orators and Thucydides*: Diss. Johns Hopkins Baltimore 1901 51 p.

BFC X 1903 98-99 Zuretti; BPhW XXIII 1903 1093-1095 Fuhr; RC 1904 43 My.

88. Nestle W., "Thukydides und die Sophistik," NJA XXXIII,1 1914 648-685.

89. Rittelmeyer F., *Thukydides und die Sophistik*: Diss. Erlangen Borna-Leipzig Noske 1915 viii & 196 p.

WKPh XXXIII 1916 532-536 Nestle.

90. Mathieu G., "Isocrate et Thucydide," RPh XLII 1918 122-129.

91. Nestle W., "Politik und Moral im Altertum," NJA XLI,1 1918 225-244.

92. John W., *De veterum rhetorum studiis Thucydideis quaestiones selectae*: Diss. Greifswald 1922 40 p.

PhW XLII 1922 1033-1041 Levy.

93. Danninger O., "Ueber das *eikos* in den Reden bei Thukydides," WS XLIX 1931 12-31.

94. Rosenkranz B., *Der lokale Grundton und die persönliche Eigenart in der Sprache des Thukydides und in der älteren attischen Redner*: Diss. Münster 1930 54 p.

JAW CCXLII 1934 3-4 Widmann.

95. Bodin L., "Isocrate et Thucydide," *Mélanges G. Glotz* (2 vols., Paris Presses Universitaires 1932 940 p.) 93-102.

96. Woessner W., *Die synonymische Unterscheidung bei Thukydides und den politischen Rednern der Griechen*: Würzburg Triltsch 1937 76 p.

MPh XLIV 1939 89 Drerup; PhW LIX 1939 33-38 Bender.

97. Finley J. H., "Euripides and Thucydides," HSCP XLIX 1938 23-68.

98. Hudson-Williams H. L., "Thucydides, Isocrates and the rhetorical method of composition," CQ XLII 1948 76-81.

99. Hudson-Williams H. L., "Thucydides and the literary speech," PCA XLVIII 1951 25–26 (summary of a paper).
100. Schuller S., "About Thucydides' use of *aitia* and *prophasis*," RBPh XXXIV 1956 971–984 (suggests influence of Antiphon, Ps.-Herodes, Lysias, and not the Hippocratic corpus).
101. Kiechle F., "Ursprung and Wirkung der macht-politischen Theorien im Geschichtswerk des Thukydides," Gymnasium LXX 1963 289–312 (on the influence of the sophists, especially on Pericles and his speeches).
102. Anastassiou A. A., "Eine *synkrisis* von Demosthenes und Thukydides bei Dionysios von Halikarnass," *Charis K. I. Vourveris aphierôma tôn mathêtôn tou epi têi hexêkontapentaetêridi tou biou autou*, ed. by Anastassiou A. A., Kambylis A. & Skiadas A. (Athens 1964 xvi & 424 p.) 297–304.
103. Gommel J., *Rhetorisches Argumentieren bei Thukydides*: Diss. Tübingen Spudasmata X Hildesheim Olms 1966 iv & 90 p.

SPEECHES AND HISTORY

The items listed under this rubric emphasize the relationship of Thucydidean speeches to external factors. Included are studies of objectivity and accuracy in the speeches (108, 112, 115, 118) and those which examine significant events involving speeches (107, 119, 127), political and social structures (116, 117, 121, 122, 124, 125, 131), and personalities, especially Pericles and Alcibiades (104, 105, 106, 109, 110, 113, 114, 120, 123, 126, 128, 129, 130). Volume III of the Athenian tribute lists has been cited here because of its great importance in setting a standard for evaluating Thucydides in terms of the background of the fifth century (111). Studies concerning individual speeches in this regard are listed under the speeches themselves, below.
104. Fokke A., *Alkibiades und die sicilische Expedition*: Programma Emden 1879 27 p.
105. Fokke A., *Rettungen des Alkibiades*, I: *Die sicilische Expedition*: Emden Haynel 1883 iv & 88 p.
106. Fokke A., *Rettungen des Alkibiades*, II: *Der Aufenthalt des Alkibiades in Sparta*: Emden Haynel 1886 iv & 112 p.
MHL VIII 1880 57 Foss; Gymnasium I Paderborn 1883 454–456

Brüll; DLZ III 1883 1508 Niese; LZB XXXIV 1883 1823; Phil. Anzeiger XIV 1884 8-12 Herbst; Phil. Rundschau IV 1884 752-757 Berg; ZOEG XXXV 1884 290; BPhW V 1885 1095-1097 Holm; LZB XXXVIII 1887 805; WKPh IV 1887 1186-1187 Holm; ZOEG XXXVIII 1887 290 Bauer; BPhW VIII 1888 782 Klatt; JAW LVIII 1889 102-104 Müller.

107. Stein H., "Zur Quellenkritik des Thukydides, I: Die erste sizilische Unternehmung; II: Hermokrates," RhM LV 1900 531-564 (int. al., on 6.32-41 and 6.76-87).

108. Ciaceri E., "Intorno alla obiettività storica nei discorsi Tucididei," RFIC XLIV 1916 67-90.

109. Doerwald P., "Zwei Reden des Perikles bei Thukydides," L&L 1929 35-48.

110. Bayer E., "Thukydides und Perikles," WJA III 1948 1-57.

111. Meritt B. D., Wade-Gery H. T. & McGregor M. F., *The Athenian tribute lists*, III: *The Athenian naval confederacy*: Princeton Amer. School of Class. Stud. at Athens 1950 xx & 366 p.

AHR LVI 1951 854-855 McDonald; CP XLVII 1952 261-263 Pritchett; CR II 1952 97-100 Meiggs; CW XLV 1952 230-231 Raubitschek; HZ CLXXIII 1952 540-549 Ehrenberg.

112. Hehn V., "Ueber die Authenticität der Reden des Thukydides," *Aus V. Hehns Nachlass*, hrsg. von Deichgräber K., Akad. d. Wiss. & d. Lit. in Mainz, Geistes- & sozialwiss. Kl. IX 1951 (Wiesbaden Steiner 1951 99 p.) 793-804.

113. Levi M. A., "In margine a Tucidide," PP VII 1952 81-112 (int. al., on the speeches of Pericles).

114. Wassermann F., "The speeches of King Archidamus in Thucydides," CJ XLVIII 1952-1953 193-200.

115. Chambers M. H., *Studies in the veracity of Thucydides*: Diss. Harvard Univ. 1954. Cf. summary in HSCP LXII 1957 141-143 (part of a chapter on the speeches).

116. Dover K. J., "Anapsephisis in fifth-century Athens," JHS LXXV 1955 17-20 (on 3.36.4-49.2 and 6.14).

117. Strasburger H., "Thukydides und die politische Selbstdarstellung der Athener," Hermes LXXXVI 1958 17-40.

118. Rohrer K., "Ueber die Authenticität der Reden bei Thukydides," WS LXXII 1959 36-53.

119. Andrewes A., "The Melian dialogue and Pericles' last speech," PCPS VI 1960 1–10.

120. Luria S., "Alkibiades," Meander XV 1960 217–225 & 275–285 (in Polish, with a summary in Latin).

121. Diller H., "Freiheit bei Thukydides als Schlagwort und als Wirklichkeit," Gymnasium LXIX 1962 189–204.

122. Wassermann F., "The voice of Sparta in Thucydides," CJ LIX 1964 289–297.

123. Delebecque E., *Thucydide et Alcibiade*: Publ. AFLA XLIX Centre d'ét. & rech. hellen. 5 Aix-en-Provence Ed. Ophrys 1965 250 p. 1 map.

AC XXXV 1966 270 Lévêque; GIF XIX 1966 161–163 Jannaccone; RecSR LIV 1966 597 des Places; CR XVII 1967 24–26 Westlake; Mnemosyne XX 1967 464–465 van Dijck; RFIC XCV 1967 463–467 Asheri; RH XCI 1967 190–192 Will; RPh XLI 1967 311–313 Weil; AJP LXXXIX 1968 118–119 McGregor; CP LXIII 1968 165–166 Oost; Gnomon XL 1968 715–717 Treu; P&I X 1968 174–175 Tagliaferro; REA LXX 1968 162–163 Payrau; RBPh XLVII 1969 629–630 Piérart.

124. Grant J. R., "A note on the tone of Greek diplomacy," CQ XV 1965 261–266 (on frankness of expression, attested in speeches).

125. Kinugasa S., "The comparison between the Athenians and Spartans in Thucydides," JCS XIV 1966 57–65 (in Japanese, with a summary in English).

126. Séchan L., "Deux grandes figures athéniennes, Thucydide et Alcibiade," REG LXXIX 1966 482–494.

127. Liebeschuetz W., "Thucydides and the Sicilian expedition," Historia XVII 1968 289–306.

128. Westlake H. D., *Individuals in Thucydides*: Cambridge Univ. Pr. 1968 x & 324 p.

AC XXXVIII 1969 647–649 Laronde; CF XXIII 1969 268–270 Marique; CW LXII 1969 336 Kleinlogel; Paideia XIV 1969 301–309 Daverio Rocchi; Phoenix XXIII 1969 395–397 McGregor; REA LXXI 1969 472–475 Delebecque; REG LXXXII 1969 649–650 de Romilly; AHR LXXV 1970 825–826 Immerwahr; G&R XVII 1970 109 Sewter; Hermathena CX 1970 91–92 Parke; JCS XVIII 1970 133–137 Fujinawa; Perficit II 1970 422–423; CJ LXVI 1970–1971 176–177 Lenardon.

129. Tagliaferro D., "Alcibiade e l'unità dei Greci in Tucidide," P&I X 1968 261–274.

130. Pouncey P. R., *Thucydides and Pericles*: Diss. Columbia Univ. 1969 224 p. (microfilm). Cf. summary in DA XXX 1970 5426A–5427A.

131. Westlake H. D., "Diplomacy in Thucydides," BRL LIII 1970 227–246.

TYPES OF SPEECH

Separate studies which deal with the internal classification of speeches and spoken *logoi* in Thucydides are listed here. General discussions of this topic may be found in Jebb (1), Blass (4), and Luschnat (37).

132. Weber L., "Perikles' Samische Leichenrede," Hermes LVII 1922 375–395 (reconstruction, using 2.35–46 and Herodotus 7.161, 9.27).

133. Luschnat O., *Die Feldherrnreden im Geschichtswerk des Thukydides*: Philologus Suppl. XXXIV,2 Leipzig Dieterich 1942 137 p.

AC XII 1943 121–122 Josserand; PhW LXIV 1944 193–197 Carstenn; DLZ LXX 1949 490–495 Patzer; Gnomon XXI 1949 78–79 Regenbogen.

134. Hout M. van den, "Studies in early Greek letter writing," Mnemosyne II 1949 19–41 & 138–153 (int. al., on 1.128–132 & 7.11–15).

135. Hudson-Williams H. L., "Political speeches in Athens," CQ XLV 1951 68–73.

136. Longo Rubbi C., "Sui discorsi scritti dal giovane stratego Tucidide," Orpheus X 1963 65–75.

STYLE

This section includes general studies of the influence of external forces upon Thucydides' style in the speeches (140, 141, 144) and investigations of the internal characteristics of that style (137, 138, 139, 142, 143, 145, 147, 148). One suggests that Thucydides has attempted to characterize his speakers by the style of oratory they actually employed (146).

137. Thulin C., *De obliqua oratione apud Thucydidem*: Acta Univ. Lundensis XXXVII,5 & XXXVIII,2 Lund Malmström 1901–1902 90 p.
RC 1903 245–246 Hauvette.

138. Lamb W. R. M., *Clio enthroned. A study of prose form in Thucydides*: Cambridge Univ. Pr. 1914 xv & 319 p.
CJ X 1914–1915 188–190 Calhoun; BPhW XXXV 1915 865–867 Hude; CR XXIX 1915 178–181 Sheppard; CP XII 1917 222–224 Smith; JAW CLXXVIII 1919 207 Widmann.

139. Lapounoff J., "Le style des discours de Thucydide," Journal du Ministère de l'Instruction Publique en Russie 1916.

140. Hofmann E., *Qua ratione epos, mythos, ainos, logos et vocabula ab eisdem stirpibus derivata in antiquo Graecorum sermone (usque ad annum fere 400) adhibita sint*: Diss. Göttingen 1921 Göttingen Kaestner 1922 iv & 123 p.
PhW XLIII 1923 950–957 Toedtmann; JAW CCVIII 1926 167 Widmann.

141. Cochrane C. N., *Thucydides and the science of history*: London Oxford Univ. Pr. 1929 180 p.
AHR XXXV 1930 584–585 Ferguson; BAGB (SC) II 1930 81–87; CP XXV 1930 290–292 Shorey; CR XLIV 1930 123–124 Gomme; JHS L 1930 177; RH CLXV 1930 352 Cloché; DLZ LII 1931 14 Jacoby; EHR XLVI 1931 151 D. C. M.

142. Lüdtke W., *Untersuchungen zum Satzbau des Thukydides (das sog. Anakoluth)*: Diss. Kiel 1930 Altona Lorenzen 1930 vi & 99 p.
PhW LI 1931 833–838 Keil; JAW CCXLII 1934 3 Widmann.

143. Ros J., *Die metabolê (variatio) als Stilprinzip des Thukydides*: Rhet. Stud. Ergänzungsbd. I Paderborn Schöningh 1938 xxiv & 512 p.
EPhK 1938 269–271 Marot; LEC VII 1938 605–606 Delande; AC VIII 1939 250–251 Henry; AGI XXXI 1939 155–156 Pisani; BSL No. 120 1939 57–58 Chantraine; CR LIII 1939 13 Powell; JHS LIX 1939 308–309 Lockwood; Lychnos 1939 474 Rudberg; MC 1939 195 Taccone; PhW LIX 1939 433–438 Bender; REG LII 1939 220–221 Mathieu; RFIC XVII 1939 267–269 Bartoletti; IF

LVII 1939–1940 152–153 Schwentner; AJP LXI 1940 96–102 Finley; MPh XLVIII 1940 35 Meerwaldt; RPh XIV 1940 178–179 Humbert.

144. Finley J. H., "The origins of Thucydides' style," HSCP L 1939 35–84.

145. Katičič R., "Die Ringkomposition im ersten Buche des Thukydideischen Geschichtswerkes," WS LXX 1957 179–196 (probable influence of the rhetoric of Gorgias).

146. Tompkins D. P., *Stylistic characterization in Thucydides*: Diss. Yale Univ. 1968 245 p. (microfilm). Cf. summary in DA XXIX 1969 3990A.

147. Parry A., "Thucydides' use of abstract language," Yale French Stud. XLV 1970 3–20.

148. Maloney G., "La fréquence et l'ordre des formes verbales dans l'oeuvre de Thucydide," RELO 1970,3 87–109.

INDIVIDUAL PASSAGES

This rubric is reserved for separate discussions, textual or historical, of individual passages, from more than a single speech. Discussions of 1.22 are also included.

149. Hoffmann E., "Zu Thukydides (I 35,5; II 41,4)," NJPhP CIX 1874 627–628.

150. Leeuwen J. van, "*Hôs* . . . *kai*, ad Thucyd. VI 36; ad Thucyd. VI 37,1; ad Thucyd. VI 37,2; *hôs* . . . *ei*, ad Thucyd. III 38,4; *megistos* . . . *pleistos*, ad Thucyd. III 45,3; III 59,2," Mnemosyne XXV 1897 85, 88, 92, 188, 348, 450–451.

151. Platt A., "Thucydides," JPh XXXIII 1914 270–277 (int. al., on 2.13.1, 6.16.2, 6.32.3, and 7.67.3).

152. Gomme A. W., "Notes on Thucydides, book VI," CR XXXIV 1920 81–85 (int. al., on 6.23.1, 24.3, 35.7, 40.1).

153. Ziegler K., "Der Ursprung der Exkurse im Thukydides," RhM LXXVIII 1929 58–67 (int. al., on 1.126–138).

154. Thompson E. A., "Notes on Thucydides I," Hermathena LVI 1940 136–145 (int. al., on 1.33.2, 70.3, and 82.5).

155. Gomme A. W., "Thucydides notes," CQ XLII 1948 10–14 (int. al., on 2.37.1, 3.44.2–3).

156. Braun E., "*Nomoi akinêtoi*," JOEAI XL 1953 144–150 (on 1.71.3, 3.37.3, 6.18.7).

157. Dover K. J., "Problems in Thucydides VI and VII," PCPS III 1954–1955 4–11 (int. al., on 6.17.3, 23.1, and 40.1).

158. Schmid W., "Zu Thukydides I 22.1 und 2," Philologus XCIX 1955 220–233.

159. Stamatakos S., "*Hermêneutika kai kritika sêmeiômata eis ton Thoukydidên*," Platon XIII 1961 252–257 (on 2.37, 3.12.3, 3.56.7).

160. Rokeah D., "A note on Thucydides I 22,1," Eranos LX 1962 104–107.

161. Glucker J., "A misinterpretation of a passage in Thucydides," Eranos LXII 1964 1–6 (on 1.22).

162. Thompson W. E., "Some Thucydidean parallels," Philologus CXII 1968 119–121 (int. al., on 1.124.1 and 3.40.7).

INDIVIDUAL SPEECHES

Separate studies of individual speeches and of individual passages within a speech are listed here. Many of the speeches, however, especially famous ones such as Pericles' funeral oration, the Mytilene debate, and the Melian dialogue, are also investigated in the context of book-length studies listed under other rubrics, above.

1.31–44   Assembly at Athens.

163. Schneider J. G., *Ueber die Reden der Kerkyräer und der Korinthier bei Thuk. I 32–43*: Programma Coburg 1880 16 p. JAW LVIII 1889 98–99 Müller.

164. Thompson E. A., "Thucydides I 36,3," CR LV 1941 27–28.

165. Büchner K., "Thukydides I 40,2" Hermes LXXXI 1953 119–122.

166. Craici L., "I *kerkyraika* di Tucidide," Acme VI 1953 405–418.

167. Fritz K. von, "*Hoper saphestatê pistis*," *Thesaurismata. Festschrift fur I. Kapp zum 70. Geburtstag* (München Beck 1954 168 p.) 25–37 (on 1.35.5).

168. Calder W. M., "The Corcyraean-Corinthian speeches in Thucydides I," CJ L 1955 179–180.

1.67–88   Conference of the Peloponnesian League at Sparta.

169. Brown E. S., "Thucydides, book I 69," Hermathena XIV 1906–1907 283–284.

170. Bonner R. J., "On Thucydides I 77,1," CP XIV 1919 284–286.

171. Bodin L., "Thucydide I 84," *Mélanges offerts a A. M. Desrousseaux par ses amis et ses élèves* (Paris Hachette 1937 502 p.) 19–26.

172. Hopper R. J., "Interstate juridical agreements in the Athenian empire," JHS LXIII 1943 35–51 (int. al., on 1.77).

173. Turner E. G., "*Philodokein dokoumen* (Thuc. I 77)," CR LX 1946 5–7.

174. Papantoniou G., "Observations on Thucydides," AJP LXXI 1950 299–304 (on 1.74.1).

175. Kamerbeek J. C., "Ad Thucydidem I 68, 1 et 3," Mnemosyne VI 1953 64.

176. Reich L., *Die Rede der Athener in Sparta (Interpretation von Thuk. I 73 bis 78)*: Diss. Hamburg 1956 115 p. (typescript).

177. Bartoletti V., "Tucidide II 73,1–74,1 in un papiro dell' Università statale di Milano," *Studi in onore di L. Castiglioni* (Firenze Sansoni 1960 1143 p. in 2 vol.) 59–66.

178. Tasolambros L., "Thucydides I 71," Platon XVII 1965 246–259.

179. Kierdorf W., *Erlebnis und Darstellung der Perserkriege. Studien zu Simonides, Pindar, Aischylos und den attischen Rednern*: Diss. Köln 1963 Hypomnemata XVI Göttingen Vandenhoeck & Ruprecht 1966 130 p. (int. al., on I.73–78).

CW LX 1967 213–214 Frost; Gnomon XXXIX 1967 517–518 Ehrenberg; Gymnasium LXXIV 1967 382–384 Radt; LEC XXXV 1967 86 Walbrecq; MH XXIV 1967 239–240 Breitenbach; Phoenix XXI 1967 137–141 Lattimore; CR XVIII 1968 79–80 Hammond; DLZ LXXXIX 1968 395–397 Barth; JHS LXXXVIII 1968 153–154 Burn; REG LXXXI 1968 257–259 Orsini.

1.128.7   Pausanias' letter to Xerxes.
1.129.3   Xerxes' letter to Pausanias.

180. Waszyśńki S., "De l'authenticité de la correspondance de Pausanias avec Xerxes chez Thucydide I 128 et 129," Eos 1900 113–117 (in Polish).

181. Olmstead A. T., "A Persian letter in Thucydides," Amer. Journal of Semitic Lang. XLIX 1932–1933 154–161.

182. Kappus K., "Der Königsbrief bei Thukydides I 129," cf. summary in *Berichte über die Sitzung des philol. Vereins* Berlin 1936–1937 19.

183. Fornara C. W., "Some aspects of the career of Pausanias of Sparta," Historia XV 1966 257–271 (against the authenticity of the letters).

184. Vogt J., "Zu Pausanias und Caracalla," Historia XVIII 1969 299–308 (int. al., discussion of the authenticity of the correspondence between Pausanias and Xerxes).

1.136.4   Speech of Themistocles to Admetus of Molossus.
1.137.2   Remarks of Themistocles to the captain of a ship.
1.137.4   Letter of Themistocles to Artaxerxes.

185. Lenardon R. J., "Charon, Thucydides, and Themistocles," Phoenix XV 1961 28–40.

1.139.3–145   Assembly at Athens.

186. Müller F., "Disposition der ersten Perikleischen Rede bei Thukydides (I 140–144)," NJPhP CXXXII,2 1885 550–557.

187. Leeuwen J. van, "*Kólyei, pou lyei,* ad Thuc. I 144," Mnemosyne XXVII 1899 336.

188. Hirst M. E., "Thucydides I 141," CR XLVIII 1934 171.

189. Nesselhauf H., "Die diplomatische Verhandlungen von dem peloponnesischen Kriege (Thukydides I 139 ff.)," Hermes LXIX 1934 286–299.

190. Zahn R., *Die erste Periklesrede (Thukydides I 140–144). Interpretation und Versuch einer Einordnung in dem Zusammenhang des Werkes*: Borna-Leipzig Noske 1934 iv & 116 p. CR XLVIII 1934 238 Powell; BAGB (SC) VII 1935 70–73; PhW LV 1935 337–345 Oetzmann; GGA CXCVIII 1936 281–300 Pohlenz; RPh X 1936 382 Collart.

191. Delachaux A., "À propos de quelques passages de Thucydide (livre I)," *Mélanges offerts à M. Niedermann à l'occasion de son soixante-dixième anniversaire* (Univ. de Neuchâtel, Rec. de Trav. publ. par la Fac. des Lettres XXII Neuchâtel Secrét. de l'Univ. 1944 208 p. 1 pl.) 63–66 (int. al., on 1.143.4).

192. Hamond N. G. L., "Thucydides I 142,2–4," CR LXI 1947 39–41.

193. Herter H., "Zur ersten Periklesrede des Thukydides," *Studies presented to D. M. Robinson on his seventieth birthday*, II, ed. by Mylonas G. E. & Raymond D. (St. Louis Washington Univ. 1953 xx & 1336 p. 98 pl.) 613–623.

194. Luschnat O., "Eine Interpretation von Thukydides I 142,3," *Rastloses Schaffen. Festschrift für F. Lammert* (Stuttgart Kohlhammer 1954 156 p.) 37–38.

195. Bickermann E. J., "*Autonomia.* Sur un passage de Thucydide (I 144,2)," RIDA V 1958 313–343.

196. Mello M., "A Tucidide I 144,1–2," PP XVII 1962 60–63.

197. Wet B. X. de, "The so-called defensive policy of Pericles," AClass XII 1969 103–119 (on 1.143.5 and 144.1).

2.10.2–11   Assembly of the Peloponnesian army at the Isthmus.

198. Nicklin T., "Nuces Thucydideae," CR XVIII 1904 199 (int. al., on 2.11.7).

2.13   Assembly at Athens.

199. Cavaignac E., "Thucydide II 13 et un papyrus de Genève," *Actes du congrès de l'Association G. Budé à Strasbourg, 20–22 avril 1938* (Paris Les Belles Lettres 1939 511 p.) 90–92.

200. Meritt B. D., Wade-Gery H. T. & McGregor M. F., "Thucydides II 13,2–9 (T 117)," *The Athenian tribute lists*, III (cf. 111, supra) 118–132.

201. Accame S., "Note storiche su epigrafi attiche del V secolo," RFIC XXX 1952 111–136 & 222–245 (int. al., on 2.13.3–4).

202. Gomme A. W., "Thucydides II 13,3," Historia II 1953 1–21.

203. Meritt B. D., "Indirect tradition in Thucydides," Hesperia XXIII 1954 185–231.

204. Gomme A. W., "Thucydides II 13,3. An answer to Professor Merritt," Historia III 1955 333–338.

205. Wade-Gery H. T. & Meritt B. D., "Athenian resources in 449 and 431 B.C.," Hesperia XXVI 1957 163–197.

206. Oliver J. H., "Thucydides II 13,3," AJP LXXIX 1958 188–190.

207. Sealey R., "P. Strassburg 84 verso," Hermes LXXXVI 1958 440–446.

208. Knight D. W., "Thucydides and the war strategy of Perikles," Mnemosyne XIII 1970 150–161 (int. al., on 2.13.2).

2.34–46 Public burial at Athens.

209. Kratz H., "Zu Thukydides," NJP CXIII 1876 111–113 (on 2.44).

210. Tyrrell R. Y., "Atakta," Hermathena III 1877 107–124 (int. al., on 2.37,43).

211. Rühl F., "Vermischte Bemerkungen," NJP CXVII 1878 311–315 (on 2.35–46).

212. Meuss H., "Zum *logos epitaphios* des Perikles," NJPhP CLVI 1897 679–680.

213. Bernardakis G. N., "*Poikila philologika*," PhSPE 1900 58–93 (int. al., on 2.43).

214. Caccialanza G., "Thucydidea. Osservazioni alla 2. Periklea di Tucidide," *Xenia Romana. Scritti di filologia classica offerti al secondo convegno promosso dalla Società italiana per la diffusione e l'incoraggiamento degli studi classici* (Roma Albrighi, Segati 1907 169 p.) 147–152.

215. Hutton M., "Notes on Herodotus and Thucydides," TAPA XLI 1910 11–17 (int. al., on 2.40.4).

216. Corssen P., "In Thucyd. II 42,4," BPhW XXXI 1911 1485.

217. Smith C. F., "Personification in Thucydides," CP XIII 1918 241–250 (on 2.36.4).

218. Kalitsunakis J. E., "Zu Thukyd. I 37,4," PhW XLIII 1923 190.

219. Hélin M., "Le sens de l'oraison funèbre de Pericles. Thuc. II 35–46," MB XXVIII 1924 223–233.

220. Doerwald P., "Die Leichenrede des Perikles," L&L 1930 47–59.

221. Schroeder O., "Zwei Interpretationen, I: Ueber einen Abschnitt aus der Leichenrede des Perikles," Hermes LXVI 1931 355–361.

222. Oppenheimer K., *Zwei attische Epitaphien*: Berlin Ebering 1933 96 p. (int. al., on 2.35–46).

AC IV 1935 498 Meunier.

223. Sinko T., "De Atheniensium studio pulchritudinis et sapientiae secundum Thucydidem," *Munera philologica L. Cwiklinski oblata* (Poznan Soc. Philol. Polon. 1936 483 p.) 23–28.

224. Colin G., "L'oraison funèbre d'Hyperide. Ses rapports avec les autres oraisons funèbres athéniennes," REG LI 1938 209–266 & 305–394.

225. Kakridis J. T., "Epitaphios-Interpretationen," WS LVI 1938 17–26.

226. Treves P., "Herodotus, Gelon, and Pericles," CP XXXVI 1941 321–345.

227. Pearson L., "Three notes on the funeral oration of Pericles," AJP LXIV 1943 399–407.

228. Phabes B., "*Analekta philologika*," Athena LIII 1949 270–296 (int. al., on 2.40.2).

229. Tabachovitz D., "Thuc. II 35,1 *en heni andri pollón aretas kindyneuesthai* und Cic. in Catil. I 5,11 in uno homine summa salus periclitanda," Eranos XLVII 1949 129–137.

230. Spyridakis K., *Ho epitaphios tou Perikleous kai hai en autôi politikai skepseis tou Thoukydidou (II 35–46)*: Leucosia 1950 30 p.

231. Oliver J. H., "On the funeral oration of Pericles," RhM XCIV 1951 327–330.

232. Bamboudakis E. G., "*Philokaloumen te gar met' euteleias kai philosophoumen aneu malakias*," Platon III 1951 109–119.

233. Georgoulis K. D., "*Thoukydideia*," Platon IV 1952 155–184 (int. al., on 2.34.2–4; 35.1,3; 36.4; 37.2; 38.1; 40.1–2; 41.3–5; 43.2,8).

234. Kapsalis G. D., *Hoi duo koryphaioi tês Athênaikês dêmokratias. Hê pompê tôn Panathênaiôn. Ho epitaphios tou Periklê sto Thoukydidê*, I & II: Athens 1952 204 p.

235. Mette H. J., "Die 'grosse Gefähr,'" Hermes LXXX 1952 409–419 (on *kindynos* in 2.35–46).

236. Michaelis S., *Das Ideal der attischen Demokratie in den Hiketiden des Euripides und im Epitaphios des Thukydides*: Diss. Marburg 1952 92 p. (typescript).

237. Dienelt K., "*Apragmosynê*," WS LXVI 1953 94–104 (on 2.40.2).

238. Gomme A. W., "The interpretation of *kaloi kagathoi* in Thucydides II 40,2," CQ XLVII 1953 65–68.

239. Korré St. G., "*Hoi epitaphioi logoi*,I: *Ho Dêmosthenous dokôn*," Platon V 1953 120–125 (on 2.35.1–3; 36,1–4; 44 and Demosthenes 60.1–10, 31–34).

240. Else G. F., "Some implications of Pericles' funeral speech," CJ XLIX 1953–1954 153–156.

241. Herter H., "Comprensione ed azione politica. A proposito del capitolo 40 dell' epitaphio tucidideo," *Studi in onore di G. Funaioli* (Roma Signorelli 1955 xii & 440 p. 1 pl.) 133–140.

242. Oliver J. H., "Praise of Periclean Athens as a mixed constitution," RhM XCVIII 1955 37–40 (int. al., on 2.37).

243. Mueller F., "Die blonde Bestie und Thukydides," HSCP LXIII 1958 171–178 (on 2.41.5).

244. Murphy P. R., "Cicero's Pro Archia and the Periclean Epitaphios," TAPA LXXXIX 1958 99–111.

245. MacDonald C., "Plato, Laws 704a–707c and Thucydides II 35–46," CR IX 1959 108–109.

246. Stamatakos S. V., "*Kritika kai hermêneutika sêmeiômata*," Platon XI 1959 169–171 (on 2.43.8, 44.1).

247. Wardman A. E., "Thucydides II 40,1," CQ IX 1959 38–42.

248. Fraenkel E., "Eine Anfangsformel attischer Reden," Glotta XXXIX 1960 1–5 (on 2.35.1).

249. Georgoulis K. D., *Philologika sêmeiômata*," Platon XII 1960 265–292 (on 2.39.4).

250. Pérez Ruiz F., "Tucídides, su modo de concebir la historia, concretamente estudiado en su narracion del primo año de guerra," Humanidades XII 1960 135–165 (int. al., on 2.35–46).

251. Kakridis J. T., *Der Thukydideische Epitaphios. Ein stilistischer Kommentar*: Zetemata XXVI Munchen Beck 1961 xii & 119 p.
CR XII 1962 206–207 Dover; CW LV 1962 120–121 Day; Gnomon XXXIV 1962 529–534 Sieveking; LEC XXX 1962 236 Moraux; CJ LVIII 1963 324 Wassermann; DLZ LXXXIV 1963 717–719 Diesner; Gymnasium LXX 1963 434–438 Eberhardt; JHS LXXXIII 1963 170 Hudson-Williams; Mnemosyne XVI 1963 309–311 van Dijck; REA LXV 1963 419–420 Moulinier; RFIC XCI 1963 88–92 Longo; RPh XXXVII 1963 297–299 Weil; AAHG XVII 1964 155–159 Braun; AJP LXXXV 1964 105–107 Oliver; RBPh XLII 1964 699–700 Peremans.

252. Adrados F. R., "Pericles y la democracia de su época," EClas VI 1962 333–403.
253. Rees B. R., "*Kakôsis* in Thucydides II 43 and elsewhere," Mnemosyne XV 1962 369–376.
254. Alberti G. B., "Note al testo di Tucidide," Maia XV 1963 129–135 (int. al., on 2.37.2).
255. Meremetis A. D., "*Epitêdeusis, politeia kai tropoi. Symbolê eis tên hermêneian tou Epitaphiou tou Perikleous tou Thoukydidou*," Stasinos I 1963 43–75.
256. Ziolkowski J. E., *Thucydides and the tradition of funeral speeches at Athens*: Diss. Univ. of North Carolina 1963 189 p. (microfilm). Cf. summary in DA XXIV 1964 3329.
257. Lacey W. K., "Thucydides II 45,2," PCPS X 1964 47–49.
258. Pagliani M. P., "Thucydidea," RFIC XCII 1964 65–73 (on 2.39.2–4, 41.4).
259. Vretska H., "Pericles und die Herrschaft des Würdigsten, Thuk. II 37,1," RhM CIX 1966 108–120.
260. Stamatakos S. V., "*Kritika kai hermêneutika eis ton para Thoukydidou epitaphion tou Perikleous*," Platon XX 1968 273–274.
261. Flashar H., *Der Epitaphios des Perikles. Seine Funktion im Geschichtswerk des Thukydides*: SHAW 1969,1 56 p.
AC XXXIX 1970 217 Roobaert; BIEH IV 1970 76–77 Alsina; CW LXIV 1970 125 Day.
262. Tourlides G. A., *Analekta philologika kai historika*: Athens 1969 32 p. (int. al., on 2.35–46).

2.59.3–65.2   Assembly at Athens.
263. Nestle W., "*Apragmosynê* (Zu Thukydides II 63)," Philologus LXXXI 1925–1926 129–140.
264. Plenio W., *Die letzte Rede des Perikles (Thukydides II 60–64)*: Diss. Kiel 1954 133 p. (typescript).

2.86–89   Preparations for a naval battle near Rhium.
265. Bodin L., "La bataille de Naupacte," REG XXVII 1914 xlix–l.

3.8–15   Conference of the Peloponnesians at Olympia.
266. McWhorter A. W., "Thucydides III 13,1," TAPA XLV 1914 xxv–xxvi.

267. Bannier W., "Zu den griechischen und lateinischen Autoren, II," RhM LXXIII 1919–1924 59–83 (int. al., on 3.12.3).

3.29.2–31   Conference of the Peloponnesians at Embatum in the territory of Erythrae.

268. Bill C. P., *"Ta kaina tou polemou,"* CP XXXII 1937 160–161.

269. Schulz H. J., "Zu Thukydides III 30,4," Hermes LXXXV 1957 255–256.

3.36–49.1   Assembly at Athens.

270. Büdinger M., "Kleon bei Thukydides. Eine kritische Untersuchung," SAWW XCVI 1880 367–412.

271. Lincke K., "Miscellanea," Philologus LIX 1900 186–200 (int. al., on 3.38.5).

272. Jessen J., *Quaestiunculae criticae et exegeticae*: Diss. Kiel 1901 Peters 34 p. (int. al., on 3.37.1).

273. Schmidt B., "Zu Thukydides," RhM LXII 1907 151–153 (int. al., on 3.39.6).

274. Stahl J. M., "Zu Thukydides," RhM LXII 1907 478–479 (int. al., on 3.39.6).

275. Bodin L., "Diodote contre Cleon. Quelques aperçus sur la dialectique de Thucydide," REA XLII 1940 36–52.

276. Mathieu G., "Quelques notes sur Thucydide," REA XLII 1940 242–253 (int. al., on 3.36–48).

277. Stevens E. B., "Some Attic commonplaces of pity," AJP LXVI 1944 1–25 (on 3.36.2).

278. Mueri W., "Beitrag zum Verständnis des Thukydides," MH IV 1947 251–275 (on 3.45).

279. Moraux P., "Thucydide et la rhétorique," LEC XXII 1954 3–23 (on 3.37–48).

280. Saar H. G., *Die Reden des Kleon und Diodotus und ihre Stellung im Gesamtwerk des Thukydides*: Diss. Heidelberg 1954 101 p. (typescript).

281. Ebener D., "Kleon und Diodotus. Zum Aufbau und zur Gedankenfuhrung eines Redepaares bei Thukydides (Thuk. III 37–48)," Wiss. Zeitschrift der Martin Luther Univ. Halle-Wittenberg V 1955–1956 1085–1160.

282. Wassermann F., "Post-Periclean democracy in action. The

Mytilene debate (Thuc. III 37–48)," TAPA LXXXVII 1956 27–41.
283. Andrewes A., "The Mytilene debate. Thucydides III 36–49," Phoenix XVI 1962 64–85.
284. Winnington-Ingram R. P., "Ta deonta eipein. Cleon's speech in the Mytilene debate. A study of Thucydides III 37–48," cf. summary in BICS IX 1962 69.
285. Wet B. X. de, "Periclean imperial policy and the Mytilenean debate," AClass VI 1963 106–124.
286. Schram J. M., "Prodicus' fifty-drachma show-lecture and the Mytilene debate of Thucydides. An account of the intellectual and social antecedents of formal logic," AntR XXV 1965 105–130.
287. Winnington-Ingram R. P., "Ta deonta eipein. Cleon and Diodotus," BICS XII 1965 70–82.
288. Christodoulou G. A, "Thoukydideia G 37–48," Platon XX 1968 113–124.
289. Grant J. R., "Thucydides III 44,2," Philologus CXII 1968 292–293.

3.52–68   Trial of the Plataeans.
290. Havelock E. A., "Dikaiosynê. An essay in Greek intellectual history," Phoenix XXIII 1969 49–70 (int. al., on 3.63.3–4).

4.10   Speech of Demosthenes to Athenian troops on Sphacteria.
291. Morel W., "Zu den griechischen Romanschriftstellern, I: Klassischen Sprachgebrauch bei Chariton und Heliodor," Mnemosyne IX 1941 281–282 (int. al., on 4.10.3).

4.16–22   Assembly at Athens.
292. Seaton R. C., "On Thucydides IV 18,4" CR XIV 1900 223–224.

4.40.2   Conversation between an Athenian ally and a Spartan prisoner at Athens.
293. Rackham H., "On the papyrus fragment containing Thuc. IV 36–41," PCPS XLVI–XLVIII 1897 17.

4.58–65.2   Assembly of Sicilian cities at Gela.
294. Stahl J. M., "Berichtung zu Thukydides IV 63,1," RhM LV 1900 160.

295. Landmann G. P., *Eine Rede des Thukydides. Die Frie-densmahnung des Hermokrates*: Kiel Lipsius & Tischer 1932 82 p.
CR XLVII 1933 65–66 Marchant; Gnomon X 1934 117–121 Nes-selhauf; JAW CCXLII 1934 4–5 Widmann; PhW LIV 1934 1075–1081 Oetzmann; RFIC XII 1934 108–109 De Sanctis.

4.84–88   Assembly at Acanthus.
296. Bernardakis G. N., "*Diorthôtika kai hermêneutika*," Lao-graphia 1923 1–8 (int. al., on 4.87).

4.126   Speech of Brasidas to Peloponnesians at Lyncus.
297. Torstrik A., "Die Rede des Brasidas bei Thukydides, IV 126," Philologus XXXV 1875 103–114.
298. Gomme A. W., "Notes on Thucydides," CR I 1951 135–138 (int. al., on 4.126.2).

5.44.2–46.3   Assembly at Athens.
299. This item has been deleted.

5.85–113   Melian dialogue.
300. Hude K., "Macht und Recht in antiken Beleuchtung," *Festschrift til J. L. Ussing, i anledning af haus 80-aarige fodselsdag 10. April 1900* (Köbnhaven Gyldendal 1900 276 p.) 110–116.
301. De Sanctis G., "Postille Tucididee," RAL VI 1930 299–341 (int. al., on 5.85–113).
302. Méautis G., "Le dialogue des Athéniens et des Meliens (Thucydide V 85–113)," REG XLVIII 1935 250–278.
303. Bartoletti V., "Il dialogo degli Ateniesi e dei Melii nella storia di Tucidide," RFIC XVII 1939 301–318.
304. Deininger G., *Der Melier-Dialog (Thuk. V 85–113)*: Diss. Erlangen Krahl 1939 144 p.
PhW LX 1940 129–136 Bender.
305. Nawratil K., "Zu Thukydides V 105," PhW LXII 1942 382–383.
306. Waltz P., "Notes critiques sur Thucydide," REG LVIII 1945 97–104 (on 5.110.2, 111.4).
307. Wassermann F., "The Melian dialogue," TAPA LXXVIII 1947 18–36.

308. Hudson-Williams H. L., "Conventional forms of debate and the Melian dialogue," AJP LXXI 1950 156–169.

309. Braun E., "Nachlese zum Melierdialog (Thukyd. V 85–113)," JOEAI XL 1953 Beiblatt 231–242.

310. Levi M. A., "Il dialogo dei Meli," PP VIII 1953 5–16.

311. MacKay L. A., "Latent irony in the Melian dialogue," *Studies presented to D. M. Robinson on his seventieth birthday,* II (cf. supra, 193) 570–572.

312. Herter H., "Pylos und Melos. Ein Beitrag zur Thukydides-Interpretation," RhM XCVII 1954 316–343.

313. Scharf J., "Zum Melierdialog des Thukydides," Gymnasium LXI 1954 504–513.

314. Treu M., "Athen und Melos und der Melierdialog des Thukydides," Historia II 1954 253–273 & III 1954 58–59.

315. Röver E., "Gespräche bei griechischen Historikern. Interpretationen aus Thukydides (V 85 ff.); Xenophon *Kyrou paideia* (I 6; VII 2); Herodot (I 86, 87; VII 101–104, 209–210)," AU II,6 1955 21–62.

316. Ferrara G., "La politica dei Meli in Tucidide," PP XI 1956 335–346.

317. Eberhardt W., "Der Melierdialog und die Inschriften ATL A 9 (IG I² 63) und IG I² 97," Historia VIII 1959 284–314.

318. Kierdorf W., "Zum Melier-Dialog des Thukydides," RhM CV 1962 253–256.

319. Méautis G., *Thucydide et l'impérialisme athénien, suivi d'un choix d'études*: Neuchâtel La Baconnière 1964 143 p.

RA I 1965 121–122 Picard; REG LXXVIII 1965 678 Irigoin; RecSR LIV 1966 595 des Places; REA LXX 1968 162 Defradas.

320. Kalliphatidis K. J., *Hermêneutikes paratêrêseis ston dialogo tôn Mêliôn*: Thessaloniki 1965 187 p.

cf. CR VIII 1958 280 Gomme (review of parts, issued separately).

321. Amit M., "The Melian dialogue and history," Athenaeum XLVI 1968 216–235.

322. Liebeschuetz W., "The structure and function of the Melian dialogue," JHS LXXXVIII 1968 73–77.

323. Treu M., "Staatsrechtliches bei Thukydides," Historia XVII 1968 129–165 (int. al., on 5.94).

324. Volk M. T., *The Melian dialogue in Thucydides. A structural analysis*: Diss. Ohio State Univ. Columbus 1970 168 p.

6.8–26   Assembly at Athens.

325. Corsini V., "Sull' interpretazione di un passo di Tucidide, VI 10,2," BFC IV 1897 185–187.

326. Münscher K., "Ein neues Wort bei Thukydides," PhW XLI 1921 163–167 (on 6.17.1).

327. Hartmann J. J., "Ad Thucydidem l. VI c. 11," Mnemosyne LI 1923 134.

328. Lorimer W. L., "Thucydides VI 11,7," CR XLVI 1932 155–156.

329. Peremans W., "Thucydide, Alcibiade et l'expédition de Sicile en 415 av. J. C.," AC XXV 1956 331–344 (int. al., on 6.15, 17.2).

330. Groningen B. A. van, "Deux conjectures sur Thucydide," Mnemosyne XIII 1960 328–329 (on 6.20.4, 22).

331. Murray H. A., "Two notes on the evaluation of Nicias in Thucydides," BICS VIII 1961 33–46 (int. al., on 6.23.1–4).

6.32.3–41   Assembly at Syracuse.

332. Marchant E. C., "Ad Thucyd. VI 37," Mnemosyne XXV 1897 332.

333. Gomme A. W., "Thucydides VI 34,7," CR XLIII 1929 15.

6.46.5–50.1   Conference of Athenian generals at Rhegium.

334. Liebeschuetz W., "Thucydides and the Sicilian expedition," Historia XVII 1968 289–306 (int. al., on 6.47–49).

6.75.3–88   Assembly at Camarina.

335. Camps W. A., "Thucydides VI 87,5," CR V 1955 17.

6.88.9–93   Assembly at Sparta.

336. Wilamowitz-Moellendorff U. von, "Lesefrüchte," Hermes LX 1925 297–300 (on 6.89–92).

337. Daux G., "Alcibiade, proxène de Lacédémone (Thuc. V 43,2 et VI 89,2)," *Mélanges offerts à A. M. Desrousseaux par ses amis et ses élèves* (cf. supra, 171) 117–122.

338. Bodin L., "Alcibiade interprète à Sparte de l'appel des Syracusains au Peloponnèse," *Actes du congrès de l'Association G.*

Budé à Strasbourg, 20–22 avril 1938 (cf. supra, 199) 89–90.
339. Pusey N. M., "Alcibiades and *to philopoli*," HSCP LI 1940 215–231 (on 6.92.4).

7.10–15.2   Assembly at Athens.
340. Widmann S., "Endliche Lösung einer Thukydides-Schwerigkeit (VII 13,2)," WKPh XXIV 1907 1099–1100.
341. Zuretti C. O., "La lettera di Nicia (Thucyd. VII 11–15)," RFIC L 1922 1–11.
342. Herbert F. J. H., "Ad Thucydidem VII 13,2," Mnemosyne LII 1924 412.
343. Phloros A. T., "*Paratêrêseis eis to 7on biblion tou Thoukydidou kai eis ton pinaka tou Kebêtos*," Platon VIII 1956 86–90 (int. al., on 7.12.6).

7.47–49   Council of generals at Epipolae.
344. Powell J. U., "Thucydides VII 47,1," CR XXVI 1912 123.
345. Felten J. N., "A note on Thucydides 7.47.3," CJ LXV 1969 80–81.

7.77   Speech of Nicias to the Athenian survivors at Syracuse.
346. Mossé C., "Armée et cité grecques (à propos de Thucydide VII 77.4–5)," REA LXV 1963 290–297.

8.45.2–3   Advice of Alcibiades to Tissaphernes.
347. Delebecque E., "Sur deux phrases de Thucydide," REG LXXVII 1964 34–49 (int. al., on 8.45.3).

8.50.2   Letter of Phrynichus to Astyochus.
348. Westlake H. D., "Phrynichos and Astyochos (Thucydides VIII 50–51)," JHS LXXVI 1956 99–104.
349. Schindel U., "Phrynichos und die Rückberufung des Alkibiades," RhM CXIII 1970 281–297 (on 8.50–51).

8.53   Speech of Pisander in the Athenian assembly.
350. Bieler L., "A political slogan in ancient Athens," AJP LXXII 1951 181–184 (on 8.53.3–54.1).

8.108.1   Remarks of Alcibiades to the Athenians.
351. Delebecque E., "Une fable d'Alcibiade sur le mythe d'une flotte (Thucydide VIII, 108)," AFLA XLIII 1967 13–41.

Index of Authors Listed in the Bibliography

(References are to item numbers.)

Accame S. 201
Adcock F. E. 28
Adrados F. R. 252
Alberti G. B. 254
Altinger J. 84
Aly W. 61
Amit M. 321
Anastassiou A. A. 102
Andrewes A. 36, 119, 283

Bamboudakis E. G. 232
Bannier W. 267
Barth K. 31
Bartoletti V. 177, 303
Bászel A. 2
Bayer E. 110
Beardslee J. W. 59
Bender G. F. 62
Bernardakis G. N. 213, 296
Bickermann E. 195
Bieler L. 350
Bill C. P. 268
Blass F. 4
Bodin L. 48, 95, 171, 265, 275, 338
Bonner R. J. 170
Bowersock G. W. 32
Braun E. 156, 309
Brown E. S. 169
Büchner K. 165
Büdinger M. 270
Bury J. B. 7
Busolt G. 5

Caccialanza F. 214
Calder W. M. 168
Cammerer C. 3
Camps W. A. 335
Cavaignac E. 199
Chambers M. H. 115
Christodoulou G. A. 288
Ciaceri E. 108
Cochrane C. N. 141
Colin G. 224
Corsini V. 325
Corssen P. 216
Craici L. 166

Danninger O. 93
Daux G. 337
Deffner A. 13
Deininger G. 304
Delachaux A. 191
Delebecque E. 123, 347, 351
DeSanctis G. 301
Dienelt K. 237
Diller H. 121
Doerwald P. 109, 220
Dover K. J. 36, 116, 157
Drefke O. 40

Ebener D. 281
Eberhardt W. 317
Else G. F. 240
Erbse H. 23

Fellner T. 43

Felten J. N. 345
Ferrara G. 316
Finley J. H. 17, 33, 97, 144
Flashar H. 261
Fokke A. 104, 105, 106
Fornara C. W. 183
Fraenkel E. 248
Friedrich G. 45
Fritz K. von 34, 167

Gardiner T. 73, 76
Georgoulis K. D. 233, 249
Glucker J. 161
Gomme A. W. 15, 19, 24, 25, 27, 36, 152, 155, 202, 204, 238, 298, 333
Gommel J. 103
Grant J. R. 124, 289
Grene D. 64
Griffith G. T. 26
Groningen B. A. van 330
Grosskinsky A. 54
Gundert H. 63

Hammond N. G. L. 192
Harrison A. R. W. 55
Harrison J. E. 6
Hartmann J. J. 327
Havelock E. A. 290
Hehn V. 112
Hélin M. 219
Herbert F. J. H. 342
Herter H. 35, 63a, 193, 241, 312
Hirst M. E. 188
Hoffmann E. 149
Hofmann E. 140
Hopper R. J. 172
Hout M. van den 134

Howald E. 10, 18
Huart P. 74
Hude K. 300
Hudson-Williams H. L. 98, 99, 135, 308
Hutton M. 215

Jaeger W. 20
Jebb R. 1
Jessen J. 272
John W. 92
Junghan E. A. 39, 41, 44

Kakridis J. T. 225, 251
Kalitsunakis J. E. 218
Kalliphatidis K. J. 320
Kamerbeek J. C. 175
Kappus K. 182
Kapsalis G. D. 234
Katičič R. 145
Kennedy G. 29
Kiechle F. 101
Kierdorf W. 179, 318
Kinugasa S. 125
Kleist H. 79, 86
Klinz A. 75
Knight D. W. 208
Korré St. G. 239
Kratz H. 209

Lacey W. K. 257
Lamb W. R. M. 138
Landmann G. P. 295
Lapounoff J. 139
Laqueur R. 56
Leeuwen J. van 150, 187
Lehmann J. 80
Lenardon R. J. 185

Levi M. A. 113, 310
Liebeschuetz W. 127, 322, 334
Lincke K. 271
Longo Rubbi C. 58, 136
Lorimer W. L. 328
Lüdtke W. 142
Luria S. 120
Luschnat O. 37, 133, 194

MacDonald C. 245
McGregor M. F. 111, 200
MacKay L. A. 311
McWhorter A. W. 266
Maloney G. 148
Marchant E. C. 332
Mathieu G. 90, 276
Méautis G. 302, 319
Mello M. 196
Menzel A. 60
Meremetis A. 255
Meritt B. D. 111, 200, 203, 205
Mette H. J. 235
Meuss H. 212
Meyer E. 16
Meyer Eduard 46, 49
Michaelis S. 236
Moraux P. 279
Morel W. 291
Mossé C. 346
Mueller F. 243
Mueri W. 278
Müller F. 186
Müller I. von 21
Münscher K. 326
Murphy P. R. 244
Murray H. A. 331

Nawratil K. 305

Nesselhauf H. 189
Nestle W. 88, 91, 263
Nicklin T. 198
Nieschke A. 85
Norden E. 9

Oliver J. H. 206, 231, 242
Olmstead A. T. 181
Oppenheimer K. 222

Pagliani M. P. 258
Papantoniou G. 174
Parry A. 70, 147
Patzer H. 57
Pearson L. 227
Peremans W. 329
Pérez Ruiz F. 250
Phabes B. 228
Phloros A. T. 343
Platt A. 151
Plenio W. 264
Pohlenz M. 14, 51
Pouncey P. R. 130
Powell J. U. 344
Pusey N. M. 339

Rackham H. 293
Radford R. S. 87
Rees B. R. 253
Regenbogen O. 22, 61a
Reich L. 176
Rittelmeyer F. 89
Rockel C. J. 82
Rohrer K. 118
Rokeah D. 160
Romilly J. de 65, 68, 69, 71
Ros J. 143
Rosenkranz B. 94

Röver E. 315
Rühl F. 211

Saar H. G. 280
Schadewaldt W. 53
Scharf J. 313
Schindel U. 349
Schmid W. 21, 158
Schmidt B. 273
Schneider J. G. 163
Schram J. M. 286
Schroeder O. 221
Schuller S. 100
Schulz H. J. 269
Schwartz E. 50
Sealey R. 207
Seaton R. C. 292
Séchan L. 126
Sinko T. 223
Smith C. F. 217
Sörgel J. 42
Spyridakis K. 230
Stahl H.-P. 72
Stahl J. M. 274, 294
Stählin O. 21
Stamatakos S. V. 159, 246, 260
Stein F. 81
Stein H. 107
Strasburger H. 66, 117
Stevens E. B. 277
Syme R. 30

Tabachovitz D. 229
Taeger F. 11
Tagliaferro D. 129
Tanaka M. 77
Tasolambros L. 178
Thody P. 71

Thompson E. A. 154, 164
Thompson W. E. 162
Thulin C. 137
Tompkins D. P. 146
Torstrik A. 297
Tourlides G. A. 262
Treu M. 314, 323
Treves P. 226
Turner E. G. 173
Turska C. M. 38
Tyrrell R. Y. 210

Uzun F. 8

Vogt J. 184
Volk M. T. 324
Vretska H. 259

Wade-Gery H. T. 111, 200, 205
Waltz P. 306
Wardman A. E. 247
Wassermann F. 12, 67, 114, 122, 282, 307
Waszyśńki S. 180
Weber L. 132
Westlake H. D. 128, 131, 348
Wet B. X. de 197, 285
Widmann S. 340
Wilamowitz-Moellendorff U. von 47, 52, 336
Winnington-Ingram R. P. 284, 287
Woessner W. 96
Woodhead A. G. 78

Zahn R. 190
Zeitschel 83
Ziegler K. 153
Ziolkowski J. E. 256
Zuretti C. O. 341

INDEX OF NAMES
AND PASSAGES

A

Acanthus, 10, 93, 102, 158
Acarnanians, 9
Admetus of Molossus, 8, 150
Aegean Sea, 53
Aegina, 73
Aegospotami, 56, 59
Agis, 11
Agrigento, 71
Alcibiades, 11–15, 30, 38, 48, 59, 61,
    64–67, 72, 75, 79–84, 93, 105–8, 110,
    113, 115–17, 118n, 120, 122, 142,
    144–45, 160–61
Alexander the Great, letters of, 120
Amphilochians, 9
Amphipolis, 11
Anaxagoras, 118
Andocides, 1.27: 80n; 1.36: 79n
Androcles, 79, 85
Antalcidas, peace of, 119
Anthemocritus, 33, 121–22
Antiphon, 126, 140, 142
Aratus, *Memoirs*, 120
Archidamian War, 55–57
Archidamus, 3, 6–9, 25, 28, 34, 73, 77,
    92, 100, 112, 143
Argos, Argives, 11
Aristarchus, 15
Aristides, 140
Aristogeiton, 70
Aristophanes, 113, 118; *Lysistrata* 387–
    98: 122; *Wasps*, 44; *FAC* fr. 81:
    79n
Aristotle, 113, 119; *Ath. Pol.* 29: 86–
    88; 29.2–3: 87n; 29.2–5: 87; 29.5:
    86; 32: 79n; *Poetics* 1450 B 7: 50;

Aristotle (*cont.*)
    1451 B 4–11: 50; *Rhetoric*, 118;
    1.7.34: 119; 3.4.3: 119n; 3.10.7:
    119n; 3.18.1: 119n; 3.18.6: 88n
[Aristotle], *Rhetorica ad Alexandrum*,
    5
Artaxerxes, 8, 10, 150
Aspasia, 119, 122
Astyochus, 13–14, 161
Athenagoras, 12, 92, 99, 108
Athens, Athenians, 5–12, 14–15, 23–
    26, 28–48, 51, 53–58, 60–61, 64–65,
    67–77, 80–83, 85–89, 93–98, 101–3,
    105–7, 112, 114, 116–18, 121, 126,
    134, 143–45, 148–52, 154–61
Attica, 18, 34, 96
Attic orators, 140–41

B

Boeotians, 10
Brasidas, 9–11, 50–51, 93, 102, 158

C

Caesar, *Commentaries*, 120
Callicles, 137
Callimachus, 37
Camarina, Camarineans, 12, 30, 36–
    37, 41, 48, 55, 68–69, 93, 95, 108,
    160
Caracalla, 150
Carthage, 116
Carystos, 42
Catana, 67–68
Ceryces, 83
Chaereas, 14
Chalcideus, 13

Index

Charinus, 33, 122
Charon of Lampsacus, 150
Chios, Chians, 13
Cicero, *Brutus* 27: 118n; 287–88: 120n;
Catil. 1.5.11: 153; *Orator* 30–32:
120n; *Pro Archia*, 154
Cimon, 41–42, 121
Cleon, 4–5, 9–10, 28–29, 79, 94, 97–
99, 102, 110, 113, 115, 156–57
Cnemus, 9
Cnidians, 13
Colonus, 84, 88–89
Corcyra, Corcyraeans, 7, 22, 24, 29, 51,
55, 64, 66, 94–95
Corinth, Corinthians, 6–7, 24–25, 43,
51, 55, 64, 110
Coriolanus, 111n
Coronea, 42
Craterus (*FGrHist* 342), 121–22; F 12:
122n
Croesus, 17
Cyprus, 41
Cythera, 110

D
Decelea, 88–89, 116
Decelean War, 56–57
Delium, 10, 22
Delos, 14, 42
Demosthenes (the general), 9, 12, 69,
72, 74, 114, 157
Demosthenes (the orator), 120, 142;
60.1–10: 154; 60.31–34: 154; 60.34:
119
Demostratus, 122
Dio Chrysostom, 140
Diodotus, 4–5, 9, 20n, 28–29, 94, 97,
102, 156–57
Diomedon, 14
Dionysius of Halicarnassus, 111n, 142;
On Thucydides 18: 120n; 44: 113n;
49–50: 120n
Diopeithes, 122
Dracontides, 122

E
Egyptian Expedition, 41
Eleusis, 33
Embatum, 9, 156
Ephorus, 122
Epidamnus, 51, 64, 77

Epipolae, 12, 114, 161
Euboea, 42, 58
Eumolpidae, 83
Euphamidas, 11
Euphemus, 12, 30, 36–39, 41, 48, 68,
93, 95, 108
Eupolis, *FAC* frs. 31, 181: 79n
Euripides, 28, 58, 116, 141, 153; *Medea*,
46
Eurybiades, 38
Eurymedon, 41

F
Fabius Maximus, 112–13
Five Thousand, the, at Athens, 57, 79,
88
Four Hundred, the, at Athens, 15, 78–
79, 84, 87–89, 96

G
Gela, xi, 10, 52, 58, 92–93, 157
Gelon of Syracuse, 71, 153
Glaucon, 122
Gorgias, 129, 147
Gylippus, 12, 69, 114, 116

H
Hagnon, 73, 122
Hannibal, 112
Harmodius, 70
Hephaestion, 79
Hermippus, *FAC* fr. 9: 79n
Hermocrates, xi, 10, 12, 52–53, 55,
57–59, 68, 77, 92–93, 95, 104, 108,
143, 158
Herodes, pseudo-, 142
Herodotus, ix, 17–18, 152–53; 1.86:
159; 1.87: 159; 6.109.6: 37; 7.20:
17; 7.101–4: 159; 7.139: 38–39;
7.139.1: 37–38; 7.139.3: 38; 7.139.5:
37; 7.161: 145; 7.162.1: 119; 7.209–
10: 159; 8.42–48: 39; 8.57.2: 38;
8.61: 31; 8.62.1: 38; 8.124: 39;
8.142.2: 37; 9.27: 145; speeches in,
130, 134
Hippocrates, 10
Hippocratic corpus, 142
Homer, 140; *Iliad*, ix, 22n; *Odyssey*,
22n
Hykkara, 67
Hyperbolus, 79, 111
Hyperides, 153

I

Inscriptions, *IG* I² 370: 79n; Meiggs-Lewis 23: 38n
Ionian War of 412 B.C., 46
Isocrates, 141
Isthmus, 8, 96, 151
Italy, 24, 66–67, 116

L

Lacedaemonians, 43, 46. *See also* Sparta, Spartans
Lamachus, 12, 67
Leon, 14
Leon of Byzantium, 114
Leontini, 11, 54, 64
Lycurgus, *Leocrates* 121: 89n
Lyncus, 10, 50, 158
Lysias, 129, 142; 7.4: 79n, 89n

M

Magnesia, 83–84, 86–87
Mantinea, Mantineans, 11, 116
Marathon, 36–38
Medes, 35–37, 57
Megara, Megarians, 33–34, 110–11, 121–22
Megarian Decree, 33–34, 110–11
Megarid, 34
Melian Dialogue, 3, 5, 29, 31, 38, 43, 72, 103, 139, 144, 148, 158–60. *See also* Thucydides 5.85–113
Melos, Melians, 22, 29–30, 36, 45, 48, 56, 72, 110, 158–59
Menon, 122
Miltiades, 37
Minoa, 110
Mnesiphilus, 38
Morgantine, 55
Mycalessus, 22
Mytilene, Mytileneans, 5, 9, 28–29, 93–94, 96–97, 99, 102–3
Mytilenean Debate, 4, 29, 148. *See also* Thucydides 3.37–48

N

Naupactus, 155
Naxos, 42
Nepos, *Alcibiades* 5, 79n
Nicias, 10–12, 20n, 31, 61, 64–65, 67–75, 77, 83, 105–8, 110–11, 113–16, 118, 122, 160–61; peace of, 43, 134

O

Oenoe, 15
Olympia, 9, 93, 96, 103, 155
Olympieion, 67

P

Paches, 97
Pagondas, 10
Pausanias, 8, 40, 46, 149–50
Pedaritus, 13
Peloponnesus, Peloponnesians, 6, 9–11, 35, 37–38
Pentecontaetia, 40–42, 94. *See also* Thucydides 1.89–118
Pericles, 6, 8, 21, 25–28, 30, 33–34, 36, 39–40, 42–43, 46–48, 55–57, 61, 73, 77, 92–93, 100–101, 103, 110–13, 117–23, 142–45, 151–55; Funeral Oration, x, 3, 26–27, 46, 91, 119–21, 139, 148. *See also* Thucydides 2.35–46
Persia, Persians, 37, 41, 45, 59, 81, 87; Great King, 82, 88
Persian Wars, 7, 17, 21, 24, 35–36, 38, 41–42
Phidias, 122
Philistus, 122
Phormio, 9
Phrynichus, 13, 80, 83, 161
Pisander, 13–14, 78–89, 161
Pisander son of Glaucetes of Acharnae, 79
Plataea, Plataeans, 3, 8–9, 22, 25, 29, 31, 35, 37, 91, 157
Plataean Debate, 35. *See also* Thucydides 3.52–68
Plato, 118, 120, 137; *Laws* 704 A–707 C: 154; *Menexenus* 236 B: 119; 245 E: 119; 246 D ff.: 27n
Plutarch, 109–23; *Lives*, 109–10, 120; *Alcibiades*, 109–10, 115, 117, 122; 2: 116; 6.3: 111; 10.4: 120; 11.2: 116; 13.4: 111; 14.8–9: 115; 15.1–2: 116; 16.4: 116; 17–18: 116; 17.3: 116; 18.3: 122; 19.2–3: 122; 22.4: 122; 23.2: 116; 41.3: 116; *Alexander*, 120; *Aratus*, 120; *Aristides* 24.4: 117; 26.4: 122n; *Caesar*, 120; *Cicero*, 120; *Comparison of Coriolanus and Alcibiades* 2.2: 115; 5.1: 116; *Comparison of Pericles and Fabius*, 117;

Plutarch (cont.)
Comparison of Nicias and Crassus
3.5: 110; Demosthenes, 120; Fabius
7.4–5: 112; Lycurgus 27: 110; 27.6:
117; Nicias, 109–10, 113, 115, 117,
122; 1.5: 114, 122; 3.5: 113; 4.1:
111; 5.7: 113; 6: 110; 7: 110, 113;
7.3–5: 113n; 8: 113; 11.5: 111; 12.2:
116n; 12.4: 114; 12.6: 122; 14.3:
114; 19.10: 114; 20.3–4: 114; 22:
114; 22.3: 114; 22.4: 114; 26.4: 115;
26.4–6: 115; Pericles, 109–111, 115,
117; 2.5: 113; 8: 118, 120; 8.7: 119n;
8.9: 119; 9.1: 111; 10.4: 121; 15:
120; 15.3: 111; 17: 121; 17.1: 43,
121; 17.4: 121; 19.2: 110; 22.1:
110; 23.3: 110; 24.1: 110, 121; 25–
26: 110; 25.1: 121; 27.1: 110; 28.1:
110; 29.8: 110–11; 30: 33–34, 40;
30.2–3: 121; 31.1: 111; 31.5: 122;
31–32: 122; 32.2: 122; 32.3–4: 122;
33: 112, 118; 33.1: 110; 33.5: 119n;
35.4: 113; 37.3: 121; 37.5: 121;
Solon, 120; Sulla, 120; Themistocles,
109; Moralia, 109; 73 A: 117; 242 E:
117; 533 A: 117; 535 E: 117; 540 C:
117; 783 F: 117; 802 C: 111; 803 B:
117; 828 B: 117; 854 A: 117; 855 C:
111; 856 A: 112n
Pnyx, 88
Prodicus, 157
Pylos, 22, 30, 57, 74, 97, 99, 102, 110,
113, 159
Pythodorus, 86, 87n

Q
Quintilian 3.1.12: 118n; 12.2.22: 118n;
12.10.49: 118n

R
Rhegium, 12, 160
Rhium, 9, 155
Rhodians, 13

S
Salamis, 38
Samian War, 110, 119
Samos, Samians, 14, 42, 79–84, 96,
119, 121
Scione, 10
Scironides, 83
Segesta, 11, 64–67, 74

Selinus, 64
Siceliotes, 54
Sicilian Expedition (War), 30, 36, 41,
57, 63, 68–69, 76, 113–14, 116, 160
Sicily, Sicilians, 22, 24, 30, 52–56, 64–
65, 67–72, 74–77, 95, 105–6, 114,
116
Socrates, 119
Solon, 88; poems, 120
Sophocles, 57–58, 88n; Antigone, 46
Sparta, Spartans, 6–13, 18, 23–25, 29,
31–40, 42–43, 45–48, 58, 64, 70, 73,
76–77, 81, 83, 88–89, 92–94, 96–
101, 103, 107–8, 110, 112, 115–16,
121, 137, 142, 144, 148–49, 160.
See also Lacedaemonians
Sphacteria, 9, 98, 157
Stesimbrotos, 119
Sthenelaïdas, 7, 24, 35, 46, 77, 92, 99–
100, 107
Sulla, Memoirs, 120
Sybota, 7
Syracuse, Syracusans, 11–12, 52, 54–57,
64, 66–72, 74–75, 77, 93, 95, 99,
104, 108, 114, 116, 160–61

T
Tanagra, 10
Teutiaplus, 9
Thasos, 42
Thebans, 3, 9, 35, 91
Themistocles, 7–8, 31, 38–39, 56, 150
Themistocles Decree, 38
Theophrastus, 120
Theopompus, 113, 118n, 120
Theramenes, 14–15
Thessalus, son of Cimon, 122
Thirty Years Peace, 42
Thrace, 110
Thrasybulus, 14
Thrasylus, 14
Thucydides 1.1–23: 17; 1.1: 20–21; 1.2–
19 (Archaeology): 17–19, 24; 1.2.4:
18; 1.2.6: 18; 1.5: 18; 1.15: 18;
1.15.1: 18; 1.15.2: 18; 1.17.1: 18;
1.18.1: 18; 1.19: 20, 21; 1.20–22:
18, 20; 1.20.1: 38; 1.22: xi–xii, 18,
23, 49, 77, 90, 125, 134, 136, 147–
48; 1.22.1: 36, 40, 148; 1.22.1 (ta
deonta): xii, 25, 31, 35, 39, 49, 51–
52, 99, 104, 108, 157; 1.22.1

Thucydides (*cont.*)

(*gnōmēs*): xii, 35; 1.22.2: 148; 1.22.4: 19n, 63; 1.23: 21, 22n; 1.23.6: 39–40; 1.31–44: 148; 1.32–36: 6n, 23; 1.32–43: 51; 1.33.2: 147; 1.33.2–3: 24; 1.35.5: 147–48; 1.36.1–3: 95; 1.36.2: 24; 1.37–43: 6n, 23; 1.44.2: 24; 1.44.2–3: 94; 1.53.2: 5n, 6n; 1.53.4: 5, 6n; 1.67–88: 148–49; 1.67.5: 92; 1.68–71: 6n, 24; 1.70.3: 24, 147; 1.71.3: 148; 1.72: 32, 34–35, 101; 1.72–78: 32–48; 1.72.1: 35, 39, 46; 1.73–78: 6n, 23–24, 34, 36–38, 101; 1.73.1: 24, 36, 39, 44, 46, 101; 1.73.2: 38; 1.73.4: 36, 38; 1.73.4–74.3: 37; 1.74.1: 38; 1.74.4: 37; 1.75: 43; 1.75ff.: 29n; 1.75–76: 29n; 1.75–77: 40; 1.75–78: 35; 1.75.1: 36, 38; 1.75.1–2: 40; 1.75.2: 40; 1.75.3: 40; 1.75.4: 42; 1.76: 43; 1.76.1: 43; 1.76.2: 19n, 24, 29n, 41, 43; 1.76.3: 43, 56; 1.76.4: 39, 44; 1.77: 44n; 1.77.1: 44–45; 1.77.2: 44–45; 1.77.3–6: 45; 1.78: 46; 1.78.1: 35, 46; 1.78.3: 47; 1.78.4: 47; 1.79.2: 92; 1.80–85: 6n; 1.80–85.2: 34; 1.80–86: 25; 1.82.5: 147; 1.83.2: 73; 1.84.2: 28; 1.84.3: 28; 1.85.3: 92; 1.86: 6n, 24, 35, 46; 1.86.1: 35; 1.86.4: 35, 46; 1.86.5: 35; 1.87.1–3: 99; 1.87.2: 5n, 6n, 100; 1.88: 39–40, 46, 94; 1.89–117: 40; 1.89–118 (*pentecontaetia*): 70, 94; 1.90.3: 7; 1.91.4–7: 7; 1.94–96.1: 40; 1.96.1: 40; 1.100–101: 42; 1.100.1: 41; 1.104: 41; 1.109–10: 41; 1.111.2: 110; 1.112.1–4: 41; 1.112.4: 42; 1.113: 42; 1.114: 42; 1.114.1: 110; 1.114.3: 110; 1.116–17: 110; 1.119: 92; 1.125.1–24: 6, 25; 1.124.1: 148; 1.125.1: 93; 1.126–38: 147; 1.127: 112; 1.127.1: 110; 1.128–32: 145; 1.128–35: 40; 1.128.7: 5n, 149; 1.129.3: 5n, 149; 1.136.4: 150; 1.137.2: 150; 1.137.4: 150; 1.138.3: 56; 1.139–2.65: 123; 1.139.3: 5n; 1.139.3–145: 150–51; 1.139.4: 92; 1.139.4–145: 110; 1.140–44: 6, 25, 39, 46; 1.140.2: 47, 103; 1.140.5: 112; 1.141–44: 117; 1.144.1: 56; 1.144.2: 47, 103; 1.144.4: 56; 1.145: 93, 103

Thucydides (*cont.*)

2.10.2–11: 151; 2.11: 6; 2.13: 112, 151–52; 2.13.1: 147; 2.13.2: 56; 2.13.2–8: 117; 2.13.2–9: 6; 2.13.3: 117; 2.13.5: 117; 2.13.9: 56; 2.34–46: 152–55; 2.35–46: x, 3, 26–27, 46, 117, 119–21, 139, 145, 148; 2.37: 148; 2.37.1: 147; 2.39.1: 110; 2.41.3: 29n; 2.41.4: 147; 2.43.1: 20n, 27; 2.59–65: 100; 2.59.3: 100; 2.59.3–65.2: 155; 2.60–64: 26, 113, 117, 144; 2.60.1–61.3: 101; 2.62.2: 139; 2.63.1–2: 29n; 2.63.2: 28; 2.64.1: 46, 101; 2.64.1–2: 30; 2.64.3: 27, 29n; 2.65: 111; 2.65.1: 101; 2.65.5–7: 56; 2.65.6: 47; 2.65.7: 28n; 2.65.10: 28n; 2.65.13: 56–57; 2.71–74: 3, 5n, 6n; 2.86–89: 155; 2.87: 6n; 2.89: 6n

3.4.5–6: 96; 3.8–15: 155–56; 3.8.1: 96; 3.12.3: 148; 3.13.3–4: 96; 3.15.1: 93, 96; 3.15.2–16.2: 96; 3.16.2: 96, 103; 3.29.2–31: 156; 3.36: 97; 3.36–49: 4, 28–29, 148, 156–57; 3.36.4: 102; 3.36.4–49.2: 143; 3.37–40: 6n, 97; 3.37.2: 28; 3.37.3: 148; 3.37.3–4: 28; 3.38.4: 147; 3.40.7: 148; 3.42–48: 6n, 97; 3.44.2–3: 147; 3.45: 19n; 3.45.3: 147; 3.45.4: 29; 3.45.5: 20n, 29; 3.48.1: 102; 3.49: 97; 3.49.1: 94; 3.49.4: 97, 102; 3.51: 110; 3.52–54: 35; 3.52–68: 157; 3.52.4: 35; 3.53ff.: 31; 3.53–59: 6n; 3.53–67: 3; 3.54.2: 35; 3.56.7: 148; 3.59.2: 147; 3.61–67: 6n; 3.67.2: 35; 3.82: 70; 3.82.8: 19n; 3.84.2: 19n

4.10: 6n, 157; 4.11.4: 6n; 4.12.3: 57; 4.16–22: 98, 157; 4.17–20: 6n, 98; 4.17.4: 102; 4.21–22: 98; 4.21.2: 102; 4.21.3: 6n, 98; 4.22.1: 6n; 4.22.2: 6n, 98; 4.27–28: 99, 113; 4.28.1–2: 113n; 4.40.2: 157; 4.41.4: 103; 4.42–45: 110; 4.53–54: 110; 4.56–57: 110; 4.58: 52, 55, 92; 4.58–65.2: 157–58; 4.59–64: 52–55; 4.65: 55; 4.65.1: 52, 93; 4.65.4: 55; 4.84–88: 158; 4.86.1: 102; 4.87.2: 93; 4.88: 102; 4.88.1: 93; 4.92.2: 102; 4.97.2–4: 6n; 4.98: 6n; 4.99: 6n; 4.126: 50, 158; 4.126.1: 50; 4.129–31: 110

Thucydides (*cont.*)

5.25–116: 103; 5.26: 134; 5.35.4: 115; 5.43.2: 110; 5.44.2–46.3: 158; 5.44.3–45.1: 6n; 5.45–46: 113; 5.45.2: 115; 5.45.2–4: 6n; 5.46: 6n; 5.69.1: 6n; 5.69.2: 6n; 5.85–113: 3, 5, 6n, 29, 31, 38, 43, 103, 139, 144, 148, 158–60; 5.89: 36, 45; 5.89ff.: 29; 5.97.1: 139; 5.105.1–2: 19n; 5.109.5: 139; 5.111.4: 158

6.2–5: 70; 6.6: 64; 6.6.1: 71; 6.8–24: 65, 71; 6.8–26: 105, 160; 6.8.2: 65, 67; 6.8.4: 71; 6.9–14: 6n; 6.9–26: 113; 6.9.2: 71; 6.10.5: 103; 6.12.2: 65, 114; 6.13: 20n; 6.13.1: 71; 6.14: 143; 6.15: 65, 111; 6.15.1: 106; 6.15.3–4: 105; 6.16–18: 6n, 38, 116; 6.16.2: 116, 147; 6.16.3: 116; 6.16.4: 116; 6.16.6: 116; 6.17.2: 65; 6.17.3: 148; 6.17.4: 65; 6.17.7: 107; 6.18.2–3: 107; 6.18.5: 65, 139; 6.18.6: 30; 6.18.7: 107, 148; 6.19.1: 6n, 106; 6.19.2: 105; 6.20: 74; 6.20–23: 6n; 6.20.2: 65; 6.21.1: 65; 6.22: 65, 67; 6.22.1: 66; 6.23.1: 147–48; 6.24: 73–74; 6.24.1: 72, 106; 6.24.2–4: 106; 6.24.3: 20n, 76, 147; 6.25.1: 6n; 6.25.1–26.1: 107; 6.25.2: 6n; 6.31–32: 73, 75; 6.32–41: 143; 6.32.3: 92, 147; 6.32.3–41: 108, 160; 6.33–34: 6n, 52; 6.33.1: 77; 6.35.7: 147; 6.36: 147; 6.36–40: 6n; 6.36.2: 67; 6.37.1: 147; 6.37.2: 147; 6.40.1: 147–48; 6.41.2–4: 6n; 6.41.4: 92; 6.42.2: 67; 6.43: 66; 6.44.4: 67; 6.46: 74; 6.46.5–50.1: 160; 6.47: 6n, 114; 6.47–50: 72; 6.48: 6n; 6.49: 6n; 6.54–59: 70; 6.62: 67; 6.62.3: 66; 6.63.3: 67; 6.65: 67; 6.67.2: 66; 6.68: 6n; 6.68.1–4: 118; 6.68.3: 67; 6.70.3: 67; 6.71.2: 68; 6.72.2–5: 6n, 52, 104; 6.74.2: 68; 6.75–88: 68; 6.75.2: 68; 6.75.3–88: 160; 6.75.4–88.2: 108; 6.76–80: 6n, 52; 6.76–87: 143; 6.82–86: 30; 6.82–87: 6n, 37; 6.82.1: 36; 6.83.1: 36, 39, 103; 6.83.2: 36, 37; 6.83.4:

Thucydides (*cont.*)

41; 6.88.1–2: 95; 6.88.2: 93; 6.88.9–93: 108, 160–61; 6.89–92: 38; 6.93.1: 93; 6.94.4: 69; 6.96–7.9: 5; 6.98.1: 69

7.2: 69; 7.10–15.2: 161; 7.11–15: 114, 145; 7.12.3: 65; 7.15.1: 65; 7.21.3–4: 52; 7.29–30: 22; 7.42: 69; 7.47–49: 114, 161; 7.47.3–4: 6n; 7.48: 6n; 7.48.2: 139; 7.48.4: 114; 7.49: 6n; 7.50.4: 69, 111; 7.52–54: 69; 7.55: 74–75; 7.57–59: 70; 7.61–64: 6n, 118; 7.66–68: 6n; 7.67.3: 147; 7.69.2: 6n, 118; 7.73: 52; 7.75: 75; 7.77: 31, 114, 118, 161; 7.77.1: 115; 7.73.2: 53; 7.77.3: 115; 7.77.7: 31; 7.87.5: 30

8.1.1: 76; 8.1.2: 58, 76; 8.2.1: 58; 8.47–49: 80; 8.48.2: 82n; 8.53: 78, 81; 8.53.1: 81; 8.53.2: 81n; 8.53.3: 82; 8.54.1: 82; 8.54.2–3: 83; 8.54.4: 83; 8.56: 84; 8.57: 87n; 8.63.3–64.1: 85; 8.63.4: 81n; 8.63.4–65.1: 85; 8.65.1: 85; 8.65.2: 85; 8.65.3: 85; 8.66.1–2: 85; 8.67: 78, 88; 8.67.1: 84, 87; 8.67.3: 88; 8.68.1: 88; 8.73.3: 111; 8.76.2–77: 96; 8.81.2–83.2: 96; 8.85: 53; 8.86.3: 6n; 8.86.6–7: 6n; 8.89: 89n; 8.89.1: 6n; 8.89.2: 6n; 8.90.1: 89; 8.96.1: 58; 8.96.2: 58; 8.96.4: 58; 8.96.5: 58; 8.97.2: 57; 8.98.1: 89

Thyrea, 110

Tissaphernes, 13–14, 53, 80, 81n, 83, 161

Torone, 10

X

Xenophantidas, 13

Xenophon, 53, 140; *Cyropaideia* 1.6: 159; 7.2: 159; *Hellenica* 2.2.3–19: 76; 2.2.3: 30; 2.2.10: 30; 2.2.23: 30; speeches in, 134

[Xenophon] *Resp. Ath.* 1.16: 44

Xerxes, 8, 38, 71, 149